Silence Broken

A Psychological Novel About
Overcoming the Impact of
Childhood Trauma

Rivcka Edelstein, Ph.D.

Reim International Associates
Noblestone Press, New York,
Massachusetts, and Israel

Copyright © 2018, by the author, Rivcka Edelstein, Ph. D and Reim International Associates. Noblestone Press.

Copyright © 2012, Revised edition, by the author, Ricvka Edelstein, Ph.D.

Copyright © 1990, by the author, Rivcka Edelstein, Ph. D and Reim International Associates. Noblestone Press.

All rights reserved by the author.

Cover photography by Amanda Nirenberg; all rights reserved, 2018.

Hebrew copyright © 1994 by Reim International Associates and Bitan Publishers

50 Yeshayaho St., Tel Aviv

Printed in Israel 1994

For more information: http://www.edelsteinrivcka.com/

ISBN # 978-0-692-86747-1

This novel is a work of fiction. Names, characters, places, and incidents are either the product of the author's imagination or are used fictitiously. Any resemblance to actual events, locales, organizations, or personals, living or dead, is entirely coincidental and beyond the intent of both the author and publisher.

This book may not be reproduced, changed, in whole or in its parts, by photocopy, mimeograph, scanning, or any other means, without the permission of the author.

This book has been edited and proofed numerous times, but despite great efforts sometimes, things slip through. If you should find any errors, please contact the author through the website above. We will both update the corrections and be incredibly grateful to you for pointing them out.

In memory of Dr. Robert Martin Edelstein,
my husband, lover, and friend;
my vital source of support, inspiration, and strength.

About the Author

Rivcka Edelstein, Ph.D., is a licensed psychologist, certified and trained mediator, and trained life coach. She works both in the United States and abroad, and she has experience teaching in universities, presenting papers, running workshops, and supervising other clinical professionals. She has worked with children, adults, couples, families and groups. She has worked in various settings, including schools, residential treatment centers, government, and private clinical and business agencies. Between 1978 to 1984, she was the clinical director of a residential treatment center. In 1986, she founded the Awareness Center: Psychological Health and Growth, Life Coaching and Mediation Services, Inc. to facilitate mental health and growth, so that clients can develop healthy relationships, constructive conflict resolution skills, and effective communication skills.

Dr. Edelstein testified in courts as an expert witness in the areas of child sexual abuse, custody, and domestic violence. She has taught both in the United States and internationally at the university level, including courses and seminars on Socialization — Parent-Child Relationships, Domestic Violence, Psychology of Women, Psychology of Race, Gender and Ethnicity, the Impact of Childhood Trauma, and the Impact of Child Sexual Abuse. In 1979, she published the therapeutic game *Everything Is Possible.*© During her career, she has written books and screenplays that, though fictional, are based on the knowledge she has acquired.

Acknowledgements

I would like to extend my gratitude to my family and friends for their support and encouragement in writing this book. Thanks to my late husband Robert, my daughter Ruth, and my son Roy, who have supported me with endless words of encouragement, emotional support, and a never-ending source of constructive criticism and editorial comments.

Special thanks to my friends Dr. Patricia Nilson, Lois Altman, Hedva Boger, Ifat Lechno, Michal Bitan, for their reading of and comments on my manuscript.

Special thanks to Yael Cohen, for reading, editing, publishing in the U.S., and who helped me self-publish this book and "rush the charts."

Last, but not least, thanks to my secretaries Jennifer Gulizia, Zhanna Alkhazova, Pooja Bachani, Kate Souls, and Victoria Gruenert for their dedicated efforts on behalf of the manuscript.

Prologue

Tel Aviv, Israel, May 2, 1991

Jeremy sat in his office after a long and tedious day. It was past midnight and into the early morning hours of May 2nd. The closer it came to his wedding day, the more irritable and moody Jeremy became and the more he felt the need to be alone. Busy with meetings and phone calls, he had not had a minute to himself all day.

Days like today made him wonder if he had chosen the right profession. Lately he found himself dealing with too much red tape and very little with the cases themselves. Everybody told him that it came with the territory and that he would get used to it. Unfortunately, after all these years, he still didn't like it. Now he doubted that he ever would.

As his colleague, Ben, poked his head inside Jeremy's office, Jeremy's phone rang. The unexpected ringing startled Jeremy and he didn't notice his visitor right away. His mother was on the line; her calls had become more frequent since his engagement to Danielle.

"Yes, Mom... I'm at work. I'm fine... No, Mom. I don't have time to think about my engagement party. I'll talk to you tomorrow. Love you," he said in Hebrew.

"Why don't you and Danielle go on a vacation? I'm sure you both could use some relaxation," Ben suggested cheerily.

"We'll see," Jeremy sighed, unmoved. Ben just shook his head and popped back out of the office.

Jeremy turned to face the window. He loved this view of the Mediterranean Sea and Old Jaffa; looking at the water always calmed him.

Rivcka Edelstein

Over the radio, Jeremy heard Yehoram Gaon's voice and those words that had such special meaning for him: *"Ah, ah, od lo ahavti dai"* — *"Oh, I have not yet loved enough."*

How true, when had anyone had enough when it came to love?

He turned, reached for the TV remote and leaned back in his recliner. He enjoyed watching the BNN news at that time of the night; it was after five o'clock New York time. A news segment was just beginning; at first, he was unsure as to what he was watching.

On the screen, there was a view of the sunset over the Statue of Liberty. The view changed to the deck of a ferry as the background noise gradually increased, ringing clearly of human voices. There were children screaming and pointing to the water. The camera moved in the direction of the commotion. Ten boys and girls, a class of first graders, and their teachers rallied at the ferry railing, screaming and pointing toward the water below. The camera followed the water — a young boy struggled to stay afloat. Back on the deck, a slim, tall, white female teenager quickly took her sneakers off, threw her jacket on the floor, and climbed onto the railing. The others tried to stop her, but she jumped into the water. The ferry's alarm turned on. She surfaced for air and circled around, searching for him. The crowd screamed and pointed in the direction of the boy as his head quickly surfaced, then disappeared. She dove again.

The boat gradually came to a halt and a few life-preservers were thrown into the water. A few seconds passed, great tension grew on the deck and then cheers broke out as the teenager resurfaced, holding the boy with one arm and swimming toward the life-preservers. She lifted his head above the life-preserver and put her arms around him. Two ferry employees jumped into the water and rushed toward them. One diver held the boy and quickly climbed the ladder; the other diver helped the girl.

Surrounded by a teacher and classmates, a doctor urgently tended to the boy who showed signs of life. People cheered and clapped. The girl's friends and on-lookers hugged her. She clutched herself, shivered, and walked toward the revived young boy.

A voice from behind exclaimed, "Good job! What's your name?"

Silence Broken

Before the girl could answer, a woman, 25, put one hand on the girl's shoulder while using the other to swat away any photographers.

"No pictures, please," she demanded sternly.

The voice from behind emerged again, asking: "What is your name? The parents might want to reward you!"

The woman pulled the girl away as the ferry stopped. The picture changed to a screen shot of the young woman and child. Jeremy heard the BNN's anchor continue:

"This clip was taken by a tourist on the ferry. The young woman was told that the child's parents would want to reward her. She reportedly responded, 'I jumped into the water because it was the right thing to do and not because of a reward.' Little is known about this courageous youth. The parents of the young boy, who was on a school trip, want to reward 'The Mysterious Rescuer,' who was part of a group of teens. If anybody knows the young woman's identity, please call 1-800-555-3636.

"Why not reveal her name?" Jeremy wondered. She had been part of a group. Does she attend some exclusive school which prohibits publicity? He looked at the picture more closely: a wet skinny girl with long straight hair stood beside a small shivering child who tightly held her hand.

The TV camera zoomed in and focused on the youth's face. Jeremy focused more closely as well... Her face looked familiar...

Jeremy turned his recliner once again, and from the 27th floor of his office he saw the antiquity of Old Jaffa blend in beautifully with the sea. He tried to relax, but couldn't. He felt a strange uneasiness. He knew what had triggered it. The picture on TV had reminded him of Beth. Scenes flooded back from the winter of 1970...the summer of 1973...

Rivcka Edelstein

Part I: 1970, 1973

Silence Broken

Long Island, New York, Winter 1970

Chapter 1

The first time Jeremy met Beth was at a ninth-grade mixer. His cousin Rami, two years his junior, persuaded him to go to the party with a promise that he would have a good time even though he was older.

Jeremy had just arrived from Israel two days ago. His Aunt Reava, Uncle Bob and his two cousins, Sharon and Rami, picked him up from the airport.

The plan was that he would live with his aunt's family for the first part of the school year until his parents, Dr. and Mrs. Offir, would arrive for the Spring Semester for his father's Sabbatical at Stony Brook University on Long Island, NY.

For two days he was very excited, but quite overwhelmed with the changes. He had to meet new people, who speak a foreign language, and adjust to a different "home." He was jet-lagged, but when his cousin invited him to the party he felt a surge of energy; it would be fun to meet Rami's friends.

Uncle Bob drove them to the party and as soon as they arrived at the school's parking lot, several of Rami's friends approached them.

Rami spoke to Jeremy in Hebrew, giving him the rundown on each of his friends and introducing him to the ones that came around to greet them. Together, they all walked to the party in the gym, and Rami introduced him to more people as they went in. Rami told each one of his friends that Jeremy can speak English quite well. However, to Jeremy's surprise and disappointment, Rami's friends chose to speak to him slowly, with only a few polite words and then moved on to talk to others at the party.

In the midst of the party, Rami walked around and talked to different friends. Jeremy didn't mind. He was completely absorbed in his hobby of people watching, observing body language and facial expressions. In the past, he had been complemented on his intuitive perceptions.

Jeremy's curiosity peaked, when Beth walked into the gym. Something stirred inside him. Her hair, straight and long, was in constant motion, sometimes because of her head movements and other times because she ran her fingers through it as she talked. She was dressed very simply with flat shoes and no make-up. Jeremy admired that. *It's refreshing when a fourteen-year-old girl looks like 14 instead of 25, like the other girls at the party.* His eyes followed her. The way she carried herself set her apart from her friends. But there was something about her eyes that captivated him. It became the focus of his attention; he couldn't pin-point as to why.

He continued to watch her as she moved around the room. At first, he couldn't hear her voice, but as she got closer he was able to pick up the conversations between her and her friends. Her voice was…musical. He noticed the commotion created around her by the other girls as much as by the boys. Almost everybody asked her why she was so late.

"I had things to do," she replied very gracefully as she pulled her hair behind her ears.

For a quick second, Jeremy noticed sadness in her eyes. The friends wanted to know if she was elected or not. Jeremy didn't know what was she running for, but it seemed important to everybody. She smiled, nodded her head and thanked them for their support. He liked what he saw and heard. There was an aura around her that he couldn't quite describe in words. He felt excited and looked for his cousin for an introduction.

Jeremy noticed her sense of relief when she saw Rami in the other corner of the room. She made her way towards him.

* * *

Beth noticed the tall handsome stranger in the other side of the room.

Who is that? I have never seen him in school before. Did he come with someone as their date?

Silence Broken

But for the moment, she decided she had too much on her mind to engage in idle conversation with him. She came to the party to see and talk to Rami, her best friend. She felt he was closer to her than her own brother, Kevin. As she approached Rami, she seemed calm and collected. She tried to keep appearances with her friends and smiled but she could not calm the bursting pain she felt inside. She could not stop the images of the conversation she had with her father a few minutes ago. As hard as she tried, she could not untie the knots she felt in her stomach. She hoped to talk to Rami alone.

On the way to the party, no more than a couple of minutes ago, tears stung her eyes. In the confines of the car, with his usual preface, "I know what is best for you, and I am only thinking about your interests…" Her father berated her choice of friends. He recited his familiar speech about how her decision, this time it was to go to the party, had disappointed him.

Once again, he reminded her how "your decisions now will define your life in the future." It ended with the usual, "the consequences are inevitable, and it doesn't make a difference how hard I try to protect you. If you decide in favor of short-term pleasures instead of the needed sacrifices and hard work, in the end, you will amount to nothing, like your friends and many others in this world."

She hated those lectures. He always spoke to her using big words. She sat quietly, afraid to speak. In her head, she was ready to scream out loud and tell him to shut up already. She was extremely angry and confused. She was trembling, afraid to protest for fear that he would turn around and drive her home — as he had done in the past when she didn't agree with him.

When it came to school, she didn't know what he wanted from her. She was a fourteen-year-old girl with very good grades who just wanted to go to the beginning of the school year party. She didn't see anything wrong with that. Since her mother was in favor of her going out and socializing and she expressed her opinion, her father had no choice but to concede. However, he was not happy about her going to the party and he let Beth know it throughout the entire ride to the school.

She tuned her father out by thinking about Rami. Beth felt warm and slightly envious when she thought of seeing him at the party. She knew that his parents had faith in him, trusted his decisions, and accepted his friends. Rami's parents didn't harass him. She wished her parents were like Rami's. Her parents questioned her constantly — especially her father. She wished they had faith in her but instead they always reminded her about her papers and tests.

She loved her parents very much, but why couldn't they see that she worked very hard to be a good student, to make them happy? But it was never enough.

Once again, she had to agree to all kinds of extra work and conditions that her father imposed on her before he reluctantly agreed to drive her to the party. She was shaking with the thought that, out of desperation to go to the party, she might have promised too much.

That morning in school, she told Rami how much she liked him, and that he was her best friend. Rami told her that he liked her too and he liked their friendship. She was disappointed. She hoped he would tell her that he loved her and would ask her to be his girlfriend. She hoped they could see each other more often. Rami was not only her best friend, but also the only boy her parents approved of. He was a good student and his parents were friends with her own.

She made it to where Rami stood. He was happy to see her and kissed her on the cheek. Rami told her that he was worried when she didn't show up. She liked what she heard. It was OK with her if he didn't want a girlfriend as long as he was her best friend and spent his free time with her.

Beth heard Rami tell her that there was someone special he would like her to meet. Her heart fell. As they were making their way toward another group of people in the room she felt tears in her eyes.

After all I have gone through to come? This is too much! She felt nervous and agitated. Her eyes were down. She was following Rami, determined not to show her disappointment. This was what she feared all along. He was too much of a nice guy not to have other girls trying to hook up with him.

She barely heard Rami's announcement, "I would like you to meet my . . ."

What did he say? What was going on? She didn't look up. She didn't want to meet her rival.

Silence Broken

"Beth, I would like you to meet Jeremy! Jeremy, this is my friend Beth."

She reluctantly extended her hand. She looked up, to see the tall and handsome stranger she had noticed before. He looked older than the others.

Thank you, God, for sparing me the humiliation. Her face lit up.

"Hello," Jeremy said excitedly as he shook her hand. He was relieved that Rami introduced Beth as "my friend" and not as "my girlfriend." The couple of minutes that had passed between the time Beth and Rami met and the time that they approached him, he observed their closeness. It had occurred to him that this stunning girl might be Rami's girlfriend.

She gave him another look and bombarded him with questions before he had a chance to speak.

Jeremy was so excited that he couldn't speak. Rami threw a snide remark at him, in Hebrew. Beth froze.

Rami took charge of the embarrassing situation. He explained to Beth that Jeremy arrived from Israel two days ago.

"He is not only my cousin — he is also my best friend." Beth felt as if somebody had slapped her hard across her face. She thought that she was Rami's best friend. Rami continued talking.

I wonder what he said, she was thinking to herself, when she heard Rami's final comment, "...When you know him you will see how terrific he is." Rami turned around and said something to Jeremy.

I don't want to know him. She dreaded her resentment. *He probably doesn't understand English. I know it's not his fault for being here but now I'm left out.*

She forced herself to smile while she patiently waited for Rami to finish his explanation in Hebrew.

Beth made repeated efforts to engage Rami in a conversation. Rami mostly spoke to Jeremy in Hebrew. Others frequently interrupted them.

She made a comment to Rami, along with other teasing remarks, "You are speaking to Jeremy in a language I don't understand."

Rami only responded by saying, "Well, Jeremy is my guest and I would like to make sure he understands what is happening around him."

By the end of the evening, Beth was extremely annoyed that Rami had brought Jeremy along. All of a sudden, she was shaking. Did she hear Rami saying that his cousin was coming with them for the ski trip? *Oh, please God, it couldn't be true.* She hoped she didn't hear Rami correctly. For the last few weeks she had been counting the days until her family and Rami's family would enjoy their traditional vacation together.

* * *

Jeremy felt a large lump lodged in his throat. His momentary hopes of striking a conversation with her were crushed. Beth only spoke to Rami — completely disregarding Jeremy's presence. He heard part of the conversation and felt it was too private for his ears. He moved away, pretending he was busy observing others. He felt ill at ease. He decided that Beth had needed an urgent conversation with Rami and that was why she was so abrupt with him. It eased his disappointment a bit, but he could not stop obsessing about her reaction. *Why did she react that way?* It didn't fit with the image he had of her from the few minutes before they were introduced.

* * *

A week later, Jeremy Offir and the Baker family arrived at the Town & Country Motor Lodge at 10 PM, completely exhausted from their ten-hour drive. Jeremy wondered how his Uncle Bob had the strength to make the trip.

Silence Broken

"Here we are," Uncle Bob proclaimed after parking the car and he went inside.

Uncle Bob returned to the car after checking in.

"Our room is next to theirs."

"You mean the Robinoffs checked in already?" Rami inquired, still half-asleep.

"The Robinoffs arrived only half an hour earlier. They are already settled in and are waiting for us."

One by one, they crawled out of the car, stretching their cramped limbs. They collected their belongings, which had been tossed around during the long drive, and dragged themselves into the motel to find the Robinoff family waiting for them.

The Bakers joined the Robinoffs in their room. Jeremy was very excited when he saw that Beth was part of the Robinoff family. He knew they were going to spend the ski vacation with the Robinoff family, but he didn't know who they were. He was glad to see her again. Her gorgeous big green eyes and beautiful brown hair entranced him. He was determined to speak to Beth this time, remembering his unfortunate muteness the last time they had met.

Mrs. Robinoff poured wine for the adults and juice for the children. She sliced several kinds of cheeses and placed them on a tray. They made a toast to the forthcoming wonderful vacation they were all anticipating.

"Sorry, sorry, in all the confusion I forgot to introduce my beloved nephew, Jeremy Offir. Jeremy, these are our friends, the Robinoffs. Jeremy has come to stay with us for a while!" Jeremy's aunt exclaimed.

Dr. and Mrs. Robinoff and Kevin shook hands with Jeremy and asked him the usual polite questions. He welcomed his aunt's handling the answers and explanations. She told the Robinoffs that Jeremy's father was on sabbatical for a year. Professor Offir and his wife would not be arriving until February. Jeremy arrived early so he would be able to start the new semester with the rest of the students and would have the chance to improve his English.

"How dreadful it must be for you to live so far from all of your relatives," Mrs. Robinoff said sympathetically to Reava Baker. "Most of our relatives live only two hours away and I find that too far. You came here and left your whole family behind in Israel."

"Yes, it was hard." Jeremy's aunt nodded her head." The kids don't get a chance to spend as much time with their cousins."

Mrs. Robinoff sighed. "I don't know if I could do what you are doing!"

"When you have to, you do." Mrs. Baker shrugged her shoulders.

At first it seemed that they were all engrossed in his aunt's enthusiastic explanations. Then Jeremy noticed that Beth had an annoyed look on her face. He wondered if she was angry about something. He was sure he hadn't done anything to hurt her.

He left the room to go wash his hands. On his way back, he overheard Beth quietly speaking to her mother.

"I was looking forward to this weekend for weeks."

Her mother gave her a puzzled look.

"So?"

"It's a disaster! I'm going to have to listen to Rami talking in Hebrew all the time. We won't have any fun like we always did before."

Dr. Robinoff chose not to comment. He was actually pleased. Kevin, Beth's older brother, frowned at her.

"What do you expect Rami to do? Try to make conversation with Jeremy."

"I met him last Friday and he didn't say a word to anyone except to Rami, and that was in Hebrew. Anyway, how could I? He seems so shy and boring. He doesn't understand the language. I tell you something else, I don't believe he's Rami's favorite cousin." Beth said angrily. As soon as the words came out of her mouth, Beth knew she sounded bratty. She was so upset, her voice was shaking, and she could barely hold off the stinging tears.

Jeremy was stunned. He stepped back into the bathroom. These comments really didn't fit the image he had of her when he saw her interaction with her friends last Friday.

How could she be so cynical and judgmental when she doesn't know me? What did she expect Rami to do? How could she jump to conclusions like this even though I didn't talk to her at the party? His initial excitement of seeing her disappeared and instead he felt knots in his stomach.

Jeremy walked back in the room soon enough to hear the rear end of the conversation.

"He probably does understand English," her mother said. "After all, the Israelis do study English in school and they use it daily. I am confident that you will find something to talk about." Beth blushed when she noticed Jeremy.

"Do you understand any English?" She turned to him when he entered the room. She spoke very slowly, carefully enunciating each word.

For no other reason than to ease her agony, Jeremy answered slowly as well, "Very, very little. I am trying to learn."

She was clearly relieved and she offered him some cookies with a smile.

Rami saw what took place. He felt for Jeremy and was surprised at Beth's behavior. He wondered what was going on. He had known her for so long and had never seen her acting the way she had been in the last couple of weeks. She seemed stressed. He didn't know what was wrong. *Worse than that, why had she chosen to act like this around Jeremy?*

Rami said to Jeremy, in Hebrew "Let her be helpful, it will make her feel good. She really is a nice person."

Jeremy played along. He wished she'd like him, even though he was still hurting. She talked to him slowly and he answered her with a nod or "yes" and "no." For his cousin's sake, he did not want to be nasty. As long as she was trying, he would not spoil it for her, but he was in pain. Despite his earlier decision to minimize her agony, Jeremy still wanted to teach her a lesson. He just hoped that his cousin didn't like her more than what he had described as "just friends." Rami was known to have a very good judgment of people, but Jeremy knew that good judgment doesn't necessarily prevail in matters of the opposite sex.

Give her the benefit of the doubt; what have you got to lose? Jeremy argued with himself. That approach, however, did not help erase the pain he felt in his stomach. He found himself degrading her in his mind. He couldn't stop his growing irritation with her giggling and everything she said. *Stop it, Jeremy.* He felt uncomfortable with his own reaction.

"A penny for your thoughts," his cousin whispered in his ear in English, and proceeded to explain the idiom to Jeremy in Hebrew.

"If you knew the thoughts I've been having, you would pay more than a penny for them." Jeremy replied in Hebrew with a forced smile. He noticed Rami's concern. He knew Rami was the type of person who wanted everyone to be happy, watching out for the best interest of everyone. Sometimes the family teasingly called him "the international peacemaker."

"When she gets to know you better, she'll change her opinion on her own."

"Who cares?" Jeremy snapped, slightly irritated, but deep down he knew that he did care.

"Nobody, but it would be simpler, since we will all be spending time together." said Rami. "I'm surprised at you. It's not like you to take a girl's comment seriously. I've seen you among your friends, even if you are somewhat shy with…"

"I am not shy with you and your family!" Jeremy interjected defensively.

"How could you be shy with my mother?!"

"I guess I do give the impression of being shy until I know someone."

"You're not the only one." Rami added with a smile.

"You? You must be kidding; you're so friendly and you always find something to say to make a stranger feel at ease. I admire you for that."

"That's on the outside, on the inside I feel anxious and uncomfortable with strangers."

"I never saw it. Anyway, I don't understand what you see in her. Even as 'just a friend,' she seems shallow."

"She isn't. She might talk a lot, but it's just a cover up when she is worried. She is really very nice." It was clear that Rami was concerned that Jeremy and Beth had begun the vacation and their relationship on the wrong foot.

Jeremy tried to accept Rami's explanation, but Beth's words were still echoing in his ears.

Beth came back with three cups of hot apple cider.

"You will never learn English if you don't speak it," she said slowly to Jeremy. She then turned to Rami and spoke in an angry tone.

"What good are you doing him by speaking in Hebrew? If you speak to him in English, he will learn and I will be able to understand what you two are talking about." She sounded like a spoiled brat.

"Now Beth, you would not want to know all that we gossip about. Anyway, it would spoil our fun." Rami replied jokingly.

"What about my fun?" She exploded loudly. She saw the others' reaction and regretted her tone of voice and her loss of control. She started to move from one foot to the other and nervously pushed her hair from her face.

"I was just joking." Rami was concerned with her reaction. "I will try to translate for you whenever possible, but you can speak to him in English. Believe me, he understands quite a lot."

Beth looked at Rami with disbelief. She thought for a second, and as something dawned on her, she blushed deeply.

Rami continued, "I'm sure you haven't said anything you wouldn't want Jeremy to hear, have you Beth?"

"Well, let's drop it," she said sharply to Rami. Turning to Jeremy she tried, "Let's start afresh. I'm Beth Robinoff."

Jeremy had to resist his first reaction to tell her off and instead responded as though he did not understand why they needed to start again. They engaged in some small talk for the remainder of the night,

At least tomorrow is a new day, Jeremy thought in bed that night. He was determined not to let the incident with Beth spoil his weekend. He decided to spend more time with Sharon and Kevin. Despite being closer in age to Sharon, Jeremy felt a special bond between himself and Rami. However, spending time with the others would give Beth a chance to be with Rami without feeling threatened by the language barrier.

In the morning, they set out to examine the lodge and found a heated swimming pool, which looked more like a misplaced green pond. The water was freezing cold and covered with algae.

"I suppose 'heated' depends on what you compare it to," Rami commented.

During breakfast Beth seemed calmer, sitting between her mother and Rami, who spoke to her in English and to Jeremy in Hebrew. Jeremy was so excited about going skiing, for the first time in his life that he refused to allow anything to ruin it.

Soon after breakfast, the two families headed up to the slopes. Rami and Sharon quickly put on their ski boots and skis, while Uncle Bob took Jeremy to the rental office and fitted him for equipment. When he first attempted walking in the ski boots himself, he felt as though he were picking up heavy weights each time he lifted his foot. Rami, Sharon, Kevin, and Beth laughed at his initial efforts to walk towards them. Uncle Bob described the first time Sharon and Rami were fitted with boots and about the pictures he took of them with their funny expressions and clumsy walk. Jeremy joined in the laughter.

The others decided to ski on intermediate trails while Jeremy walked toward the ski instructor for the beginners' lessons.

As they moved toward the chair lifts, Jeremy heard Beth ask Rami, "How is he going to understand the instructions?"

"Well Beth, first, he is innately intelligent, second, he can watch and then do as the instructor illustrates, and third, he does understand English. Why don't you believe me?"

"I'll believe it when I hear it," she answered.

"Sarcasm doesn't suit you." Rami said with a shrug and moved forward on his skis toward the lifts, leaving Beth frozen in her spot, clearly insulted. *There is no question Rami is right,* Jeremy thought to himself. *She really is very sensitive.* He realized that despite the need to teach her a lesson for her attitude, he really didn't want to see her hurt.

Rivcka Edelstein

Kibbutz Nof-Golan, Israel, 1973

Chapter 2

"Down, down, down Rona . . . down." The young lady knelt down to pat the Collie that was jumping at her. She looked at her wet shoes and added, "Could it be you? You still respond to English? You remembered me! My God, I'm talking to myself. How could it be...?!"

With an untrimmed beard, Jeremy was reading the newspaper when he heard the voice near him. He looked up from where he was lying on the grass and was surprised to see a pair of long and shapely legs. Jeremy never saw the dog so affectionate with anyone except very close family members. He raised his head a little higher and saw a young woman petting the dog, the expression on her face was that of disbelief.

He remembered his aunt telling people how excited the dog got when she saw somebody she really liked and had not seen for a long time. "When Rona is happy, she loses control and pees!"

"Do you know the dog?" Jeremy asked in Hebrew. A second later he repeated the question in English.

"Actually, I don't. When the dog jumped on me I... I remembered a collie a friend of mine used to have back in the United States, but... When they lived in Israel they stayed in the city of Be'er Sheva... Now..." She stopped. She felt silly and sensed that her explanation didn't make any sense. "Forget it. Say, this dog is really friendly. Does it jump like this on everybody?"

"No, only special somebodies."

"Then I guess I'm special," she said with a smile.

"I guess so! What did you call her?"

"Oh, it's silly, forget it. I told you, I was just talking to myself. What's her name?"

Silence Broken

"Rona."

"Rona?" She was speechless for a moment. "The dog I used to know was named Rona too."

"No kidding!" he laughed. Then, with a second look at her, he added curiously, "Do I know you from somewhere?"

"How could you? I just arrived from the United States about a month ago."

"Seriously, I have met you before."

"Is this your line with every new girl you meet or just American girls?" she asked cynically. She had been warned about Israeli guys.

Sparked by her cynicism, Jeremy suddenly remembered. He was actually surprised it took him so long to remember — she really had changed. She was not the fourteen-year-old skinny girl he had met in the U.S.A. in the winter of 1970…

She had grown up, matured; nonetheless, her sharp tongue had not changed.

Jeremy ignored her comment and continued, "Don't you see? The dog's name is Rona. You used to know a dog named Rona in the United States; your friend's family moved to Israel for two years and just recently returned to the United States, and I say I've met you before…"

"You are serious, aren't you?"

"Beth. That's your name."

"That's right. Now the mystery almost is complete — except that I still don't remember ever seeing you before."

"My face is not as memorable as yours," he said. After a short pause, he decided to pay her back for the past and continued, "Or maybe you've met so many young men that you don't remember who's who!"

Beth was stunned by his presumptuous comment.

She took a deep breath, and calmly inquired, "Where did you learn to speak English so well? The other young Israelis I met didn't speak this well."

"I spent some time in the United States about three years ago. Most of my cousin's friends were friendly to me and tried to be sociable. Of course, they all spoke to me in English and gave me a chance to practice the language."

She looked at him closer and blushed.

"You're Rami's 'shy cousin.' Now I remember you! I met you as soon as you arrived. You hardly spoke a word the few times I met you."

Jeremy did not especially care for the label which she gave him. The memories of her initial impression of him were still vivid, but he decided to remain pleasant.

She was looking at him, waiting for a response to her realization, and finally commented, "You've changed."

"So have you."

"Should I take that as a compliment?"

"It depends — how am I to understand your comment?"

"Does an Israeli ever answer a question or does he always respond with another question?" she asked sarcastically.

Jeremy stared at her blankly. *Why am I letting her comments upset me again?* he wondered.

"You are cross." She barely uttered the words and her voice was shaky. "I didn't mean... sometimes, when I feel awkward or uncomfortable, I become cynical."

Her unexpected honesty touched him. "Okay, let's start afresh, from the beginning," he offered. "I'm Jeremy."

She laughed, relieved, recalling her similar gesture three years ago, "And I'm Beth."

"What are you doing here, Beth?"

"Here at the kibbutz or Israel?"

"Both."

"Well, I…" She was about to explain when he pointed to the grass and suggested they sit. She settled down, crossing her long legs beneath her and then continued. "I came here because I needed a vacation."

"Here in Israel or at the kibbutz?"

"Both," she laughed. "Actually, Israel."

"When did you come to Israel?"

"At the end of May."

"In the middle of the school year you needed a vacation? Aren't you supposed to be in your junior year in high school?"

"Yes, but I completed all of my requirements for high school graduation and…" Beth took a deep breath, "my guidance counselor came up with the idea of an independent study abroad in Israel as an honors project that will enable me to graduate a year early."

Jeremy's mind was racing but he didn't dare pry.

"What is the project about?"

"The education system in Israel."

"So, what brought you to the kibbutz?"

"In my project, I am comparing different educational systems in Israel as well as making comparisons between Israel and the United States." She stopped, but it was clear that she had more to say. Jeremy motioned her to go on.

"My guidance counselor wrote to a number of kibbutzim including Nof Golan. Your kibbutz responded favorably."

"And others?" Jeremy asked curiously.

"Well, it seems they are tired of being cooperative and being observed, only to find out, later, that inaccurate publications have been published and circulated about them."

"I've heard that from my aunt."

"So, if this is true, why did your kibbutz invite me to come?"

"This kibbutz is new. It was established by young families who left urban living and came here. Since it is a young kibbutz and on the Lebanon border, *really* on the border, they have not had the same experience with researchers that other, more established kibbutzim have."

"Why did you say 'they?' Wouldn't that include you?"

"Well, I am not a member yet, although I hope to become one. I am here as part of my army service. Our youth movement was sent here to help cultivate the land and to serve as a military force on the border. We serve the country and stay together as a group called Nachal, short for *Noar Chalutzi Lochem*, which means 'fighting pioneering youth.'"

"Is that an easy way to meet your military obligations?"

"No, it's actually hard, but we chose it. It includes difficult, ongoing, and extensive training. But, the fact that we grew up together, as children and as young men and women, makes it easier and fun."

"What is your primary task?"

"What do you mean by 'primary?'"

"Are you here first for fighting or first for pioneering?"

"Army training takes place outside of the kibbutz. Here, we work at whatever the kibbutz assigns to us. During the evenings, we have group programs and we socialize," he explained patiently.

Recalling what she had read about the Israeli military and mobilization, she wondered how the soldiers stationed on the border were affected.

Silence Broken

"What happens to your group in a national emergency?"

"Why, do you expect one?" Jeremy asked jokingly, quite surprised at the question since there had been no wars in Israel for six years.

"My father said that a war could break out at any time due to the hostility in the region."

"I see," he replied, impressed with her awareness of Israel's constant security problems. After a moment he continued, "We undergo intensive training as one large troop and, in an emergency, we are mobilized to wherever we are needed. In the meantime, the kibbutz is our home and we assist in guarding the border."

"Well, I hope you will not need all of your training."

"Believe me, so do I," he smiled.

There was momentary silence.

"How is your project coming along?" he asked in an attempt to resume the conversation.

"Quite well, actually. I interviewed some of staff and students at a *moshav* (a semi-cooperative farm) in the north. I visited religious and non-religious schools in the cities of Tel Aviv and Tiberias, as well as two special education schools, and now this kibbutz."

"It seems like you've covered a lot of ground. Would you say that your goals have been accomplished so far?"

She looked him straight in the eyes, paused, and then said, "Not completely, not as much as I had hoped."

He decided to ask directly. "Do you mean as far as your project or your vacation?"

She was surprised at his comment and the astute interpretation of her remarks.

"A little bit of both. As far as the project is concerned, so far, I have seen and heard a lot and I kept notes and a daily log. I still need to sit down and organize them. I hope I can do that in the next few weeks. Then I can see if I need to collect any more data." She stopped.

It was clear to Jeremy that she was not about to respond to the second part of his question, so he asked another. "Where did you stay when you were in the different locations?"

"I wanted to live the life of the people in Israel and not that of a tourist, so different families were contacted in each location to be my hosts. My guidance counselor felt that the kibbutz would be the most convenient location as a center for my project. I could also help out by teaching English to the children who need it."

"Is the kibbutz your final stop?"

"Yes. The kibbutz, with Mrs. Eben's help…"

"Mrs. Eben?"

"Yes, the principal of the school."

"Oh, you mean Ruth."

"I guess so. She invited me to stay as long as I need and to take advantage of the available transportation to other cities in case I want to go back for any reason."

"That was very nice of her." Jeremy paused. "Aren't you quite young for all of this?"

"Age is a state of mind," she stated and then added, "My school didn't think so. My guidance counselor suggested it and planned the entire project."

"What about your parents?"

"That was the hardest part. My father simply objected; he never liked me going anywhere out of his sight. My mother knew in her heart I had to get away, but did not know why… You might say I was 'burnt out.' Both of them were quite opposed to the idea of my going all the way to Israel…"

Jeremy felt confused. He was moved by her honesty, and yet the contrast between her words and her facial expression and her nervous body's gestures convinced him that many important details were being purposely omitted. His train of thought was interrupted when he heard Effrat, one of the *gar'in* members, calling him in Hebrew from her room.

"Jeremy, can I have the paper now? I want to read the headlines before we go to the dining room."

"I haven't read it yet."

"All of this time? You said you wanted it for half an hour…"

She came out, saw Beth, and smiled.

"I see why you didn't get to read it yet. A nice distraction," she commented in Hebrew, smiling at Beth. Effrat then spoke to Beth in Hebrew, asking her who she was, where she was from, and whether she was visiting Jeremy. She spoke very quickly, not letting Beth respond, unaware of Beth's confusion.

When she finally stopped, Beth held out her hand and said quite slowly and carefully in Hebrew, "My name is Beth."

Effrat continued in Hebrew until Jeremy intervened, noticing Beth's apprehension.

"She doesn't understand you, Effrat. She's a student from the United States and what you heard in Hebrew is probably her total vocabulary in our language."

Effrat turned to Beth and said in English, "I'm sorry. I assumed you spoke Hebrew because you look like an Israeli."

"I'll accept that as a compliment," Beth answered, relieved that the language issue had been cleared up and that Effrat spoke English. Effrat restated the questions and Beth answered them patiently. It was soon time for dinner and the three of them headed toward the dining room.

"She is *beseder (okay)*," Effrat mumbled into Jeremy's ear on the way to the dining room. "What were you talking about all this time?"

"Her research project."

Effrat put her hand on Jeremy's elbow, suggesting more than a casual friendship and Beth's eyes followed her every move. Effrat asked Beth questions about the project and the different schools she had already seen. Beth found Effrat's questions helpful in shaping her own thoughts.

Knowing Effrat, Jeremy anticipated that she was going to "adopt" Beth. She had already appointed herself Beth's personal hostess and treated her as though she were her responsibility. On the way to the dining hall, Effrat introduced Beth to everyone who joined them. Jeremy realized that the *chevreh* (group of friends) were under the impression that Beth was a college student doing a project, but he didn't bother to correct them. *She certainly is mature for her age, both in looks and behavior. Maybe Beth was right — age is a state of mind*, he thought to himself.

While Beth was socializing with Effrat's help, Jeremy stood to the side, taking the opportunity to see things from a different perspective. He liked what he saw: Beth was pretty and had beautiful eyes. He really had enjoyed speaking with her. Although their conversation had been interrupted in the middle, he was not sure whether Beth would want him to interrupt her socializing. Maybe this was what she wanted, to meet as many people as possible. He didn't like the sadness lurking in her eyes.

Ruth approached the group. "Beth, I see you have met our new gar'in."

Beth was obviously puzzled.

Ruth went on to explain, "The *gar'in* is the whole age group which comes to Nachal together from the same youth movement. We refer to them as the *gar'in* until they become members of the kibbutz. You will probably find their activities and leisure time even more appealing than spending time with my family. Have you had dinner already?"

"She will eat with us as soon as the rest of the *chevreh* arrive," Effrat volunteered.

Silence Broken

"OK, I guess I'll see you when you come back tonight."

"Mrs. Eben, I'll return after dinner so we can talk." Beth reassured her.

"Please, not Mrs. Eben. Call me Ruth. Nobody would know who you were talking about if you called me by my family name. We can talk in the morning, there is no rush for it tonight. Have a good time." Ruth said in a motherly tone of voice. She turned away and called her husband, and their two sons over to an unoccupied table.

The *gar'in* finally gathered and sat down to dinner. Beth observed and followed the procedures of the dining room and commented on this to Jeremy as they prepared to leave.

He smiled at her. "Seems like you did well with the *chevreh*."

"Effrat deserves the credit; she did most of the talking. She seems like a wonderful person. How long have you known her?" She followed Jeremy out the door and down the main path.

"Since kindergarten; we were in grammar school together, joined the youth movement together, and went through the same high school classes."

"I like the system here more than the one in our schools."

"In what way?"

"We change classmates and teachers every year. You are probably more able to form lasting friendships this way."

Jeremy didn't respond; he was still thinking about their earlier conversation.

"I was sorry we were interrupted earlier in the middle of discussing your project."

"Oh, we've been talking about my project all along; all those questions really help me crystallize my ideas."

"How long do you intend to stay in Israel?"

"A few more weeks… Two months maybe… It all depends on the progress I make."

"So I guess I will be seeing you when I return."

"Return? I thought you are stationed here?"

"I will be going to Tel Aviv for a short seminar as part of our youth movement."

"When will you be leaving?" she asked anxiously. Beth felt embarrassed over her reaction and decided to explain. "I can imagine it might not sound logical to you, but meeting someone I knew gave me a sense of self-confidence about my stay here."

"You could have fooled me. The way you handled all those questions before, I wouldn't have thought for a minute that you lacked confidence."

"I don't go out and advertise it. Anyway, you shouldn't let appearances fool you. It's been my best defense for years. My sarcasm helped me to cover up my own feelings of inadequacy. I never feel that I am as good as I should be." She saw his surprised expression and added, "I mean, according to my own standards."

"Maybe you should modify them," Jeremy joked.

"Don't laugh, that's exactly what my counselor told me."

They strolled quietly, enjoying the fresh air. Beth finally asked where they were headed.

"Do you want to go back to Ruth's house now?" He asked.

"Not particularly, but maybe I should."

"Should? Would you like to go to Ruth's house now or would you like to go for a walk?"

"Don't you have things that you have to do?"

"Not especially. Usually after dinner I like to take a short walk, then I go to my room and read or join some friends for coffee. I'm asking what you want to do."

Silence Broken

"Would you like to continue to walk?"

"You are avoiding the question. Do you want me to make the decision?"

"You're being… Okay, I would like to continue our walk." There was silence. They continued to walk. After a while Beth said, "For years I haven't considered what I want, but rather what's expected of me. Challenging it seemed too difficult; it took too much energy to resist."

Jeremy heard her but chose not to ask questions.

Rivcka Edelstein

Kibbutz Nof-Golan, Israel, 1973

Chapter 3

After the walk around the kibbutz, Jeremy had an idea.

"If you'd like to walk outside of the kibbutz gate, we could stop and tell Ruth that you'll be late."

"Splendid. I wanted to continue talking, but I thought that I..."

"I wish you had said so before."

"I'm learning, I'm learning."

Jeremy accompanied her back to Ruth's house. Beth apologized about not continuing to work that evening. Ruth was pleased with the change of plans. She heard that Beth was a hard worker; she tried to persuade Beth that having some time off from work was healthy.

"Life should be enjoyable, not just productive. It's OK to relax!" Ruth had noticed sadness in Beth, but did not know what it stemmed from. Neither she nor Jeremy could have anticipated what was to follow.

"You know, I've been in this country for only a few weeks and I have seen a number of people take interest in my well-being. People accept me as if I am at home among friends... I am not used to that. Sometimes I feel awkward, not knowing how to react to being accepted. For years, Rami, Jeremy's cousin, a classmate of mine, encouraged me to be open and to be in touch with my feelings. You're all very perceptive. I *am* driving myself too hard. Life is more than projects and papers. I accept your comments; heaven knows I've heard them before. Unfortunately, my academic achievements were my only source of pride; the only things that received any recognition and approval." She went forward and kissed Ruth on the cheek and hugged her.

Silence Broken

"Thank you."

"You are more than welcome and please excuse my forwardness. That's me! For better or worse, that's me."

They all smiled and Ruth added, "Since you've got the whole evening to chat, why don't the two of you stay for coffee and dip into some of the goodies I received from my mother?" Beth and Jeremy agreed and Ruth put water on to boil.

"I didn't realize you knew Jeremy from before," Ruth wondered.

"I didn't know he was here; we met accidentally earlier this evening. Would you believe it was because of a dog?"

"Rona, my aunt and uncle's dog," Jeremy explained. "She isn't friendly with everyone, but she greeted Beth like a long-lost friend." Jeremy went on to describe in detail what had happened earlier.

"Incredible!"

"In short, we realized we had met about three years ago during the winter I was at my aunt's house on Long Island. We've both changed quite a bit," Jeremy laughed. "I recognized Beth rather quickly, but it took her longer to recognize me... Maybe because when I met her three years ago, I didn't have the beard," Jeremy added as an afterthought.

"Speaking of your beard, you looked better without it," Ruth commented. "I don't know why you men think a beard makes you more attractive. Anyway, like I said..."

"You're not the first woman to disapprove of my beard, but it's easier than shaving every day." He looked at Beth, but she responded only with a smile.

Rivcka Edelstein

Kibbutz Nof-Golan, Israel, 1973

Chapter 4

Jeremy and Beth enjoyed the visit with Ruth. They were in the yard saying good night to her when Saul, her husband, returned from accompanying the children to their respective dorms.

Ruth introduced Beth and then added, "Beth decided to relax for the evening, so why don't you and I go read a story to the children while they take a stroll?"

Jeremy and Beth headed out toward the fields. It was quiet and there was a sense of tranquility. They were close to the border and Jeremy decided there was no need to alarm her as long as they stayed within a safe limit. They didn't talk for a while. It was so peaceful. Jeremy felt that words were not necessary, and it seemed that Beth was content and absorbed in her own thoughts as well.

They arrived at an observation point over the valley with a small path leading to it. Jeremy stepped forward and then extended his hand to Beth for support to climb. The touch of her fingers was like electricity on his palm — shaky and warm. He held onto her fingers and was very much aware of his own reaction. They kept holding hands even though it was no longer necessary.

When they stopped walking, Jeremy pointed out to Beth the different sites in every direction. The sun was setting, reflecting warmly on the village below them.

Jeremy explained, "This is a Lebanese Village. Not long ago, they lived in peace with its Israeli neighbors. Things changed recently…"

"Can we sit here? It is a beautiful site," Beth whispered.

They sat silently and then Beth started, "I have not felt relaxed like this for a long time. Here, I'm able to avoid thinking about the many things weighing on my mind… I feel good. I don't know if I am expressing myself clearly."

"You're doing a good job so far."

"Jeremy, when your fingers touched mine, a few moments ago, I knew you did it out of courtesy, to help me climb, but it felt good. I…"

"I felt the same way. It's strange since we just met."

"Correction: we met over three years ago. You were shy and quiet, but not unnoticeable. I felt you didn't like me and that we were in competition."

"I was not in competition. Rami likes you a lot and my aunt likes you, too. I don't think she ever accepted the fact that you and Rami were 'just friends.'"

"Your aunt is great; I think most of Rami's friends would agree. I really missed them when they left for Israel."

"I missed them when they returned to the United States. Even though Sharon and I are closer in age and are good friends, Rami and I share more interests. We became even closer the year I was in the United States since Sharon was already away at college. When we meet, it's as though we have just seen one another the day before, even when we haven't seen each other for months. They are supposed to be coming for a visit soon. Maybe you will still be here."

"It depends on when they are coming. Anyway, if I don't see them here, I will see them as soon as I get back."

It was getting dark.

"We should go back inside the gate. It is not safe…"

Beth quickly stood up. "I wasn't aware that we were that close to the border. I've heard stories about terrorists. They give me the chills. Where's the border?"

"The observation point we sat on is the border." He paused. "You should become familiar with the different border markings in case you decide to go for a stroll by yourself. Be sure not to stay out of the gate after dark."

By now they had already reached the bottom of the hill heading back to the kibbutz. They walked hand in hand, naturally, unlike earlier when her hand was merely placed in his. Once they entered the gate, he closed it behind them with the lock and explained that anyone who arrived would now have to ring the bell and identify themselves before the gate would be opened by the guards.

"This is quite an experience for me. I hope my parents don't find out about this; my mother would remain sleepless until I returned."

"Are you going to be sleepless now that you know?"

"Are you kidding? Why should I be nervous? I trust that the guards are doing a good job. Anyway, I feel safer here than walking in New York City, where crime has been running rampant. I knew that the kibbutz was close to the border, but I didn't realize just how close."

They were walking quietly again, each immersed in their own thoughts. Jeremy questioned his interest in Beth, but he knew he wasn't just acting out of a sense of responsibility to his cousin. He tried not to read too much into it, knowing it was going to end in a few weeks. *Friendships can last beyond Beth's stay here.* At that point, friendship was the right word he sought. There was a girl he saw on his leaves to the city. Nothing serious and no commitment, but they were considered to be "going together" and not what his cousin would call "just friends."

"It has been a long day for you. Would you like me to walk you to Ruth's or would you like to come to my room?"

Beth shot him a look of surprise and Jeremy quickly clarified.

"You can meet my roommate Ben; he is supposed to be arriving later tonight from Tel Aviv."

"Your room is fine if you're sure I am not keeping you from your work."

"What work?" he asked smiling.

Silence Broken

"I don't know; I just don't want to impose."

In Jeremy's room, Beth felt very self-conscious. She looked at the books and records on the shelves and then noticed an anthology of poems on the night table near one of the beds.

She reached to pick up the book and Jeremy explained, "That is my nightly reading. Every night I read a few poems before I fall asleep. Each time I read them, I find new meanings in each."

"I love poetry," she said enthusiastically, as if answering a question. They were sitting close to each other, reading and talking about one of the poems that were familiar to both of them. The time passed quickly.

Ben entered the room unannounced, looked surprised when he noticed the guest, and began to excuse himself. Jeremy called after him to come and meet Beth. Ben, having noticed how close they were sitting, felt as though he had interrupted them. Ben was attentive as Jeremy told him how he had met Beth this afternoon and also three years prior. Ben made a few comments and then tried to pick up some necessities to leave and find an empty bed for the night. He would expect Jeremy to do the same if he were in a similar situation.

He was on his way again when Jeremy asked him in Hebrew not to leave and added, "It's not what you think."

Beth tried to figure out what was happening. Jeremy noticed her apprehension, and, turning to Ben, explained in English, "Beth is sleeping at Ruth's place. It is late and we all have to get up in the morning." He turned to Beth and continued, "Why don't I take you back?"

Beth looked at her watch and was surprised to see that it was close to midnight. They had read and talked for hours. She really was enjoying the evening.

"Nice meeting you, Ben."

"Likewise," he replied when she shook his hand.

Beth followed Jeremy outside. They walked quietly. She finally broke the silence.

"I really had a great evening. I'm glad you suggested the walk." After a moment of silence, she added, "I hope we can do it again."

"You bet," Jeremy smiled.

They arrived at Ruth's cottage. He stood there not knowing what action was appropriate to take under the circumstances — to act on what he felt or on what was expected of him. Beth felt uncomfortable just leaving. Yet she did not feel comfortable doing anything else, despite her racing heart. She finally leaned forward and kissed him lightly on the cheek.

"Good night, Jeremy. I am glad I had the chance to meet you again and see for myself what Rami was telling me during the winter break in 1970." She ran toward the entrance before he could respond.

"Likewise," he whispered after her.

He walked back to his room slowly. He felt strong excitement. Although he tried to quell it, he knew that if someone had told him earlier that afternoon that something like this might happen to him he would have said it was impossible.

* * *

Over the next few weeks Beth and Jeremy spent a great deal of time together. After his return from the seminar in Tel Aviv, he worked during the day while she spent the time at the school or in Ruth's office. They would meet in the afternoon, chat, go to dinner, and take long walks.

The members of the *gar'in* accepted Beth and Jeremy as a *zoog* — a couple — even sooner than Jeremy and Beth saw themselves as such. Effrat was especially nice to Beth, feeling that Beth was a terrific choice for Jeremy if she could not have him herself. Ben tried to make himself scarce as to give them some space and privacy since they could not use Ruth's house for being alone together.

Jeremy recognized the strength in his feelings toward Beth from the first night when they took their walk together. However, he was confused about Beth's reactions to his physical advances. She responded excitedly to his hand touching hers, but closer moves on his part caused her to withdraw. She seemed uncomfortable with such intimacy. He was not sure how to act. He definitely did not want to offend her. Her behavior, it seemed to him, suggested that she looked for more intimacy, but when he tried to accommodate her, she pulled back embarrassed, shivering and shaking. Sometimes she even looked frightened.

"I feel I owe you an explanation, but I don't know how to start." Beth said one evening. It was about a month after her arrival at the kibbutz, and two months since she left her home. Beth and Jeremy were taking their nightly walk. She started the conversation after a few minutes of silent walking.

Jeremy not knowing what was coming next decided silence was the best approach for the moment.

"I know I want to be close to you, to be touched by you, and to feel safe and secure in your arms, but when you get closer, things happen to me that cause me to pull away. I don't want to pull away, but my body takes over. It has nothing to do with you, it's me. I hope you don't think that I'm a tease." She stopped and turned to look at Jeremy.

Jeremy felt as though she had read his thoughts during the last few weeks. He was pleased that she approached the topic, even admired her for it. He put his arms around her and pulled her close.

"I do feel you pull away, but I don't think you are a tease and I don't want you to do anything that makes you feel uncomfortable."

"It is not that I feel uncomfortable; I want to be closer to you, but for some reason, I fight myself." The words came out as she meant them, but he did not understand.

"Why fight yourself? We don't have to do it. We can wait." Jeremy said, gently stroking her hair. He had wanted her long ago, but had restrained himself. He did not know how she felt about the future. He realized that for him, however, Beth was not a summer affair. He knew it when he broke up with his girlfriend on his last trip to Tel Aviv. He wanted Beth for life and, despite his overwhelming desire for her, he was willing to wait. He wanted her to set the pace and if it meant months, or longer, he was willing to wait until she was ready.

"You don't understand," she said pulling back and looking at him. "I don't want to wait!"

Jeremy leaned down to kiss her and she watched him as she moved her lips toward his. There was no doubt what she had in mind and he was neither ready, nor willing to resist. They kissed, first gently and then hungrily as they gave in to their desires. He hugged her tightly and it felt as though she had always belonged in his arms. This was how he dreamed it would be.

Jeremy was glad they waited — it was better when Beth seemed to want him and wasn't fighting him. Strong urges stirred in them.

Jeremy finally pulled away and in a hoarse voice he said, "I think we should turn back."

Beth was too aroused and not prepared to listen. A few minutes ago, she finally was able to fight off the frightening and intruding thoughts. Temporarily, she was able to block out the frequently tormenting images that rushed into her mind. At last warmth flooded her body from head to toe. Now she didn't want to stop. She felt that Jeremy loved her and that she was safe to feel the way she did with him. His arms were a source of strength for her. She wanted to be even closer to him. Despite the "brainwashing" by her father, she sensed that feeling like this with

Jeremy was healthy. Beth ignored Jeremy's hesitations and got closer to him again, but he was persistent.

"Let's go back before we do something we might regret."

"Would you regret it?" she asked.

"It is different for guys," he said quietly.

"Not if we both want the same thing... Unless you don't feel the same... Maybe I am assuming..." She stopped, but Jeremy could no longer hold back. He pulled her close to him, kissing her passionately, until she responded as strongly, moving her hands down his back and up inside his shirt. The touch of her hands on his bare skin excited him even more than he could bear.

He whispered into her ear, "Beth, this is not the place."

"Why not? I think it is the perfect place." She was surprised by her own comment. For a split second, she wondered what it was about this place that made her feel this way. She felt excitement and desire when Jeremy's hands touched her skin. She felt good about her feelings. Unlike the other times, the other places, the other hands where she felt shame and disgust.

"Beth, are you sure?" he asked again, but she responded only with her body, pressing herself closer to him. The closer she got to Jeremy, the calmer she felt. Those horrifying images that repeatedly interrupted her when she got close to anybody were not there. She welcomed their absence. She didn't want to think; she was afraid that thinking would bring them back. She just wanted to feel Jeremy's warmth and closeness.

Jeremy did not need any further encouragement. What followed neither one of them could have expected earlier that evening.

He gently pulled her down; she was glued to him as though afraid he would change his mind. She knew that she did not want the beautiful sensations inside her to stop, only to grow. She took his shirt off and with one hand he put it on the ground, spreading it to cover as much of the earth as possible. She lay down on the shirt, pulling him along with her...

His fingers roamed between her legs and he felt her stiffen. He stopped. Beth shivered. *Oh my God, they are coming back... Please make them go away.* She prayed for strength to win in her fight against the intruding images. She took hold of Jeremy's hand, placing it back where it belonged... She knew he understood because he continued...

* * *

They continued to lie in each other's arms, neither of them wanting to move, both satisfied. There was no need for words.

The sun, once a big red ball in the western horizon, had completely disappeared.

Jeremy was the first to speak. "Beth, we should move indoors; it's not safe for us to be here this late." Reluctantly Beth got up. She watched him as he pulled his shirt from the ground. Just before he put the shirt on she reached for him, pushing her breasts against his chest and kissed him. He responded, loving every move of her touch. He kissed her breasts once more before she put on her bra.

He knew he loved her before they had even touched one another, but now he knew he didn't want to be without her.

Holding each other as closely as possible, they walked toward the gate.

Near Ruth's house he pulled her close, kissed her, and whispered, "You've released an insatiable thirst in me; I don't know what I am going to do when you're not near."

Silence Broken

Kibbutz Nof-Golan, Israel, 1973

Chapter 5

She approached the tree trunk and, as she expected, he was already there looking across to the other side of the valley. He seemed content. She glanced in the same direction as the sun set over the horizon. In the distance, the top of the Galilee Mountains looked like a picture painted with orange and gold colors. It was a breathtaking sight and she felt at peace.

He noticed her approach, reached his hand towards her, and pulled her down to sit beside him. The sun gradually disappeared behind the distant mountains and the lights from the scattered settlements slowly replaced those of nature.

"This country is my home," Jeremy said after a long silence. "I couldn't be happy any place else." He leaned against the tree and continued to stare into space.

"I know how you feel. It might sound strange, but I would like it to be my home too." Beth was speaking very quietly.

He turned to her and she was looking at him, clearly waiting for a response. He finally spoke, carefully selecting his words.

"I want to believe it very much; it's very important for me. I know you feel you mean it now, at this moment, but I wonder how you will feel once you go back to the United States."

"Believe me, I mean it; I'm happier here than I have been in years at home."

He looked at her intensely and reached his hand out to lightly touch her cheek.

"I love you Beth, very much . . ."

"I love you, too," she whispered back shyly.

He put his hand behind her neck and drew her face closer to his, gently kissing her and then, his voice barely audible, he whispered, "I think I've actually always loved you."

"Always?" she asked in a surprised and teasing tone.

"I am known to be accurate in my use of words. I meant always, even when you behaved like a spoiled brat who quickly jumped to conclusions; I loved you even then. You had some attractive qualities in you, despite your quick lashing tongue. I guess your words hurt me even more because I loved you."

"I am sorry. I was a spoiled brat, but you were an obstacle in my path to victory. It wasn't you, I would have been against anyone who stood in my way; Rami was my friend and your presence drew his attention away from me."

"Did you have a crush on him?"

"Yes, but only for a short time. He was absolutely my best friend. In those far away years, he knew all my thoughts, feelings, and experiences — good and bad — I shared everything with him. He had such good insight and was a great listener. He supported me when I was right and argued with me when I was wrong, and I was wrong a lot of the time. He was the only one I could talk to. When we went to high school, things changed in my life, things I couldn't share." Her tone changed and she was close to tears. He heard the choked sadness and tried to break the silence.

"Rami is very fond of you. Even when I was deeply hurt by your comments, he did not let me say anything bad about you; he defended you."

"Rami is still my best friend, but things have changed in my life and I am not as free . . ."

"What do you mean?" Jeremy asked curiously, especially since she had commented twice about the change in her life. During her silence, Beth's facial expression changed and Jeremy looked back into the distance. By now he was more than curious about what happened in Beth's life to make her run away. Beth broke the silence only with a comment about the beautiful colors on the distant mountains.

It was clear that Beth wanted to avoid the previous subject, obviously not willing to discuss it further, at least not now. He sensed it was something very painful and maybe even embarrassing, because, aside from this issue, she had been very open with him. He was not about to push her. He hoped that in time she could tell him everything without reservations. He loved her so deeply that he was sure that, whatever took place before that summer, they could overcome it and move on.

"I saw my parents while I was in Tel Aviv," he said, trying to lighten the mood.

"How are they?" From her tone of voice, it was clear that she was thankful for his understanding and not pressing her to answer his question.

"Actually, I only saw my mother since my father was meeting with a guest lecturer from the United States. They are both doing fine. She and I had a very interesting talk . . ." He looked at Beth mischievously as he put an extra emphasis on the word "interesting". She waited curiously for the rest.

"We talked about you."

"Me?!"

"Yes" he said, satisfied with himself.

"How did you come to me? Did you run out of other topics? I heard about you and your mother from Effrat. She told me that you like to tease her about her belief in the medicinal value of different herbs, about her cooking, and about her political views."

"You mean her lack of political views," he smiled remembering lively discussions he had with his mother. He loved his mother very dearly, but did not agree with some of her extreme opinions on several issues, some of which Beth had just mentioned.

"No, we didn't discuss any of these topics. As a matter of fact, I was there for only a few minutes when your name came into the conversation."

"What did I do to deserve that?"

"It wasn't what you did, it was what I did."

"Jeremy Offir, would you please make some sense. You have already triggered my curiosity…please," she added, when she realized that he was just looking at her and smiling with no intention of saying anything.

"When I showed up at the front door without calling, my mother was surprised to see me and commented that I seemed different. I entered the apartment and she began with the interrogation. She decided I was calmer and more content, obviously, the effects of a woman. When I didn't deny the accuracy of her insight, she became excited and after bombarding me with questions, finally said, 'I must meet any girl that has this kind of effect on you.' She was very happy with the way I described you, her only concern was that you were not Israeli."

He noticed Beth's facial expression; she was waiting to hear the rest, so he continued.

"I assured her about your excellent 'breeding.' She always had great respect for psychiatrists. My father used to tease her that she has a blind admiration for the profession since, from his experiences, it bore no resemblance to reality. I vividly remember the first time they met your parents — at my aunt's house in 1970. Later that evening, my mother didn't stop making comparisons between my father and yours, in fun of course, but my father didn't see it that way. He got very upset and walked out of the room. All joking aside, my mother feels Dr. Robinoff is a super guy, very intelligent and warm."

Beth started to feel very agitated. "What did you tell your mom about me?" she interrupted in the middle of Jeremy's reminiscing.

Jeremy was confused by her tone of voice and obvious agitation. He moved to the end of his story.

"We concluded the conversation with her comment, 'He must have done a good job raising her — look at her excellent effect on you.' Well, I couldn't argue with that."

Beth felt her stomach and her throat tighten. *Little did they know about her father, "the psychiatrist."*

Jeremy noticed the change in her face and he suddenly felt uncomfortable. He would have given anything to help her with whatever was tormenting her but how could he if she didn't tell him what it was.

Beth regained her composure and asked, "So what did you tell her about me?" She felt and sounded anxious.

"Do I sense somebody fishing for compliments?" He said, trying to lighten up the situation.

"I am trying to find out what you see in me."

"I love you. I love everything about you. You are in my thoughts all day and all night. Beth, I feel good all over and I guess it is reflected in my face; my mother saw it."

"How could you love *everything* about me without knowing anything about me, I mean prior to my arrival here?"

Once again, he realized there was something from the past that was haunting her. He tried to reassure her.

"You are wrong; what must I do to convince you of that? Whatever happened before you came here is in the past and is behind us; I know what I've seen since you arrived. I've seen you with my friends, with the children of the kibbutz, at work. In short, I like everything that I saw. I love you. I don't care what may have happened before you arrived here, please believe me."

The last few words were said very softly while he held her face close to his. He kissed her on the forehead and when he noticed that she was crying, he kissed her eyes, slowly and tenderly.

"Beth, on more than one occasion I have sensed that something from the past is tormenting you. I pray that one of these days you will trust me enough to tell me. I want you to know that whatever it is, I am here and I love you. I don't know what else to say or do to convince you of that."

He bent down and kissed her on her lips with a long and reassuring kiss. She was responsive and he felt her tight muscles finally relaxed. He held her close and she rested her head on his shoulder.

* * *

As the days passed, Jeremy noticed that, though she still was not sleeping or eating well, most of the times Beth seemed less tormented. Beth herself felt that when she was with Jeremy, most of the time she felt quite relaxed and had some relief from her haunting memories and thoughts. At other times, the horror she experienced in her dreams terrorized her and ruined her temporary peace of mind. At those times, she had to try hard to cover her fear and pain.

However, when she was alone, the old doubts crept in and forcefully intruded upon her beautiful moments. She dreaded the possibility that her past would be disclosed. She constantly was afraid that someone would find out what she had done. She knew she had not wanted those things to happen, but sometimes she doubted herself: had she done anything to encourage it? Was she guilty for letting it continue?

Whenever these thoughts were present she started to cry, first softly and later uncontrollably.

I don't deserve love and I certainly don't deserve happiness. How could Jeremy and his friends like me when I don't even like myself? Look at me, full of horror and ghosts. Can't they see it is all an act? Can't they see beyond the mask I am wearing? I know what would happen if the mask were removed. Nobody would like me. They would despise me if they knew the truth. I wouldn't blame them . . . Look at me, what am I? Who would want damaged goods like me?

Silence Broken

The memories of all those moments, days, and years flashed in front of her during those hearty crying periods, like film strips from a fast movie. She was in the center of it, the young innocent Beth that was dragged into filth and shame by someone who betrayed her. She would cry even louder as she saw herself in the movie strip as the powerless young teenager torn by the conflicting emotions she felt against those who took charge of her feelings, used her unconditional trust, and manipulated her love. Then, towards the end of the film was a sign "No Exit." She cried even more. She knew for the last few years that she was trapped in her past without hope of escape.

The nightmares she had for the past three years continued, but less frequently. There were variations, but in each case she was running from one room to another being chased by this big headless monster who blamed her for being a spiteful nuisance . . .

She remembered what she was told would happen if she ever chose to reveal her secret. It scared her enough that she didn't tell. She didn't dare remove the mask, even for Jeremy. *How could he, or anyone, understand?*

* * *

Beth and Effrat watched as Jeremy and Ben played paddleball on the beach.

"They are good," Beth commented.

"Yeah!" Effrat agreed whole-heartedly. "They've played together since they were seven or eight."

"I met Jeremy's mother. She was wonderful to me."

"Why wouldn't she be? I thought you had met her three years ago."

"I didn't. I met Jeremy with his cousin Rami. My parents met his parents at his aunt's house."

"What are you doing about your parents' pressure?" Effrat knew about Beth and Jeremy's situation, and felt frustrated with Beth's parents as well.

"I told them I would like to start college later. I'm too young."

"And?"

"And nothing. I'm here."

* * *

The sun poured down over Old Jaffa, filling the streets with warmth. Jeremy and Beth walked, holding hands, along the narrow streets of the rehabilitated section. They approached the edge of the park where they can see the sunset over the Mediterranean Sea and stood in each other's arms, soaking in the sunlight.

Silence Broken

Kibbutz Nof-Golan, Israel, October 1973

Chapter 6

There was a loud pulsing sound coming from outside… Beth woke in a sweat. At first, she thought it was one of her nightmares, but even when she was completely alert the shrieking and rhythmic noise continued. The sirens were real, like the familiar fire house sirens in the United States.

Where do they keep the fire engines on the kibbutz?

She covered her body with a blanket and looked out the window nearest the bed. People were running in all directions with apparent apprehension, but no fire or even smoke was visible. She grabbed her jeans and shirt, and started dressing while making her way to the window at the opposite end of the room. She stopped for a second, making sure her shirt was buttoned, and then opened the blinds. She only saw people running with no sign of a fire.

"I'm glad you're dressed already," Jeremy said as he burst into the room, "You said you'd like to spend most of Yom Kippur sleeping and I was afraid you would still be asleep."

"You must be kidding, with these sirens?!"

"Well, I guess they did their job — to alert people." He smiled tensely, but it was clear to Beth that he was worried about something.

"You'd better get moving; we don't know how close it is."

"Where is it?"

"We really don't know."

"What do you mean 'you really don't know?'" she asked, surprised.

"You don't need to worry, just stay with the women and children until you hear the sirens again. You do know where to go, don't you?"

Beth noticed that the sirens had stopped and it was quiet outside. She noticed that Jeremy was digging in his closet, pulling out different items.

"Why don't you know where it is, just look for the smoke." She mumbled wiping the sleep out of her eyes. "Why do I have to stay with the women and children and where am I supposed to be going? Don't they need you to help with the fire?" Beth took a deep breath to go on when Jeremy lifted his head out of the closet.

"What are you searching for in the closet?" she asked impatiently.

"Beth, *what* are you talking about? What fire?" He was looking directly at her trying to figure out what he had missed.

"What do you mean 'what fire'?" Beth looked at him. He was obviously still waiting for an answer to his earlier question. Completely confused, she was no longer sure what they were talking about.

"The sirens… The fire…" she hesitated.

"Beth, there is no fire; there is a war!"

Beth froze.

Jeremy went on. "The sirens were not a call to the fire fighters, but to the people to run for the shelters, as soon as possible; these sirens are an 'air-raid'. Nobody knows the extent of the war, but it's clear that we are in the midst of it. We were all called to our units earlier this morning"

Jeremy noticed that Beth was still motionless. He moved closer to her, placing his arms around her shoulders in a reassuring manner.

"I'm sorry, Beth, but I must leave you and I don't know when I'll return. Are you OK? You haven't said anything."

Silence Broken

She didn't respond.

He continued, "Beth, you must hurry to the shelter. Please remain there until you hear the 'all-clear sirens'. The closest shelter is near the Gordon's living quarters; when you have the chance, ask where the other shelters are. It is important to run to the nearest one, depending on where you are when the sirens sound."

"You're saying there is a war?" She finally grasped the information. She was shaking and sweating profusely. "The Arabs attacked Israel?" she said in disbelief, trying hard to control her shaking. She grasped the significance of the news. She started pacing the room and moving her hands through her hair restlessly.

"You are going and you don't know when I might see you? We are only a few feet away from the border." By now she was hysterical and looked pale. It was clear that she had comprehended the details and was making an effort to evaluate the ramifications of the situation.

"Beth, I hate to leave you like this."

She motioned to him that she understood.

"I must pack my basic gear and meet the army truck at the dining hall in a few minutes. Effrat will keep you informed as the situation becomes clearer." He paused. "Have you seen my tall paratrooper boots nearby?"

With no intention of running for the shelter before he left, Beth began looking around for the boots. Jeremy realized what she was doing and he didn't stop her; running to the shelter now might be even more dangerous. Beth returned from the hall holding the boots and handed them to Jeremy without meeting his eyes.

How could I be useful?

Beth stood for a second as Jeremy got dressed.

It's Yom Kippur and he's fasting, but...

While he was putting on his boots, she rushed to the kitchen and started packing some food for him.

Rivcka Edelstein

Her hands were shaking. The only scenes of war she had ever experienced were in movies that she had seen about England during World War II and news clips about the war in Vietnam. She started to cry quietly.

Jeremy stood behind her. He noticed her body shake, and saw the tears roll down her cheeks. He hated leaving her like this, in the midst of a war that was not hers. Not wanting to startle her, he touched her shoulders lightly and turned her to face him. She seemed embarrassed that he caught her crying. With her left hand, she attempted to reach the wet cheek and wipe her eyes, but Jeremy held her hand in his and bent down to kiss her tear-filled eyes.

"Don't worry, Beth. The whole thing will be over before your letter even reaches your anxious parents."

"My parents!" She screamed, awakened. "I didn't even think about them; I guess I should call."

"I doubt that you'll find any international lines open; your best bet would be a letter." He whispered and brought her closer to him, kissing her with long gentle kisses which would hold him for a while.

Despite what he had told Beth, he was not so sure himself what was happening or how grave the situation might be. The *chevreh* had speculated about it in the first broadcast earlier that morning. Everyone was aware that this conflict was different from the war in 1967. At that point, it wasn't even clear how many fronts were involved. They had heard that the Syrians and the Egyptians attacked Israel's northern and southern settlements.

"Take care of yourself, please…" Beth gasped when Jeremy released her momentarily.

Her mind was overwhelmed with concern for Jeremy. He was going to the front and risking his life; it was possible he wasn't coming back.

"Don't worry, I'll be back soon. Take care of yourself," he said as he took her in his arms, giving her one last long and tight squeeze.

Silence Broken

"Wait for me, Beth," he whispered tenderly in her ear. He was worried about something else. He was aware of the pressure Beth felt from her parents to return to the United States.

Jeremy picked up his gear and was approaching the door when he noticed that she was following him.

"Don't! It's not safe for you to walk outside now before the 'all-clear sirens' sound. Lie down against that far wall, away from the windows. Remember Beth, when you hear the air-raid sirens, run to the nearest shelter. Keep yourself busy, time will pass fast, and soon it will be over."

He paused to look at her. "You know I love you very much. I want you to remember it because I won't have the chance to say it to you during the next few days."

Jeremy opened the door and in one quick motion he closed it behind him. He ran toward the dining hall.

Beth felt isolated and afraid. Time seemed to crawl and she fell asleep still waiting for the "all-clear sirens." She woke up to a gentle touch on her shoulder and immediately opened her eyes. She didn't know how long she had been asleep and if she had missed hearing the "all-clear sirens." Disoriented, and hoping it was all a bad dream, she heard Effrat's voice.

"We were worried about you. When we realized that you hadn't made it to the shelter, I decided to come and see if you were OK. What was holding you back? I hope you aren't too scared. I guess it is your first taste of a war. It will be over soon, you'll see. Come, let's go. The rest of our friends are still in the shelter, it will probably take a while yet because we are on the border..."

Effrat went on as usual, without allowing time for Beth to respond. However, Beth didn't hear a word after the second sentence. She realized it was not a dream at all. *There is a war, and I am in the middle of it. And Jeremy was on his way to the front.*

Effrat's voice was coming in and out of her thoughts... What was she talking about?

Beth couldn't make out her words, but it was clear that she was rushing her to move.

Effrat suggested she take sleeping garments and bedding, just in case…and maybe some arts and crafts to pass the time. In a daze, Beth finally started to gather some of the items Effrat had mentioned and then followed her, running to join the others in the shelter. She found herself wondering about food for the break-the-fast at sundown. With all the commotion, she thought no one else had taken care of it. She hesitated to ask and decided to wait and see; there were still many hours until the end of the fast.

When she was with the other young women, the hours moved faster. Conversation in the shelter was intense and Effrat translated as much as possible. Everyone was confident it was going to be over soon. Beth started to believe it too. *After all, this was not their first war. They had experience waiting for their loved ones in the past,* she thought to herself.

Despite the community's confidence, Beth found the waiting excruciating, praying that it would, indeed, be over soon.

However, for the people in the northern settlements, it was a long day and a very long night in the shelters, but it was only the first of many such nights to come.

Silence Broken

Kibbutz Nof-Golan, Israel, October 1973

Chapter 7

The first few days of the Yom Kippur War were very confusing, especially with the sporadic and incomplete news broadcasts.

After a number of chaotic days, Jeremy's unit was ordered to the Egyptian front. The transfer was delayed until the next morning to give the soldiers a break. It was a short break before their deployment to the new destination. Considering the distance to where they were being sent and the length of time they might be away, a few hours would serve well in the long run to re-energize the young men and to boost morale. The soldiers were surprised since "urgency" had been the motto of the week, but their commander was thinking ahead. They had been on duty with no relief of any kind for a number of days.

Also, the commander gave permission for two soldiers from Jeremy's unit to go back to their individual kibbutz, each one from a different kibbutz. Jeremy was the one selected from his group.

Jeremy was delighted with the unexpected break before the scheduled departure. He hoped to bring back a supply of care packages from the kibbutz. He knew the kibbutz members would be very generous in their preparation of care packages for the soldiers. He was also happy to have a chance to see Beth.

He was concerned about her, a foreigner in the middle of a war that wasn't hers. When he left on Yom Kippur, at the outbreak of the war, he didn't know what to expect. Now he knew better; the scenes of blood and destruction he witnessed were horrifying. He didn't know how long it would last, but knowing Beth was waiting for him helped him endure the savagery of the battlefield and the endless stretches during which they had to forego sleep.

* * *

All of the male teachers had been mobilized. Ruth was happy to accept Beth's help at the school and with the children. Beth had already completed her project and was eager to be useful and busy.

Beth had been staying in Jeremy's room while both he and Ben were away. Jeremy headed to his room as soon as he made arrangements with the kitchen to prepare the care packages for his unit. Beth wasn't there. He backtracked to look for her and found her sitting beside the shelter, surrounded by a group of children.

Beth looked up, unable to believe her eyes. She ran toward him, but hesitated a few yards short of where he stood, unsure of expressing affection in public. Jeremy continued toward her and scooped her up from her spot, hugging and kissing her without restraint. Beth was caught up in his desire.

She was not able to express in words her aching for him. She desperately wanted to hear his voice and to feel his arms around her. Since the war had broken out, Jeremy's female friends were taking good care of her. They invited Beth to join them in every activity and trying to reduce her apprehension about the war. Regardless of how much she tried to get involved, she missed Jeremy.

Beth released herself from Jeremy's tight hug, went into the school building. She requested relief from her supervision of the children so she could spend a few hours with Jeremy. Ruth was happy to oblige and went outside to welcome Jeremy.

Holding Beth's hand, he guided her toward the secretarial office while telling her of his longing for her. He did not want to talk about the front or his experiences and traumas; he wanted to fill himself with Beth and his love for her. As they walked, her gaze was fixed on his face, still unable to catch her breath from her initial excitement.

Jeremy and Beth approached the kibbutz switchboard. Jeremy took a folded piece of paper from his pocket. Beth noticed that there was a long hand-written list of names and phone numbers. Jeremy dialed one number after another as he delivered the messages his friends had asked him to communicate to their families. His last call was to his parents.

Beth waited patiently beside him, as her head leaned on his shoulder. When he finished, she heard him say, *"Shalom, Ema, V'lehitrao Bekarov. (Goodbye, Mom, and see you soon.)"* Jeremy replaced the receiver and looked at his watch, which read 9:30 AM. He put his arm around Beth and led her to his room. Before the war, Jeremy realized that, although in social situations, Beth came across as assertive and friendly, she was actually shy, timid, inhibited, and hesitant in intimate situations. Once she overcame her initial impulse to withdraw, she was actually very receptive, giving, and loving when he was affectionate with her. Jeremy remembered how difficult it was for Beth to let him get close to her earlier in their intimate moments. It took a lot of reassurance on his part. His actions, support, acceptance, and, most of all, his love encouraged her to open up and trust him.

Now, Jeremy noticed that some of Beth's shyness had returned and he realized it would take her time to become comfortable in their intimacy again. He didn't expect to make love to her.

Beth had a long time to think while Jeremy was gone. Now she felt the urgency to clarify a few things before he rejoined the unit and headed south. Beth feared that Jeremy believed she had previous sexual experiences — but she hadn't, at least not in the sense he might be thinking. In the past, whenever she tried to say anything about it, Jeremy didn't let her speak. He made it quite clear that it didn't matter to him what happened before he met Beth that summer; he loved her and he wanted to hear that she loved him. The rest was irrelevant.

Now, again, Beth barely managed to say a few words before Jeremy realized where her comments were leading. He was disappointed. He thought she had understood that he did not want to waste time, energy, or words on this with the short visit he had. She stopped.

He decided to take a shower — fresh warm running water was a luxury he did not expect to have during the coming days.

"Would you like to join me in the shower?" he asked.

"You aren't serious?!" She said in a tone that left him unsure of how she meant it.

He decided not to pursue it; he didn't want Beth to withdraw into her emotional shell. He would be happy to lie down and hold her while he closed his eyes for a couple of hours before he had to leave.

He came out of the bathroom dressed comfortably and sat beside Beth on the bed. With one arm, he held her tightly and close to him; with the other, he removed a lock of her hair from her forehead. She noticed the tension and pain on his face and reached out and touched him tenderly. She loved him so much.

Under her breath she whispered, "I want to feel closer to you."

Those words were the warmest and the most forward Jeremy ever heard from Beth since they met. He responded immediately. Jeremy kissed her intensely and she responded. They were both hungry for each other, and their mouths, hands, and bodies expressed it.

They made passionate love.

* * *

Later, while they rested in each other's arms, Jeremy told Beth, again, how much he had missed her. Beth talked very little but she said enough to reassure him that the feelings were mutual.

Time passed and Jeremy looked at his watch and whispered to Beth that he had to go back to his unit. They dressed quietly. Beth put fresh clothes in his gear, along with a variety of fresh fruits, a few packages of gum, and a big bag of sunflower seeds.

He turned her toward him, hugged her, and hoarsely whispered in her ear, "I love you, Beth Robinoff. I need to see,

Silence Broken

hear, and touch you. I love you very much. Never have doubts about that, never! Beth, I'll be back, please be here. Don't give in to your parents' demands. Don't disappear from my life."

She gazed up at him and didn't say a word.

Although she knew what Jeremy meant, she thought, yet she wanted to scream, *the only one disappearing these days is you.*

Since the end of August, her parents were pressuring her to return home. Afraid with every letter that she received from them, Jeremy dreaded that her parents would finally convince her to return. Now, with the outbreak of the war, American tourists and citizens were encouraged to leave Israel, and the U.S. embassy had provided special flights evacuating those who were stranded. Beth told Jeremy earlier that she hoped she could convince her parents to let her stay awhile longer. Although they never spoke about the future, Jeremy prayed Beth saw it as he did.

They walked in silence toward the dining hall where Jeremy picked up the packages for his unit and meet his ride. Before he boarded the waiting jeep, Jeremy hugged Beth tightly.

"I heard what you were trying to tell me earlier. I want you to believe me; I don't care about anybody or anything that happened before we met on the kibbutz. I know you love me. In the last few days, all of my thoughts were about my love for you. Although I have to go now and I don't know for how long, I do know that I'm coming back to be with you. Write to me. Remember, I love you very much; you should never have doubts about that — never! Beth, I am coming back, please be here."

He wiped the tears from Beth's cheeks and climbed onto the jeep. She cried and waved until the jeep was out of sight.

Rivcka Edelstein

Kibbutz Nof-Golan, Israel, October 1973

Chapter 8

Beth wrote every day. It took more than a week before Jeremy's letters began to arrive, but from the first five letters she received it was clear that he wrote daily. He wrote only about his love and longing for her and did not mention the horrors of the war, the lack of equipment, the casualties, and the rest of the grueling hardships. Those details she learned from the BBC News and stories from visiting soldiers. The military had been noticeably unprepared for the outbreak of a full-scale war. There were not enough supplies or ammunition, the equipment was old and poorly maintained, and the soldiers were fighting without relief and without sleep for days.

In the beginning, Beth was very worried about Jeremy, but became optimistic when she heard that Israel was "recovering" on the Egyptian front. Though there were still a few pockets where the Egyptians surrounded the Israeli forts, the Israeli army was able to halt progress of the Egyptians toward the Israeli settlements. She later heard that, not only had the Israeli army crossed the Suez Canal and moved toward Egyptian cities, but that the Egyptian Third Army was surrounded. She was filled with hope that Jeremy would return home soon.

Then the letters stopped coming. A few days went by without a word from Jeremy. Kibbutz members reassured Beth that it was common; sometimes there were delays in the collection and the delivery of mail from the soldiers.

She begged Effrat to call Jeremy's parents to see if they had any news from him. Effrat made several calls and the answers were always: "No news" or "Nothing yet."

She continued to write to the military address Jeremy gave her, but as the days passed, Beth fears intensified.

Each day, before she went to lunch, she stopped to pick up the mail, with great expectation. *Today his letter will be there!* And each day, for more than two weeks, there was nothing from Jeremy. On the seventeenth day since his last letter, there was still no word from him. Beth's tears came down and she rushed to the bathroom, to hide her tears, her disappointments, and her fears.

The Offir family, in Tel Aviv, and the kibbutz members were also very concerned. Finally, Professor Offir used his military connections to get in touch with the headquarters of Jeremy's unit. Even they had no information. He was told that the unit had been sent south to the Egyptian front. He already knew that fact. Also, he was told that as soon as there was more information he would be contacted.

A few days later, an army representative, accompanied by a military medical staff member, informed Professor and Mrs. Offir that their son was missing in action.

Effrat, with Beth's insistence, made her daily call to the Offirs. When she heard the news that Jeremy was M.I.A, she barely could talk. She took a deep breath before she turned to Beth. When Beth saw how distraught Effrat was, she feared the worst. Beth started to cry. Effrat hugged her. They both cried.

"He is alive!" Beth proclaimed to Effrat after a few minutes. "I know it!"

* * *

At nights Beth had a recurring dream with some kind of variation every night. In the dream, she wore a night gown and walked, barefoot, through war debris. She heard Jeremy calling for her. She walked towards his voice, stepping on black, burnt objects and trying to avoid stepping on body parts. As she neared the source of the voice, it drifted away, leaving a hollow echo in her ears. Finally, she saw Jeremy being grabbed by soldiers wearing different uniforms and being dragged away. She struggled to reach him but couldn't. She woke up each night screaming his name in terror and cried. *He couldn't be dead. He just couldn't be dead.*

News reports stated that many of the dead were buried and that there were still numerous unidentified bodies in the Sinai

Peninsula, east of the canal in the territory occupied by Egypt. Beth couldn't concentrate on her work with the children. She jumped whenever someone came in with news. She felt empty and alone.

To add to her stress, her parents insisted that she return back to the United States immediately. Since the end of the summer, her parents had been pressuring her to return home. She refused to return. They were not used to her disobeying them. When the war broke out their requests for her return were increasingly forceful. She was determined not to go back until she knew that Jeremy was safe.

In mid-November, the Offir family was neither among the families rejoicing for their returned sons nor among those grieving for their lost ones. Jeremy's name had not been listed with the names of prisoners of war submitted to the Red Cross by Egypt. His name wasn't on the list of the dead soldiers either. The Red Cross cautioned that the lists weren't complete since the field troops on both sides held prisoners whose names were not yet reported. Nobody knew when the complete lists would be ready and when the exchange of prisoners between Egypt and Israel might take place. It could be days or even months.

The phone calls from the United States became more and more threatening. Beth understood why her parents were pressuring her. Finally, her mother informed her that if she didn't return on the next available flight, her father was coming to Israel to get her.

With the state of uncertainty about Jeremy, Effrat suggested it might be best for Beth if she went home for a while. Beth understood that it would be the "mature step," as Effrat put it, to go home to straighten out her affairs. Yet, at the same time, she wanted to stay in Israel and wait for Jeremy. She chose to delay making a decision.

Effrat, as Beth's closest friend, was very concerned about Beth's state of health. Beth seemed paler than usual and was very agitated, snapping at people without provocation over even "the little things."

Finally, Effrat decided to ask.

"Beth, you seem listless, lethargic and have been looking quite ill and you... Are you OK? You should see the doctor."

Beth shrugged her shoulders.

"I know! I'm sorry I've been lashing out at you. I guess the stress and frustration of not knowing is getting to me." Beth decided to see the doctor to get something to reduce her constant irritability and crying. In answering his questions and elaborating upon her symptoms, she attributed her poor health to her constant stress.

"You said you are usually irregular," the doctor noted. "Your symptoms can, in fact, be explained by the extreme stress you are under," the doctor added, "Let me examine you..."

* * *

Her visit to the kibbutz doctor ended with Beth making the decision she tried to postpone for weeks.

She decided to listen to reason, both to Effrat's and her parents, though the reasons each side gave her were different. Now Beth was even more determined to confront her parents about her intentions. She felt that her plans to go to college and later to law school could wait.

"Plans were made to be changed. Nobody planned or foresaw the events that took place these last few months," she had said to Effrat

She missed Jeremy with every inch of her body. Though they hadn't spoken about marriage, they did talk about love and being together. She wasn't sure if it meant the same thing to him. Once again, she felt the need to tell Jeremy the truth about her past, her haunting nightmares and fears. She knew he must be told why she ran away from Long Island in the middle of the school year. *If we are to have a future together, there should be no secrets.* She knew, deep in her heart that he loved her. *But would he love me if he knew everything about me?* Most of all, she wanted to hear that he was alive and coming back, as he had promised.

With a hope that things would work out once Jeremy returned, Beth told Effrat that she decided to go back for a few weeks and would return as soon as possible.

Beth spent half of the night attempting to write a letter to Jeremy. Draft after draft she crumbled and threw it to the trash. With tears in her eyes, she wrote another draft.

She only had a couple of hours left before she had to leave for the airport, yet she still worked on a "proper" draft. She finally wrote a letter, smeared with her tears, folded it and placed it in a place she was certain Jeremy, and no-one else, would find it. After all, the content of the letter was intended for Jeremy's eyes only.

She jolted up by surprise when Ben knocked on the door that morning. He entered with Effrat following close behind him. Ben picked up Beth's two suitcases. Beth put a copy of her research paper into a folder, grabbed her carry-on bag and the three walked out. Beth said a tearful good-bye to the *chevreh*, ended by a long, tight hug from Effrat.

Effrat whispered in her ear, "He is OK; I can feel it in my bones. I know you do too. Stay strong my friend, don't let the sadness eat you alive. I'll miss you terribly, but I know you'll be back."

She told everyone that she would return soon and boarded the van to Ben Gurion Airport at Lod. As she pulled away from the kibbutz, she watched Effrat waving at her and mouthing the words "Come back soon!" Tears filled both the young women's eyes.

* * *

On the twenty-sixth day of the Jewish month of Heshvan, November 25, 1973, 50 days since the beginning of the war, Beth was headed back to New York.

Only a couple of hours after Beth had boarded her plane, Professor Offir received an early morning phone call which broke the news: "Be prepared for Jeremy's immediate return. You should know, however, that Jeremy's name is on the revised wounded list," the officer continued. "We don't know, at this point, how seriously he is hurt. Since he is coming from prison and not the hospital, we might assume his injuries are minor. He will be taken directly from the airport to Tel-Ha-Shomer hospital. You will be able to meet him at the airport."

Jeremy's parents were relieved to hear that he was alive. Professor Offir hoped the injuries his son sustained were indeed minor, but there were no guarantees.

"The doctors at Tel-Ha-Shomer perform miracles," he consoled his wife. "He will get the best medical care and social support there is — you know that."

He called Nof Golan, told the secretary of the kibbutz their news, and requested that he inform Jeremy's friends.

"We are hoping the injuries are slight; until we know more I suggest you tell only Ben that Jeremy is wounded; there is no need to worry the rest of the group."

* * *

The news of the returning prisoners of war from Egypt reached every home in Israel. Thousands of Israelis were at Ben Gurion Airport to cheer the returning heroes. Two hundred and thirty-two Israelis were exchanged for eight thousand and four hundred Egyptians. The strong sense of hope and faith that had gripped the Israeli public during the war weeks continued to sustain the public throughout the negotiations. It continued that November day as the crowd awaited the arrival of the first group of prisoners.

Everyone was kept at a distance to allow the planes to land safely and to secure the proper and immediate transfer of the wounded.

Rivcka Edelstein

Kibbutz Nof-Golan, Israel, November 1973

Chapter 9

The Red Cross planes landed at Ben Gurion airport carrying the released war prisoners. Jeremy's plane was second to land. Those who could walk unaided came out first, followed by the wounded who were helped along by Red Cross volunteers. Jeremy was carried on a stretcher towards the waiting helicopter and the medical staff paused to allow his group of relatives and friends to approach.

Jeremy's eyes searched anxiously among those who approached his stretcher. He was glad to see the familiar faces again; there were moments in the last few weeks when he didn't dare dream that he would be back alive. He looked around and started to shake. He wanted to ask, but was afraid to hear the answer.

He looked around to see as much as he could from his position on the stretcher. *Maybe in all the commotion I missed her face in the crowd.* Then he thought, *No way. I couldn't have missed that face. Where could she be?*

The whole time he was in prison he was sure that she would be there if and when he returned. The thoughts of her kept him going in captivity, despite the pain from his injuries and the torture of the endless humiliations and interrogations. In the darkness of his cell he had been comforted by the memories and images he had of Beth. The knowledge that she was waiting for him helped him endure the worst.

Where is she? He could hear his own strong and fast heartbeat.

He raised his head and gazed once again, in vain — he did not see her. He motioned for Ben to approach him and Ben came near the stretcher and bent down to hear Jeremy's whisper.

"Where is she? Where is Beth?" he asked slowly, trying to control the shakiness of his voice. There was no doubt in Jeremy's

Silence Broken

mind that Ben recognized his anguish, but he did not want the others to be aware of his despair.

"She left. From what I understood, she had to."

"What do you mean 'she had to?'" Jeremy said faintly. He wasn't sure he was ready to hear the reply. Ben put a hand on Jeremy's shoulder.

"Pressure from home; she waited as long as she could." Ben stopped. He hoped that was enough for Jeremy, but Jeremy's sad eyes sought more from Ben. He continued.

"Beth kept calling the States to delay her return while waiting for news about you, but up to the moment she left, the news about the prisoners and wounded was vague. She called several times from the airport to find out if you were listed as one of the returning prisoners, but nobody knew yet. You do know, old buddy, that we weren't sure you were among the living for weeks. Beth looked like walking death once it became clear that you were missing."

Ben was explaining as fast as he could so Jeremy could be transferred to the hospital. There were whispers among the women about another piece of news, but Ben did not mention it. There would be time for everything and some news should come directly from the source.

Jeremy's head fell back to the stretcher and he closed his eyes. Earlier, Jeremy refused morphine for the pain; he wanted to be alert when he saw Beth again. Now, the pain was unbearable. The medical personnel approached the stretcher again indicating that it was time to move on; he needed care and the sooner the better. For Jeremy, the ordeal was not over yet.

While awaiting the Red Cross plane to bring Jeremy back to Israel, the Israeli medical staff debriefed his parents about his condition. The doctors had received the information gathered by the Red Cross in their latest visit to the prisoners of war.

Jeremy had been wounded in a battle near the Suez Canal in the Sinai.

"Unfortunately, the severity of his injuries wasn't identified in the battle field, so he ended up in prison instead of a hospital," a medic explained to Jeremy's father. "The only medical help he received was just before the Red Cross's visit. He's in bad shape, but we can help him. He'll need a series of surgeries and it's very possible he may lose his leg."

Now, there was no time to waste. His hands and leg were severely injured and at risk. The medics raised the stretcher and started moving toward the waiting helicopter. Jeremy was the last to be put on the helicopter.

Everyone moved aside a few steps to allow the helicopter to take off; the wind and sand blew into their faces as they shielded their eyes and waved toward the departing helicopter. Jeremy's relatives and friends were the only ones left on the field.

As Ben approached the kibbutz van, he saw Deborah, Jeremy's mother, approaching and he walked toward her.

"What was all of that about?" she asked with a shortage of breath. Then she looked at Ben's face and added, "I'm worried, Jeremy seemed very agitated despite the medication. Ben, is there something I should know? Is there something I can do to help?"

Ben shrugged his shoulders and said, "You know I can't speak for him, Deborah. Why don't you ask him? "

"Ben, at this point we have to help him in whatever way we can — you know it and I know it. Jeremy needs a lot more than the help of surgeons to heal what happened. Would you please let me do my share?" she breathed deeply and somewhat desperately.

"You're right." he nodded.

There were a few seconds of silence. Ben was deep in his own thoughts, wondering how to help his friend. While waiting for Jeremy's plane to arrive earlier that morning, Ben was shaken by the description, given to him by another returning POW, of Jeremy's non-stop torture at the hands of his captors. He knew that Jeremy needed much more than surgeries. He didn't know how to tell Deborah about the extent of her son's suffering.

Silence Broken

"Well," she said impatiently.

"Listen, why don't I go with you to Tel Aviv? You can give me a ride, so I can be at the hospital as soon as he gets out of the recovery room, and we can talk on the way"

"That's a good plan. He needs both of us, we'll work together," she responded, relieved. She always liked Ben; he had been Jeremy's best friend for as long as she could remember and Jeremy was very lucky to have such a good friend.

During the ride to Tel Aviv, Ben told Deborah Offir what he could, carefully selecting his words, attempting to provide facts and skip rumors. He told her that Beth left for the U.S.A. earlier that morning.

Deborah knew about Beth and she liked her a great deal. However, she hadn't realized that Beth had to return home and how great of an impact her absence would affect Jeremy.

Rivcka Edelstein

Kibbutz Nof-Golan, Israel, November 1973

Chapter 10

Jeremy felt drained. With his eyes closed, he made a desperate attempt to sort things out, but couldn't.

Early that morning, he found out that he was going home. He knew all along that his country would do everything possible to get its soldiers back, no matter what the price; every soldier in Israel knew that. When he was being tortured, he sometimes felt he might never make it home alive, while at other times his faith was unshaken. No matter what the Egyptians did or said to him, he knew he was on the winning side.

During the last few weeks, his love for Beth and knowing that she was at Nof Golan among his friends helped him more than he could ever describe. His images of her were vivid and he held on to them through his torture and pain. He strongly believed that he remained alive and sane mostly because of her. Beth was woven into his plans, dreams, and hopes for the future. At no point did he seriously entertain the possibility that Beth might not be at the kibbutz.

Sure, at times of despair in his cell he feared the possibility that he might not see her or anybody again. He also assumed that she might be pressured to go home and he might not be there to help her fight the pressure. Yet as these negative thoughts came to him, he repeatedly fought them off.

He and Beth had an understanding. He had told her how deeply he loved her and he believed it was mutual. Although they never said as much, he counted on a lasting relationship with Beth.

Now he was no longer sure. He sought clues in Ben's words and in Beth's past behavior. His pain was overwhelming and he could no longer ward it off.

* * *

Silence Broken

His weakness got the best of him and many hours passed before he was alert and had a chance to try to sort things out again. He passed in and out of consciousness, waking to the unfamiliar voices of nurses and dryness in his mouth.

He opened his eyes and looked around. He noticed that both his hands were bandaged completely. He assumed that he received some needed care. He wondered if the operation on his leg had taken place, but he was afraid to look. Earlier it had been made clear to him by the doctors that he would have to lose part of his leg. He prayed for a minimum loss.

A tall nurse approached his bed,

"You finally woke up! We began to worry," she smiled as she wetted his lips with moist cotton.

Jeremy attempted to respond, but no sound was uttered by his lips. Again, the nurse wet his lips and forehead.

He fell back into another deep sleep. When he awoke, he found himself in another room, the orthopedic ward, surrounded by several other wounded soldiers.

"Good morning. Welcome back. It certainly took you a long time to return to us," a nurse cheerfully commented.

"I'm sorry the Egyptians were not more accommodating," he said, wondering what she had heard about him.

"I was not talking about the Egyptians, but about you. Do you know how long we tried to wake you from the anesthesia?" He noticed that her earlier smile disappeared.

"I guess I needed the sleep. You do know they didn't let us sleep much," he tried to lighten the mood.

"Or maybe you just didn't care to be back," she responded rather seriously.

What nerve! He tried to find an appropriate response to her comments, realizing that her tone of voice was neither sarcastic nor malicious. Truthfully, when he had gone to sleep his thoughts had not been positive. He didn't feel that was necessarily the reason why it took him so long to emerge from the anesthesia. He remained silent.

"No answer, I guess I was right." The nurse walked to the other side of his bed, taking his pulse.

"You did talk quite a lot while you were delirious. I'm not sure what happened to you before, during, or after the Egyptian's escapade, but consider yourself a lucky person — you are alive. The marvelous doctors worked with determination to enable you to keep your entire leg. They used new microsurgery techniques which will make history in the treatment of war injuries. So, whatever else is on your mind, believe me, it's minor and you should consider yourself a very lucky person," she concluded with confidence.

He looked at her in disbelief.

"You mean my leg was saved?"

"As I said, 'your whole leg.' I am not surprised you find it hard to believe; they did perform a miracle. Your leg presented a real challenge to the team of surgeons that operated on you. You might say they cut and pasted, filling whatever was missing with other material, and now you have a whole and, we hope, completely functional leg. So, you see, you have a lot to be thankful for, no matter what else you might be feeling. Understand?"

She looked at Jeremy and smiled, moving his hair from his forehead. He nodded his head. Despite the misery he felt, he was grateful for his leg; at least he was a whole person, if only on the outside.

"And how is our hero? I see you are back with us." He heard a male voice approaching his direction.

"You certainly took your time," the man continued.

"So I've heard. Well, I am back. It is certainly good to hear I still have both my legs," Jeremy said gratefully, waiting for the stranger to identify himself.

Silence Broken

"I'm Doctor Shamer, a member of the surgery team which had the pleasure to be challenged by your case. We did an excellent job, considering what the Egyptians left for us."

"That's what one of your admirers has been telling me."

"Which one? I do have so many of them," the doctor looked around and saw the smiling nurse.

"You heard it from Nurse Rina; I was not aware that she was one of my admirers," he laughed, looking at her with a questioning gaze.

"It was not admiration, only a statement of facts," she hastened to correct.

Jeremy was told that there would be more surgeries to follow. He didn't care to ask questions about it. He was glad to be home, glad to be alive, and as for the rest, he concluded, things would work out. A sudden surge of strength and optimism filled him. He also made a resolution to find out all he could about Beth once he was better. For now, he firmly believed that things would work out for the best. With this thought, he dozed off again and hours later woke in yet a different room to be welcomed by other soldiers.

A few days after Jeremy's first operation, Ben made a short visit to the kibbutz. Upon his return, he gave Jeremy two messages from Effrat. The first he understood — that Beth had called as soon as she had arrived in the United States in order to find out if he was alive and back in Israel. Effrat was careful not to mention that he was wounded as not to alarm her. The second message was that Effrat believed that Beth had left a letter for Jeremy before she returned home.

Jeremy tried to guide Ben's efforts to find the letter. A few days later, back on the kibbutz Ben looked everywhere he could think of, but no letter was found.

With the letter still missing and the long hours of the night allowing the imagination to do its best creative work, Jeremy explored all the possibilities. He could not, however, console himself over Beth's disappearance from his life.

On the ward where he was being treated, he didn't have access to a telephone and even if he had, he didn't know her number or her address. His cousin Rami might know how to reach her, but he was in the United States. As Jeremy dictated, Ben wrote the letter to Rami, posting and mailing it as soon as he left Jeremy's bedside. Ben then told Effrat to let Beth know where he was, if she called again, but not to alarm her.

Beth didn't call again once she had heard that Jeremy was back and this worried him. *I don't understand. Why had she kept calling until she found that I was back and alive, but not after? Why?*

* * *

During the weeks following his second surgery, Jeremy became depressed and was easily irritated. When he opened his eyes, he had the reality of pain to deal with, when he closed his eyes the memories of the past few months were there to haunt him. His nights were one long nightmare. In his dreams, he vividly relived the fighting, the explosions, the smoke… He saw his friends killed beside him… Then he was wounded… The medics who creatively gave him first aid… Being captured… The prison and the torture of interrogation… In his dreams, back in Israel, he didn't have an image of Beth to help him through; he didn't have the strength to withstand the pain and the enemy got to him and broke him.

The physical wounds and the pain in his heart were fused. He often woke screaming and sweating and the nurses had to hold him down. It was all so vivid that it took him time to realize that it was over and that he was safely back in Israel.

Not hearing from Beth worried him. His mood deteriorated as he was wheeled in and out of operating rooms. Opening his eyes after each procedure and seeing each additional contraption to which he was attached made him feel even more helpless then he was prior to the surgery.

He heard that he had several skin and bone grafts. Once he even made the mistake of asking the nurse about the purposes of the hooks and wires.

Silence Broken

He looked at his scars. *All I am left with are the "zippers" scattered around my body.*

He felt the tears and he closed his eyes and turned his head to the wall, letting the tears fall. He knew that he was not crying for those visible scars, but for the invisible ones.

It was clear to his family and friends that he was severely depressed. They spoke highly of his doctor's competence and fame, but he wasn't interested in hearing how lucky he was. Between the on-going physical pain and the non-stop emotional turmoil, there were days when he truly wished he was dead.

One afternoon, two days after his latest surgery and eight weeks after his return from prison, his friends from Nof Golan came to see him for their weekly visit. They told him of the return of the bodies of friends from his unit who didn't make it. Jeremy was very uncomfortable hearing the bad news; he had hoped that some of the others, who were not in prison with him, had been saved. Tears stung his eyes. He couldn't take any more of the misery and pain caused by the war. He wished he was by himself, free to scream and cry, but the room was full of visitors.

"You are lucky to be alive. Some of them would have been happy to change places with you," he heard one of his friends say. *That did it! I am tired of pretending!*

"Out! Leave! Enough! I can't take it anymore!"

No one moved, but they stared in surprise. Jeremy was always calm and rational. In all the years they had known him, they never saw him lose control of his emotions.

As a last attempt to hold back his tears, Jeremy tried to explain, "I know you are trying to help me, but I can't take it anymore. I feel like shit." He couldn't hold off any longer and let his tears flow freely.

Ben approached the bed. He had been expecting the outburst for quite a while. In fact, wondered why Jeremy hadn't done it earlier.

Since Jeremy's return, Ben was beside his bed every free moment he had. He waited along with Dr. and Mrs. Offir outside the operating room during Jeremy's various surgeries, anxiously anticipating the nurse's updates on his condition. It happened so often that he and the Offirs no longer counted the procedures. He doubted whether he himself would have the courage to take the ongoing pain that Jeremy endured. Ben took his turn sitting with Jeremy during the first twenty-four hours after each operation. He clearly saw Jeremy's pain even though his friend never complained. The sadness in Jeremy's eyes was enough to communicate his sense of helplessness. When Jeremy would drift back to sleep from the effect of the drugs, Ben would allow his own tears to roll down his cheeks. There wasn't much he could do or say to ease his friend's suffering.

At one point, Ben questioned himself, *Why am I holding back my tears in front of Jeremy?* The answer was clear. Society didn't yet accept that men need to cry. Yet, he felt that this was very unfortunate. From his own private experience, he knew how crying helped him relieve stress, though he didn't dare do it in public.

Now, Ben let his tears fall freely. He couldn't hold back and didn't want to hide it any more. He didn't care what the others might think of him — it no longer mattered.

"Jeremy, we know you are suffering. We don't know how to help you. It is easy for us to say, 'Try to get over it,' but we're not the ones going through any of it. Don't pay any mind to our mumbling words; it's our feeble effort to help you without really knowing how."

Ben looked around to see some of their friends nodding in agreement, also with tears in their eyes. Ben felt better seeing the reactions of his friends, both the men and the women. He was proud to belong to this group; they were his real family.

Jeremy cried openly and it seemed that his friends' expressions of unconditional support gave him the shot of encouragement that he so desperately needed.

Silence Broken

Although his friends were sympathetic and warm, they were frustrated with his lack of progress. In fact, what they were concerned with most was his deep sadness and some even felt that he seemed almost ready to give up.

* * *

That evening, when nobody was beside Jeremy's bed, his roommate Jonathan finally expressed his feelings about Jeremy's behavior. He was sick and tired of Jeremy's self-pity and the pain he was imposing upon his friends and relatives. He also knew all about Beth.

"If it is the last thing you hear from me, let it be, but I am going to say it anyway. Nobody is worth that much — no matter who she is. Act like a man; you're not the first one to lose a girlfriend."

By the time Jonathan finished, it was a long and harsh speech. Jeremy was not pleased to hear what Jonathan had to say and he was annoyed at the intrusion. Yet, he knew it was meant to help him. The two shared a room since Jeremy's third operation and during those long days Jeremy developed great admiration for Jonathan and his positive approach to life despite the current pain. Apparently, the doctors were pleased with Jonathan's progress and he was soon to be released.

Jeremy didn't respond, however, his actions showed that he had heard. Soon after the unsolicited sermon, Jeremy asked to be wheeled into the dining room. He talked with people in the hall and he met other wounded young men. Each had his own injuries, his own stories about what had happened and about the miracles the doctors had performed.

From the other wounded soldiers, he also learned how his mother and Ben spent the time during the days and weeks when he was totally incapacitated. They took turns sitting in his room. Jeremy also heard about the despair experienced by his parents and Ben when he appeared to be giving up.

Other soldiers in his ward shared their thoughts and concerns. They had heard about the heroism he had shown on the battlefield before he was captured and of the inner strength he manifested in the face of torture by his captors. All these stories did not fit the image of the motionless withdrawn lump they saw lying on the bed, day after day, for weeks.

Gradually, Jeremy viewed the current events in his life in a different light. Jonathan had told him that positive thinking could have an impact on physical recovery. Now he experienced it for himself. He kept busy socializing and the days passed faster; his mood improved and he made physical progress. He made several efforts to locate and contact Beth but had no luck. Neither Jeremy nor Rami could get through to her. They left endless messages with her mother to get a response, any response, but elicited nothing. Despite the enormous pain, he was not ready to give up. He mustered new strength from within to continue his search. Jeremy needed closure thus searching for her was his only way.

In the weeks to come Jeremy was moved back and forth between the various orthopedic departments and finally to the rehabilitation center. Jeremy received a great deal of support from his friends and family as his quest continued. There was a great deal of work to be done — and he did it.

Silence Broken

Kibbutz Nof-Golan, Israel, April 1974

Chapter 11

Jeremy had mixed feelings when he returned to Nof Golan. Five months had passed since his return from the Egyptian prison. It was good to be back among friends and on his own two feet, away from the hospital and the rehabilitation center's routine. At the same time, it was painful to look at all the places and things which so vividly reminded him of Beth. Every corner he turned, he remembered a laugh, a joke, or a gesture from months before. The worst part was being in his room. So far, he had not heard a word from Beth despite his and Rami's efforts to contact her.

On the day of his return, friends were in and out of his room to welcome him, to talk, to have coffee, and to eat sunflower seeds. It was OK then; the room was occupied and busy for hours and he didn't have an opportunity to withdraw to his own private thoughts for more than a few seconds at a time. But when the last person left and he was alone in the room, he was very lonely, longing for Beth even more than before.

Ben had gone to pick up Jeremy's medicine and dinner, leaving Jeremy alone for some time. To escape his loneliness, he reached up to the shelf where he kept his favorite poetry book. He hesitated, hand hovering over the book's spine, remembering the evenings he and Beth used to read poems out loud and talk about them. Finally, he picked up the book and, as he opened it, he noticed the folded papers which had been inserted inside it. He unfolded the papers, discovering the long-lost letter from Beth for which everyone had been searching. His hands shook as he lay down on his bed to read it.

Rivcka Edelstein

November 24, 1973

Dearest Jeremy,

I am leaving this letter in a place where you would be the only one to find it.

When you read this letter, I will be home with my family. I waited as long as I could, but my parent's pressure intensified. They demanded I return to the States to continue my education.

I will keep in touch with the kibbutz until your whereabouts are known. I pray that you are alive and well. As I write this, we do not know what has happened to you but I am sure you are alive.

I would have preferred to talk to you instead of writing this letter and I delayed putting it on paper until the last possible minute, a few hours before my flight. Since we did not have control over the events which took place during recent weeks, I have to resort to writing rather than talking.

I know you told me that you don't care about the past and who I was with before I met you. However, I think you should know the truth, since it has affected me in more ways than one.

When we met this summer, I told you I needed a vacation and that was the reason why I was in Israel while my classmates were still in school. You wondered whether I accomplished my goals in coming to Israel, yet you never pressured me on why I felt the need to "run away," as you put it, and for that I was grateful. From a passing comment you made, I guessed you probably assumed that I had a very painful love affair. I wish it had been so, because after being with you, any painful love affair could have been overcome and long forgotten. You were very encouraging, supportive, and understanding of my mood changes. You never tried to push me or be demanding of me. You just accepted me and loved me for who I was. However, a painful love affair was not what I was escaping.

I did not think I would ever tell you what I am going to write. Judging from my experience with other guys in the last two years, I did not think that our relationship would reach the level of intensity that it did. It surprised me, more than I imagine that it surprised you, but I fell in love with you. I am ready to make a commitment to you if that is what you want, but first you need to hear me out.

I was used by somebody I had trusted. It started before we ever met. If you found my body used, it was without my cooperation or my consent. I cannot tell you a lot and I'd rather that you don't ask. Despite my sense of betrayal, I still feel I ought to keep this to myself and protect innocent people from being affected by it. Nonetheless, the effects are still part of me. At times, I am very depressed. I blame myself for what had happened to me and for allowing it to continue.

As you noticed, I become irritable very easily. The least provocation can bring tears to my eyes; most of the time I feel powerless.

I tried to devote most of my time to my academic work in an effort to erase the nightmarish experience from my thoughts and in an attempt to compensate for my inadequacy in other areas. I have recurring nightmares and sometimes when I get up in the middle of the night, I am not sure if it was just a bad dream or reality. It has affected my social life, even my wanting to date and my ability to deal with intimacy. My head told me that not all men are like that, but I could not control my gut emotional reactions to closeness. I could not trust other people's intentions. I know you noticed my reactions to your initial attempts at intimacy. Although I wanted desperately to be close to you, there was always something that pulled me back.

My guidance counselor read my earlier school records and noticed a dramatic change in my behavior and grades. We discussed these changes, but I couldn't tell her the real reason. She spoke to my Junior High School counselor and, they agreed that there had been a gradual change in me since the beginning of ninth grade (actually shortly before you and I first met in 1970). Things became worse towards November 1972; my marks dropped drastically and I became very nervous and highly agitated. I made an extreme effort to concentrate on my courses, taking as many classes as I could to keep myself busy and out of trouble, but I could not forget. I limited socializing to a minimum to avoid any embarrassment or incidental disclosure. I slowly became completely isolated...

The idea of the honor independent study had merit in more than one respect. For me it meant getting away. I would not need to be on guard and could rest my mind and body for a while.

My parents, especially my father, objected to the overseas plan for the project. My counselor did a very good job of persuading them. She convinced them about the supervision I would be getting and emphasized the academic honor. That persuaded my parents, since academic accomplishments were always top priority to them, especially to my father. He was the one who grieved my deteriorating grades the most.

Now, as I write this, I am more hopeful. I was able to be intimate with you and I will never regret it. You cannot imagine how important and monumental this was for me. It is a big step toward overcoming the emotional scars of my past. I do hope that, in time, the past will truly be behind me and will cease to affect me. I can only say that you are the best thing that happened to me in the past four years.

I did not think in the beginning that I would tell you what I just wrote. Since you repeatedly reassured me of your love for me, I felt that you should know the situation before you make a decision.

My dearest, I love you and want to be with you for the rest of my life. My doubts are not about my love for you, but about your continuous love for me, given the fact that you loved me without really knowing me. The "me" of the last four years.

I would like to remove the mask I've worn for so long; I want to be me and still be accepted. In the past, it was difficult for me to express my feelings in so many words, but I am sure about my feelings for you and I can sum them up in five simple words: I love you very much.

In writing the above incoherent statements, my greatest hope is that you feel about me the same way I feel about you. Please think about it. You should be aware that the "me" you met is the "me" out of context or at least in a different context. If you decide that you are *able to accept me as things stand now and with the understanding that only time and support can help heal my past wounds and diminish some of their negative effects, please contact me as soon as you can, by phone if possible. I will return soon after I hear from you.*

If you don't get in touch with me one way or the other, after your return, I will understand that you are having difficulty dealing with what I have told you. I know I took a risk of losing you by writing this, however, I do believe in honesty if we are to have any type of relationship.

I have other news for you, but it can wait until you have thought things through. I hope this letter finds you in good health and the events of the war behind you.

Love always,

Beth

* * *

Jeremy clutched the letter to his eyes and tears poured down his face and onto the paper. He had not cried like this since he was a child and he made no attempt to stop.

"Poor Beth, you did not think about all the options; you only thought there was a 'yes' or a 'no' to my accepting you. You did not take into account that I might not see this letter for months after my return from prison. You did not take into account that I would be incapable of writing or calling for weeks." He found himself talking to the letter.

The months of questioning and doubts and the sense of betrayal were over for him now. Although he did not accept or agree with her decision, he understood why he didn't hear from her. His heart ached for her. *What was she thinking when she did not hear from me for the first few weeks. She must have felt that I betrayed her as she had been betrayed in the past.*

The letter answered some questions and raised new ones. He remembered what Effrat and Ben had told him in their visit to the hospital. They said that Beth had called once after he returned, verified that he was back, but left no message and no telephone number. He also recalled Ben telling him that out of a desire not to alarm her, Effrat did not tell Beth that he was wounded and in the hospital. *What a mess!*

* * *

After putting the letter down and wiping away his tears, Jeremy stared at the phone that was newly installed in each of the rooms. He ached to speak to Beth and need to untangle this web of miscommunication between them. He knew who he needed to call to get started.

He dialed quickly, fingers tapping as he impatiently waited for a voice on the other end to pick up.

"Hello?"

"Rami! It's Jeremy!" he exclaimed, grateful his cousin had answered the phone.

The excitement in Rami's voice made Jeremy feel better. Rami bombarded him with questions about his recovery and what had happened to him — and Beth.

"I'm back at Nof Golan, I just returned from rehab. I found Beth's letter. I've tried calling the number you gave me and writing to Beth's address that you told me. All of my letters have been returned back to me. I don't know if her mother has been giving Beth my phone messages, even though she said she would. Please help me find her, cousin. I love her. I'll fly to New York to see her as soon as I'm discharged," Jeremy declared.

Rami could hear the urgency in Jeremy's voice and knew his cousin was desperate. Jeremy was devastated without Beth. After talking to Jeremy in the last few months, Rami understood how passionate Jeremy was for Beth and how much they loved each other. Rami pledged to his cousin he would do everything in his power to find Beth and get her in touch with Jeremy to hopefully reunite them.

Part II: 1990

Rivcka Edelstein

Tel Aviv, Israel, September 1990

Chapter 12

Jeremy looked out the window in his office. The southwest view of the Tel Aviv shoreline relaxed him as it always had. Ben, his partner in the law practice since their swearing in to the bar, had recently commented that Jeremy was overworked. He thought Jeremy needed to take personal time to relax. Jeremy knew well why he buried himself in his work.

Deborah Offir, his mother, was concerned as well. She called weekly, asking how he was doing and what was new. She managed to always slip in a few questions regarding his social life and the young ladies he was dating. She also made sure to update him on the latest marriages of his close friends and family members.

Jeremy was not angry with his mother; she was only trying to encourage him. How could she know, as he did, that any attempt at involvement was futile? Anytime he was close enough to becoming serious with another woman, he felt like a traitor. With the past so unsettled, how could he move on? *I don't think that I'll ever feel about another woman the way I feel about Beth.*

He rationalized to himself thousands of times that if Beth cared for him or wanted him she would have shown signs of it. Yet, in her silence, he felt the pain of the unresolved mystery. He knew that his cousin Rami had received occasional notes from Beth over the years. There were no return addresses on any of them. The only thing they concluded from her writing was that she was still not married as of 5 or 6 years ago. He comforted himself with the knowledge that another man was not the reason for her silence.

He removed her seventeen-year-old letter, now tattered and fading, from his wallet and read it yet again, trying to find a missing clue that could explain her disappearance. *Why hadn't she answered my letters or returned my calls?* He knew that raising these questions was fruitless. After he read her letter in April 1974, he called her several times and left messages with her mother, but she never got back to him. He sent her many letters; all were returned, unopened. He knew he had to be realistic and move on as well. *Her message is clear. She moved on.*

He looked at his watch and decided to leave for court earlier than originally scheduled.

Jeremy headed toward the Shaar Zion Public Library Beit Ariela, across from the Regional Court Building. He had promised Yael, Ben's fifteen-year-old daughter, that he would stop there on his way to court to locate a book she needed. Jeremy smiled at the thought of Yael; he always felt closer to her than to Ben's other children. She was born a few months after Ben's discharge from the military and was among the first children born to his friends from youth. He often wished he, too, had a daughter like Yael.

He quickly located the book Yael had requested and glanced at the table of contents as he waited to check it out. *The apple does not fall far from the tree,* Jeremy chuckled to himself, noting Yael's own interest in Ben's field of study. Walking across the courtyard, passing the Tel Aviv Museum of Art, he noted the announcement for a new art exhibition. He recalled hearing positive reviews about it and made a mental note to return to see it for himself.

Jeremy entered the central hall of the court building from the west side and was once again struck by the architectural similarity of this building with one on Ben-Gurion University Campus in Be'er Sheva.

He looked around for his client and could not find him. He leaned on the reception counter, admiring the large sculpture to his left. Despite his frequent visits to this building, Jeremy was still puzzled by this particular piece of art. Each time he saw it, he vividly recalled Beth's admiration of the odd sculptures Sammy made at Nof Golan. Although he, himself, was unable to grasp their meaning, Sammy was always able to communicate to Beth his intended symbolism.

He realized that recently his thoughts turned to Beth quite frequently. He had experienced periods like this in the past, especially when he became more seriously involved with another woman. These memories always detracted from his present pursuits; having them was hopeless and led nowhere.

He heard a familiar voice from the Weitzman Street entrance and he turned his head to see his client, Raffi, rushing towards him, apologizing.

"You know how traffic is at this hour, especially when coming into town from the North. I wonder why they didn't build this court building out of town or at least some place where there is ample parking."

Jeremy smiled, "It was built here for the convenience of the people — all the people, even those who didn't have cars and relied on public transportation."

They glanced around for a quiet corner and finally settled to talk. Jeremy pulled a few thick folders from his briefcase and went over some points, explaining the other side's strategy. After a nod and smile from Raffi, they approached the elevator and eventually entered the courtroom.

Twenty-five minutes later they emerged from the court room; Raffi was impressed, and Jeremy was pleased, noting how his early legwork paid off. The insurance company was evidently clear on the fact that the law firm was out to win big and asked for a postponement after hearing some of the allegations, proposed witnesses, and documents Jeremy intended to present.

Jeremy and Ben's law firm, unlike others, only claimed a small percentage from the settlement, giving the client as much money as possible. Jeremy believed that the lawyer should not be paid out of money which was due to the client, but rather should get a percentage based on whatever extra was obtained because of the legal advice provided. This way the client was protected and would not be left with less than he might have had without a lawyer.

Raffi was glad he hadn't approached the insurance company directly for a settlement. He had previously wanted to settle for damages alone, but now it was a question of fighting for a principle. As Jeremy explained to him in their earlier meetings on this case, it was time the insurance companies recognized that they were in business to serve and ensure the safety of the people, not just build their own empires. Raffi now understood why Jeremy was known among his colleagues as the "Justice Fighter." They had known each other for a number of years since Raffi had established his business and Jeremy handled all his legal matters. Raffi knew that Jeremy's competence, sharpness, and awareness of the law were all outstanding. But what Raffi admired above all was Jeremy's integrity — and that merited his high recommendation.

Raffi had noticed deep sadness in Jeremy's eyes when he entered the court building earlier and had watched him silently before calling to him. Raffi remembered Ben telling him that Jeremy was involved with a lovely woman and was soon to be engaged. Yet, Jeremy's expression did not reflect the expected joy of such good fortune.

"It is clear you've done a lot of work in preparation for today's court hearing," he said to Jeremy. "When do you find time to do all of this work for each case, you have so many cases?"

"Paralegals," Jeremy smiled as he shrugged his shoulders.

Raffi knew that despite the help of assistants, Jeremy was conversant in each of his cases down to the smallest details. This was the impression he had from all the legal work Jeremy had done for him. He was personally involved and that's what made him such an incredible lawyer.

They discussed a few more details and what was to be expected. With a quick summary and handshake, they left the court building together through the Weitzman street exit. Raffi went to his car and Jeremy crossed the street to Bank Ha-Poalim before closing time.

Jeremy was not one to discuss his problems, but when he spoke he did so clearly with conviction and his actions proved him true to his words. Although his social and political views were not those of some of the firm's clients, even they had to admit he had sound support for his beliefs. Jeremy didn't fear expressing opposing and controversial views.

"I blame the people, not the government," he would say assertively, "How could there be so many rich people in a country that is so poor?"

* * *

Although Ben accepted Jeremy's social and political views and he knew Jeremy was right, he did not feel it was appropriate to mix business with personal political points of view, especially considering their population of clients.

Ben understood Jeremy's decision to leave the kibbutz after the military service and to go to law school. Jeremy believed that he could serve his country better applying himself as a lawyer than as a physically handicapped kibbutz member. The war injuries still bothered Jeremy even after all those years. He was probably right in being concerned that the kibbutz would have made special allowances due to his injuries and physical limitations. The Nof Golan kibbutz also held memories of a lost past from before the war, and of the girl Jeremy used to love. Ben knew Beth and understood how very special she was to Jeremy. He knew how the mystery surrounding her disappearance from Jeremy's life ate away at him, and thus why Jeremy could never accept her loss.

Jeremy had been telling Ben about the woman he was currently seeing — a very attractive and desirable woman named Danielle. She was the most recent in Jeremy's long line of acquaintances, girlfriends, and affairs. Ben thought about the volume of phone calls Jeremy used to get from attractive women who were waiting for him at lunch time or at the end of the work day. Yet, Jeremy never expressed enthusiasm about any of them. During the last few months, Danielle was the only one Jeremy was dating. Ben was hoping that it meant something. Ben had noticed that Jeremy made a conscious effort to call her, pick her up, and order tickets for the theatre in advance. He wanted to see Jeremy happy, but down deep he knew Jeremy was not. Jeremy's underlying sadness worried Ben continuously.

Silence Broken

Finally, a few weeks earlier, Jeremy announced to Ben that he planned to be engaged to Danielle. Ben believed Danielle was the best choice in every respect. Even Ben's wife had commented how wonderful and interesting Danielle seemed. Coming from her, it was a sincere compliment, since she was not one to find great virtues in other women. Despite all this, during the last few days Ben noticed the "security symptoms" were on again - Jeremy's deep sadness, restlessness, and long work hours to escape his emotional pain. At that point, Ben knew that this relationship was another one that just wouldn't last.

Rivcka Edelstein

New York, New York, September 1990

Chapter 13

At the law firm, Ms. Beth Robinoff, a specialized youth lawyer, had many acquaintances but no close friends. The only one whom she could consider somewhat of a close friend was Debbie, a patent lawyer she met over the course of her work in the firm. Debbie was married, had two children, and was very outgoing.

"You look very tired; is it the job?" Debbie asked Beth one day during lunch, noting that she looked even more sad and distracted than usual.

"Oh, nothing new, the same clients, the same frustrations," she sighed.

At first Beth hesitated to talk about the case which worried her, but she then felt the need to discuss it and she believed that talking to Debbie might help.

"Yesterday afternoon," she began, after a few seconds of silence, "I was called to the hospital as a court-appointed guardian in a situation involving a teenager. The police had brought in a girl who had been picked up on the street a few days earlier; she lost consciousness on her way back from school. In the hospital, they had to tie her hands to the bed to put her on IV." Beth was still very shaky as she recalled the specifics.

"What's wrong with her?" Debbie noticed that Beth seemed extremely distressed.

"She is 16, suffering severely from anorexia."

"It is terrible. These girls are killing themselves. How much did she lose?"

"We don't know how much she lost, but now she hardly weighs 80 pounds at five foot eight. I don't know if she'll make it..." Beth's voice cracked.

"The worst thing is that she has no desire to live. In cases like this, we can only pray. In cases like this, the hospital will work as a team with the mental health staff, but she needs help beyond their medical capabilities."

She took a long, deep sigh to stable her voice.

"When they will discharge her she probably will continue to starve herself and the next time it may be too late."

"Eighty pounds for her height is atrocious!" Debbie was shocked.

"Why wasn't she stopped earlier? How could a parent ignore such an extremely low weight." she asked angrily "Is this her first hospitalization for the anorexia?"

"Yes! Her parents were aware of the fact that she was not eating enough and that she was 'attempting to lose a couple of pounds!'"

"How could they not notice?!" Debbie was angry and amazed.

"The kids these days wear oversized clothes; it is not easy to tell their actual size. The young lady wore several sweaters, a scarf, and baggy pants that easily disguised the weight loss. It was really difficult to tell how thin she had become except from her face," Beth explained sadly.

"The hospital called her parents after they were able to find some identification," Beth added as an afterthought.

"And…"

"Her mother said that the girl had refused to eat for months and when they forced her to eat, they would later hear her vomiting. Still, she was shocked to hear her daughter's actual weight. I asked her if they had noticed any behavioral changes and the mother said she had become a complete stranger."

"Did you talk to the rest of the family?"

"Yes, of course. The whole family quickly rushed to the hospital in a panic, carrying a heavy load of guilt, especially when they heard the conditions under which she was picked up. I looked at them and could not stop thinking to myself — what was going on in that family?"

"What do you mean?" Debbie asked curiously.

"Well, her mother said, 'She never gave us any problems. We never had to bother with her because she was "the good one."'"

"The father interjected, 'All the free time we had, we spent on our son, "the troublemaker." We really hardly knew she was around; she never asked for anything. We really are shocked at her behavior now.'"

Beth recalled the knots in her stomach when she talked to the family.

"What are you going to do about her?" Debbie inquired.

"The hospital feels she needs her own lawyer to make sure her welfare is protected. They feel her family is not enough to help this sixteen-year-old." She nervously put her hand through her hair.

"Some people don't know how to appreciate what they have when things are going well," she said sadly.

Beth's voice and face suggested there was more on her mind than this case. Debbie looked at her with concern.

"You do seem to take it to heart. I mean, beyond the attorney-client relationship."

Beth was quiet for a few seconds. Then she said, "I guess you're right. There was something about her age…"

"What about her age?" Debbie asked, not even sure why it mattered.

Beth replied automatically with her thoughts clearly somewhere else, "February 1974…" she caught herself in time before she went on.

Silence Broken

Debbie noticed her hesitation. "What's special about February 1974?" Debbie asked more out of a desire to help than out of curiosity.

Beth didn't answer.

"Do you want to talk about it?" Debbie asked after a moment of silence.

Beth was alarmed. "No!" After a pause she finally added, "Not yet, anyway."

Debbie wished Beth would open up. It was clear to her from various comments Beth had made in the past that there was something she needed to share with someone. Debbie did not want to push her. She hoped that Beth would trust her, but Beth sat quietly, her mind was miles away, her face creased and sad.

To change the subject, Debbie told Beth details about the past weekend.

"Beth, why aren't you going out, mingling, meeting people?" she eventually asked.

"I just don't want to get hurt again."

"I don't know how you got hurt in the first place, but you know, not all guys are creeps, even if you happen to meet one or two along the way."

"One of the two people who hurt me was sick and the other was not even aware that I was hurt and he was definitely NOT a creep. With others, I was the one that severed the relationship and maybe I even hurt them." She replied carefully selecting each word.

Debbie noticed Beth's eyes roaming around the restaurant. It was obvious that she was trying to avoid eye contact. Debbie noticed Beth's eyes began to shine and tears were about to follow. For a second, she wished she never asked Beth the question, yet she uttered the next question.

"What happened?"

"They were empty relationships, unsuccessful efforts on my part to get over earlier pain."

Once again Debbie encouraged her to talk and offered to listen, but it was clear that Beth was not yet ready.

Just then Debbie's secretary approached her, telling her she was needed in the office.

As Debbie got up, she said sweetly and reassuringly, "Well just remember, I'm here whenever you are ready."

"I know. Thanks!"

They decided to meet later that evening, after work, at their favorite, coffee shop.

* * *

Beth arrived first. She leaned back, slowly sipping her coffee, and stared into space. Her eyes didn't focus on anything in particular and she let her thoughts wander back to her last conversation with Debbie. She never opened up to anyone about her pain; she never put it into words. Beth believed it would be safe to get closer to Debbie, yet she was not ready. It had become clear to her now, as it was clear to her all these years, that she would never tell a soul about her life as a teenager. Nobody! She felt that nobody would understand her feelings of betrayal, anger, and her sense of shame and guilt. *How could anybody accept me if they knew the truth?*

As for Jeremy, she couldn't explain that either. Nobody would understand her strong love for him, despite her anger and disappointment for what had happened. What puzzled her was her own comment about her other relationships. *What am I doing? Am I really using these empty, frivolous relationships to get over my pain from the past? I've never thought about it like that… Maybe it's true.*

Since her relationship with Jeremy, she made three attempts at semi-commitment and intimacy. Each time the relationship developed only up to a point and then there was a period of standstill, followed by a time during which she started feeling empty. She would make a few attempts to revive the relationship and to overcome the sense of emptiness, but to no avail — she needed space. That was when she ended each of the relationships. It was a clear pattern and each time she believed she was at fault. *Maybe I'm not capable of having a successful long-term, intimate relationship.*

She never looked at those relationships as a process of getting over Jeremy, until now. The more she thought about it, the more she felt that it was a possibility. Not one of the three men was an adequate replacement for Jeremy. In many ways, however, each one was a very suitable potential husband, but no man was Jeremy. *Still,* she reminded herself now as she had many times before, *you don't have the option of choosing Jeremy over the others. The choice is from those available to you. Be realistic and select.*

Over the years, she occasionally heard about Jeremy. The last time she heard anything was three years ago. He had been engaged, but at the last moment the engagement was called off. She wondered why he wasn't getting married and settling down.

"A penny for your thoughts," Beth heard Debbie's voice.

"They aren't worth even a penny. I was just thinking about our conversation at lunch," Beth said gloomily.

"Me, too! Beth, I've known you for years and I hope we can talk openly."

"I think so," Beth agreed, wondering what Debbie was going to say next.

"Don't be offended Beth, but did you ever think about going for counseling?"

Before Beth could respond, Debbie continued, "I've been going now for a few months and I really feel it is helping me. Please, Beth, think about it. What have you got to lose? I put off starting therapy for a long time and I was sorry for that. If I knew then what I know now, I could have made changes long ago. I don't know what happened to you in the past, but I have a feeling… Don't misunderstand, you are an excellent lawyer and you've accomplished a lot, but what about you, as a person? Do you feel complete? Are you happy or are you just letting life pass you by?"

When she didn't get a response, Debbie was afraid she had crossed the line without permission. Beth looked as though lightning hit her.

"I'm sorry, Beth. Forget I said…"

"No! Don't apologize, you are absolutely right, it's only that you are the first person to say something like that to me. I have been thinking about seeking professional help, but I've never followed up on it. I do need to deal with my pain."

"So you aren't angry with me?"

"No! To prove it, I'll pay for the coffee and in exchange you can give me the telephone number of your therapist and I'll get in touch with him," Beth said, smiling with some relief.

"My doctor is a 'her,' not a 'him,'" Debbie corrected as she wrote the number.

"Tell you what; we can ask her to arrange our sessions one after the other and then afterward we can go out — a ladies' night out."

"You've got a deal." Beth was pleased and she looked forward to spending time with Debbie outside of the law firm.

"Leave the planning to me; I'll show you a good time."

"Thanks, Debbie, I mean it."

"No trouble at all; you'll like her — she is a nice person and her strategy is 'cooperative effort' — client and therapist are partners; it really works."

Silence Broken

New York, New York, September 1990

Chapter 14

Beth met with Dr. Noble twice a week — once on Tuesday evenings, just after Debbie's session, and again on Sunday mornings. She was finally telling somebody the things she had never dared share before. At the end of each session she felt relieved, as though her load were actually becoming lighter. On the wall of Dr. Noble's office was a poster which read: The truth will set you free, but first it will make you miserable. Beth looked at the poster each time she was in the office and felt it specifically applied to her. She was grateful to Debbie for encouraging her to seek professional help.

During one of the sessions, Dr. Noble asked Beth why she became a lawyer.

"What do you mean? It is something my parents always had in mind for me."

"You probably wanted to do it; you didn't always do what your parents wanted."

"Actually, that isn't true. When I look back and see what I had done with my life, it was always what my parents wanted."

"To some degree you probably agreed with them."

"Well, I always liked helping people, solving their problems."

"From what you have told me earlier, I gathered that you are often inconvenienced by the other lawyers who ask you to cover for them. Aren't you burning yourself out?"

"I get tired, but I don't mind."

"And what are you getting from . . ." She stopped searching for the word.

"Do any of them reciprocate? Do for you . . .?"

"No... Not really."

"Do you ever feel resentment toward those lawyers, or people in general, who aren't there for you when you need them?"

"Sure, who wouldn't? But I don't let it bother me."

"Why not deal with it?"

"What can I do about it, confront them? Add more rejecting people to my life?"

"Why should they reject you because you express yourself?"

"Isn't that what my parents did?"

"Is it?"

Beth stopped. Her eyes dropped and she fought back tears. Dr. Noble pushed a box of tissues toward her and pointed to it.

"That is what they're here for; crying is healthy."

* * *

Beth was looking forward to the sessions with Dr. Noble, but deep inside she believed that if Dr. Noble knew all about her, she would join the 'Let's-Reject-Beth Club'. She knew that holding on to some of her thoughts or events from the past didn't help the therapy, yet she couldn't open up completely. In one of her sessions, Beth started her routine self-degradation, listing her recent failures and mistakes.

Dr. Noble stopped her. "Why do you go out of your way to devalue yourself?"

Beth stopped. "What do you mean? I am trying to tell you who I am."

"Beth, there is more to your life than your perceived mistakes."

Beth looked at her perplexed.

"What about your accomplishments? What about things you do which make you proud of yourself? I see a very successful person, one you should be proud of."

"For what?" Beth stopped.

Moments later she looked up and realized that Dr. Noble was waiting for her to continue.

"My mother never told me that she was proud of me. Not even once! My father did… But that was for his own ulterior motives… In my life, I have been rejected numerous times, especially when I was younger… I blame myself for what happened to me… If I were a good person maybe my mother would have liked me. My life changed after my brother Kevin was killed. My mother had no use for us. She became involved in everything she could to keep herself out of the house. My father was lonely and I was his only companion at home… It seemed that he only cared that I would be there for him and that I do well in school."

Beth started to cry. Dr. Noble waited.

"My parents didn't accept me for who I was. My parents…my friends, my home… everything changed after… I did well in school because it was expected of me. School served as an excuse for me to be out of the house, but I was so miserable and lonely that I wasn't fun to be around. I was ashamed of myself and afraid my friends would find out what I had done. I was so concerned about being rejected by my friends that I proceeded to reject them first." Beth paused again, but Dr. Noble was still waiting.

"You see, I know I am not loveable."

"Why?"

"How could I be loveable if my own parents, who were supposed to love me, didn't?"

"How did you come to that conclusion?"

"My parents' behavior, then my first boyfriend's behavior, and my own behavior…"

"What did you do that made you unlovable?"

"I'd rather not talk about it."

"You're holding on to several irrational beliefs that have led you to irrational decisions and defensive behavior. I think you should re-examine and dispute them one by one. Replace them with effective beliefs which can help you lead a happier and more adaptive life," Dr. Noble finally explained.

"For our next session, think about your various accomplishments and make a list." Dr. Noble smiled, "I would like to see a long list. If you are fair with yourself, the list will be longer than the list of mistakes you dug out. Just for the record Beth, I think you are very loveable. If you give people a chance to know you, the real you, you might find that many people think so."

* * *

It took a number of sessions before Beth was able to speak about her trip to Israel when she was seventeen. She noticed Dr. Noble was not surprised. Beth was not receptive to Dr. Noble's efforts to convince her that she could have called one more time, that she could have tried to get an explanation from Jeremy for his silence. There were other things she could have done.

Dr. Noble said, "You know Beth, it isn't too late to learn more about that chapter of your life. It might do you some good."

"And get hurt yet again? No thanks, I've had enough."

Silence Broken

New York, New York, November 1990

Chapter 15

The shrill loudspeaker announced the boarding of American Airlines Flight 19, non-stop to Los Angeles. People got up from their red seats in the waiting room at Kennedy Airport and approached the gate area.

Then the second announcement, "Passengers in rows twelve to twenty-four, would you kindly board the aircraft at this time."

Beth remained seated. There was no rush. She watched the faces of other passengers — some looked tired, exhausted, and drained while others seemed fresh and alive.

Recently things seemed to be going right for her. New hopes and new energy gave her a sense of excitement; today she was on her way to a professional conference. She liked going to conferences; they gave her a stimulating break from the day-to-day routine at the office. In addition, she had a chance to socialize with colleagues from school. During the conference days, she went to as many sessions as possible and during the evenings, she met old friends from law school and college.

"Last call for passengers on American Flight 19…" Beth got up. *Now it's time.* She didn't like sitting on the airplane waiting for others to board; it always reminded her of her first overseas flight in 1973. Despite the many years that had passed since that day, she still remembered the trip in detail — all the stated and unstated reasons for the trip, traveling to the airport, and the sense of choking she felt during the last few minutes before she said goodbye to her parents.

"Beth, what is the sudden rush? Your plane is not going to leave without you. You've got your reserved seat and nobody is going to take it away from you. Stay with us longer. You still have an hour." Her mother pleaded with her.

Rivcka Edelstein

Beth had worried about what might happen if she didn't leave soon. She felt that she might be unable to hold on any longer... She might burst wide open and speak about things ...events... she already had resolved were better left untold.

"I have to get moving," Beth replied nervously, moving away after a momentary look at her mother and a swift glance in her father's direction. She avoided his eyes. Her father had made several efforts earlier to get close to her.

He hugged her and quietly whispered, "Remember, I love you." Those words echoed in her ears for months and it made her shiver to think about it. She repeatedly asked herself one question: why?

"Have a good time, dear. Write often," her mother had called after her. "Look in this direction when you take off, we will be waving to you."

Beth boarded the plane in May 1973, hoping that this trip was going to be a turning point in her life.

She sat for more than an hour while other passengers boarded. She had hoped that the physical separation would minimize the intensity of her pain. The events which had taken place, especially during those last few weeks and months, kept intruding into her thoughts. In a sense, she was hoping a magic wand to make all the unpleasantness disappear, but that did not happen.

That trip had changed her life. She still remembered the hours of crying...the relentless efforts of the El-Al stewardess to cheer her up. The poor stewardess couldn't even begin to imagine what Beth was running from or why she was crying and Beth couldn't tell her — she couldn't tell anybody, ever.

Beth started to cry. She couldn't shake the memories of those years before Israel and the pain of the years after Israel. It seemed to her that her entire life was one big lie, full of fear.

She was told that she came across as aloof and cynical for such a successful, bright, young woman. Beth recalled one of her classmates saying, "Beth, excuse me for saying it, but you are so cynical about life. From the way I see it, you have no reason to be so bitter."

No reason, she thought. *What did he know about my reasons?* But that comment had made her think about seeking counseling, though she shied away from it for years not wanting to expose herself.

To her colleagues and friends, it seemed that she had it all. She was beautiful and intelligent. She had earned prestigious degrees from very well respected universities. She had the career she always dreamed about. She had the wealth to do what she wanted. Over the years, she also had three suitors who were interested in marrying her — until she had rejected them. The truth was that underneath it all, she felt hollow inside and was in constant fear that the others would discover it.

When she met Jeremy, she was so vulnerable and scared. She risked it all by getting close to him and got terribly hurt. Now, each time she became involved with another man, she felt something was happening to her when he got too close. The fear brewed inside her: she did not want to get hurt again.

Rivcka Edelstein

San Francisco, California, November 1990

Chapter 16

Beth Robinoff sat in the Crown Restaurant on the top floor of the Fairmont Hotel located on Nob Hill. Seated near a window facing San Francisco Bay, she could clearly see Alcatraz Island, where the infamous maximum security penitentiary had been until 1964. From the other window, she easily saw the Transamerica Pyramid, the Financial District, and the Embarcadero Center. In contrast, because of the mist, the Golden Gate Bridge in the distance was barely visible. The sun was sneaking behind a cloud and the view of the landscape and buildings became sharper as the light changed. Beth wondered how long it would take for the sun to warm the air and clear the mist over the two-mile bridge. At this point she could only see part of the middle pillar of the bridge as though it were suspended in midair, with neither end of the bridge truly visible.

A thought crossed Beth's mind. The bridge resembled her life at that point; she just existed now, here in the present. The past seemed so far behind her, ambiguous, and she simply could not see the future.

She kept looking through the window at the city below. She smiled, recalling a conversation from long ago. Indeed, it seemed like ages since she and Jeremy had been at Nof Golan.

Jeremy had commented on the breathtaking view of San Francisco.

She replied, "You know it's my country and you've seen more of it than I have."

He answered jokingly, "Don't feel bad. I'll take you to our own San Francisco. The view of Haifa from Mount Carmel down to the Hadar and the lower city with its shore line looks much like San Francisco. The lack of uniformity among the houses and the saturated colorful facades reminds me of the rich colors of Haifa."

Silence Broken

He never did take her to Haifa. A few days following that conversation the Yom Kippur War broke out and he was called to the front. However, she did get to Haifa when the emergency of the war passed and before she left Israel to return to the States.

The memories of that trip were as vivid as though they had just occurred…

She was very lonely when Jeremy was in the war; the days seemed to pass very slowly. Ruth was the one to suggest that Beth join David, the kibbutz buyer, on his next trip to Haifa.

On the way from the kibbutz, she remarked to David how grateful she was that he agreed to take her.

"By now you should know that nobody dares say 'no' to Ruth. I'm glad you came along."

She thought he was only trying to be polite. After David finished his errands, he asked Beth if there was any special place she wanted to visit in Haifa.

Beth hesitated and then asked shyly, "Do you mind driving to the Carmel? I would like to see the city from there."

"You read my thoughts," he responded enthusiastically. "I was going to suggest that. It will be nice to see the city in the daylight and then after sundown."

During the trip to the Carmel, they spoke about things in general; he asked her what she was doing in Israel and she told him about her project and a little about her home.

When they arrived, there was still daylight. The view of the city from the Carmel during the day was serene and beautiful.

At dinner, the conversation became more personal. After ordering, David shared with her the struggles of the kibbutz during its early years in 1967 to 1968. He was from the founding group of Nof Golan and he felt that Jeremy and his peers were the best of the bunch of the younger groups to arrive there since its founding.

Rivcka Edelstein

After they finished the soup, he admitted that he had been angry with her when she first arrived.

"Why?" she immediately asked

"Well it is hard to say. At first I was annoyed that Jeremy created a distance between himself and Effrat by playing host to you. Before you had come to the kibbutz, Effrat was after him. Although he liked her a lot, it was only as a friend. Effrat figured out that Jeremy was in love with you even before he realized or was willing to admit it. I told her to fight for him, that he was worth fighting for, but she only said, 'He would be worth fighting for if there was hope. He cares very much for me, but as a brother to a sister, not as an intimate partner. I am glad he likes Beth. She is quite lovely.' I thought to myself, 'They are both dopes. Both of them are nice people from the same culture, no complications, and they deserve each other.' I did not like Effrat's resignation and I tried to put some sense into Jeremy, but I realized I was too late. He was in love with you. Now that I know you better, I see why Jeremy fell in love with you… Please excuse my boldness. How do you feel about him? Is it a summer fling or do you see this as love with a long path?"

"Well put. I don't mind your question. I'm glad you said what you felt. I did sense some hostility at first, but I dismissed it. I know that Jeremy likes you a lot and apparently, it is mutual. As for your question, I can only speak for myself. We did not speak about the future in so many words, but I hope it is with a long path. As a matter of fact, if it is up to me, an endless path."

"What about your home country? You do know Jeremy loves his country."

"I know that, and I hope, with time, that I will love Israel, too."

"What did your parents say?"

"They don't know any of this so far. Jeremy and I have to talk about things before I tell my parents anything."

"How would they feel about it?"

"Shocked. They had my life mapped out since I was nine years old. They have saved monthly for my education since then; I'm supposed to be a lawyer."

"Are you willing to give up that dream for Jeremy?"

Silence Broken

"I don't have to. Israel needs lawyers too… I could be a lawyer here! At the moment, my only wish is for Jeremy to come home safely."

It was dark by the time they finished dinner and they drove back to the observation point on the Carmel. Beth got out of the station wagon and walked toward the spot where she and David had stood just two hours earlier. The view was magnificent. During the day it had been beautiful, but at night it was breathtaking.

On the way back, David had said, "Beth, let me say, Jeremy is a lucky guy and I agree with Effrat."

Tears filled her eyes; she had neither seen nor heard from Jeremy since that time. She got the message loud and clear — he did not care about her. Maybe it was only a summer fling for him. Maybe her letter discouraged him. Maybe… Who knows? She had built so many dreams around him during the war and months afterwards. They were dreams and she knew she had to wake up and face reality.

Looking now at the city below, San Francisco did remind her of Haifa and all of the memories. The houses were painted colorfully in contrast to the impersonal and nondescript skyscrapers and business buildings.

Saul approached her table with a smile. They had been dating for the last few months. She had flown from her meeting in L.A. to San Francisco to spend four days with him while he attended a conference at the Fairmont Hotel. They had a good time together and all was well — until her memories started haunting her.

Saul kissed her on the cheek and sat down. He told her about the events of the morning, while she wondered in distress. *Why is it happening again and when will it end?*

"Is something the matter, dear?" Saul looked concerned.

"No, why?" she answered abruptly.

"It seems like you are a million miles away in another world. You weren't listening at all, were you?" he asked, disappointed.

He had waited the entire morning to join her. Beth felt guilty.

"I am sorry; just memories that flooded me while I was sitting here and looking at the bridge." She pointed in the direction of the Golden Gate Bridge.

"That's not a good view of the Bridge; you can't see it clearly from here; it is barely visible," Saul said matter-of-factly.

Good ol' Saul with two feet solidly on the ground, she thought.

"Just what I was thinking," she replied, hoping he was not that upset.

"Anyway, I thought you said you never saw San Francisco before?" he said questioning.

"I haven't seen San Francisco before, but I saw her twin sister in another time and place," she replied, trying to hide her stirred emotions.

"Nothing like San Francisco," Saul interjected with one hundred percent assurance.

Beth chose not to argue.

"Tell me about the meetings this morning," she said, making an effort to pay attention and not let her mind wander. It was strenuous, but she really tried. She recognized the signs and she was scared. She really liked Saul; he was good for her. He loved her, but he did not know all about her and she did not know if he would understand. Besides, he was not Jeremy.

* * *

Beth saw Saul a few more times after their trip to San Francisco, but a breakup was inevitable; the relationship was not going to work. In fairness to Saul, despite her earlier resolution to make things work, she suggested a separation. She could not explain herself to him and she barely understood it herself. She only told him that she was haunted by memories from the past and until she was freed from them she would not be a whole person to anybody. He was surprisingly nice, sad to hear it, and asked if they could still be friends.

Silence Broken

Long Island, New York, September 1990

Chapter 17

The ride to The Reach Center was hard on Sophie, the probation officer. She had to deliver Karen Burg to the Reach Residential Treatment Center. The judge had been very harsh in her words to Karen, but her expression communicated that she cared.

Sophie empathized with the judge's feelings. She also had ambivalent feelings. Karen's actions caused her to be placed out of her home, but no child deserved to be treated the way she was by her parents. Karen was a child, no matter what she said or did. Sophie knew how hard it was for Karen to hear the judge and to see the rejection from her parents, yet Karen held on — she didn't cry or even show signs of remorse. One would suggest that she was actually happy to be placed, once again, outside of her home.

Following the court decision, her parents announced that they could not afford to miss any more days from their jobs. They also said that they would be unable to take Karen to her new placement. The judge ordered that the probation officer and the sheriff take her.

The Reach Residential Treatment Center program, as it had been outlined to Karen in her placement visit, had a reputation for having the toughest clientele. Even though Karen was only sixteen years old and had no criminal record, there were no other choices. Her parents insisted that the court place her away from the county where they resided so that they would not be subjected to any further embarrassment. This condition prevented the probation department from looking into other possibilities. Sophie believed this program was the one most suitable for Karen, and she recommended it in her report to the judge.

The ride to The Reach Center seemed endless. The sheriff drove quietly — he was used to making this trip and listening to the conversations that took place in the back seat. He was also used to the answers given by the rebellious adolescents. To him, Karen was no different from the rest of the teenagers he had driven to The Reach Center in the past: a scared youth who was rejected by the system on her way to meet other youths who had been rejected by the same system. He looked in the mirror at Karen's expression and wanted to say something to help her, to give her friendly advice. He didn't. He knew she, like the others, was not ready to accept any sympathetic words at this point. He empathized with Sophie who was making unsuccessful attempts to engage Karen in conversation. Karen looked straight out the side window of the car and responded to Sophie's questions with only a "yes" or "no."

Sophie didn't hear a response to her last question, so she repeated it more assertively. She waited for a response as she looked in Karen's direction. She noticed tears slowly rolling down Karen's cheek. Karen quickly turned her head to the side even more. She had fought back her tears the entire morning — she'd just have to continue. Sophie sighed quietly, thinking to herself, *the girl does give a damn! She's human after all.*

"Do you have all your clothes with you?"

"For the thousandth time today — YES!" she answered coldly. "But don't think for a second that I intend to stay long enough to wear them."

"You heard what the judge said."

"You heard what I said. You can't force me to stay there."

"You heard the judge…"

"Fuck the judge; I can run away."

"It would not be good for your records."

"Fuck the records. You better look for another place for me."

"Karen, give the program a fair chance. You might like it."

"What for? I already know I don't like it."

Silence Broken

"Give it a chance. When I come to visit you next time we'll talk . . ."

"Forget it! I want you to find me some place else. I only agreed to come here so I didn't have to go home with them."

"Karen, you didn't have a choice. The . . ."

"I always have a choice; you should remember that. I am not going to be pushed around anymore, not by anybody. I aim to please me! Let the middle class stuck-ups see I can make it without their damn . . ."

Karen was very agitated and she felt the tears coming. She turned her head again. The pain was too much.

Sophie did not respond immediately. She noticed Karen's efforts to maintain the facade. She didn't want to be trapped in a no-win argument with Karen. After a few minutes of silence, Sophie started again, quietly and assertively.

"You think living in other places will be any different from living with your parents? Every place has rules and expectations. Even when we grow older and become responsible adults, we still must act according to the rules."

"Not like theirs. You don't know what it was like to live under their rules."

"Maybe not, but wherever you go there are going to be rules. The sooner you accept that, the sooner you can repair the damage that was done and maybe go home."

"Home?!" Karen shouted. "You call their house home?!"

"What do you call it?"

"PRISON!"

"I hope you never go to prison and observe for yourself the differences between it and your parents' house, no matter how strict they are."

"Stop calling them parents. They're not parents."

"They are still your parents; they have the responsibilities of parents..."

"Maybe they forgot; they certainly didn't behave like parents."

"Maybe you gave them a reason..."

"Fuck you! Everybody cares about what I've done; nobody asks 'why.' It's so typical! Just drop it. It doesn't make a difference. Don't forget what I said. Look for another place and fast, otherwise you might come here next time and not find me."

"I am asking you, for your own good — give this place a chance. There are not many other options and none are as good as this place. You'd benefit from it, but you have to work on it."

"Give me a break," Karen burst out. "What do you mean 'work on it?' They could beg me to stay and I wouldn't."

"With this attitude, you might beg The Reach Center staff to let you stay and *they* wouldn't. Most of the girls were tough before, but..."

"I don't want to hear about how tough they were. I don't give a damn about these girls. They better not mess with me." Karen was already very scared about it as it was and she did not need an extra reminder from her probation officer about how tough the girls were.

"Nobody will unless you give them reason to. What I was about to say is that these residents have changed... Promise me you will give it a chance."

"Sure, sure." Karen was angry, but said it sincerely.

They finally reached the gate. The sheriff parked the car and Sophie noticed apprehension on Karen's face as she tried to prepare herself with a last-minute makeup job and an adult-looking hair style. Karen took a deep breath, opened the car window, and waited.

The probation officer and the sheriff got out of the car.

Silence Broken

"Karen is going to be a new challenge for The Reach Center staff. For her sake, I hope they are up to it," Sophie sighed as she whispered to the sheriff.

Rivcka Edelstein

Long Island, New York, September 1990

Chapter 18

From the parked car, Karen Burg heard noises. She turned her head in the direction of the noise and saw a group of residents playing soccer. The cheering and booing was so loud one might think it was a national game. The coach was running and making calls. The game was moving fast.

Karen heard about The Reach Center's soccer team back in the juvenile shelter. It was referred to as "The Mixed Team" because the boys and girls played together, but once a week the boys played against the girls. Everyone looked forward to that game.

Karen recalled the conversation she had with Dina, one of the residents. Dina had tried to convince her that she was really lucky to be accepted to The Reach Center. Both girls had been waiting for their respective hearings and Dina was giving Karen some tips. Dina herself was in court for the extension of her placement at The Reach Center for another year. Karen was shocked that the girl seemed elated with the prospect of the extension instead of her other option of going to a group home.

While looking out the car window, Karen's mind wandered back to the court room. The judge's final words were as audible to her now as when they were in the court room earlier that day.

"I hope you will take advantage of the fine program offered in your next placement. Other girls like you did, and I pray you will, too. You are an intelligent young lady; it would be beneficial for you to start utilizing your intelligence for good purposes. I have faith in you and I do hope that your parents' action in filing this petition is enough of a message to you that your past behavior and attitude were not and will not be acceptable."

Karen was disappointed. Dina's comments about the judge had led her to believe that this judge was fair. *She certainly was not fair with me. The court only dealt with this situation from my parents' perspective;*

they didn't give me a chance to tell it the way it is. This is not fair. She believed she knew the reason for the judge's partiality.

Let's face it, I was labeled in the petition as a Conduct Disorder adolescent and my parents were described as upstanding members of their community. They have done all that was humanly possible to control their daughter's behavior, she thought, mimicking some of the comments made in the report to herself.

If this is how the justice system works, who needs it? Definitely not me!

Karen looked at the mirror as she put more makeup on her face and rearranged her hair to a funky style. She wanted to be seen as a tough street-smart teen.

Karen got out of the car and marched in defiance around to the trunk. The sheriff unloaded her belongings. She noticed two residents coming up from the soccer field approaching the car. Earlier, she made up her mind not to let anybody know how scared she was. She didn't want any help and she didn't need anybody.

As the two residents came closer to the car Karen noticed that the others, on the nearby field, stopped the game momentarily and looked in her direction.

I don't belong here among these street-wise delinquents. She started to shake. *The only thing I did was rebel against my parents' hypocrisy.*

She decided to let the residents perceive her as tough. That strategy had been very useful in the shelter where she spent a number of weeks.

There was more than the usual conversation among the residents about the arrival of a newcomer. They had heard rumors that "a tough one" was coming today to The Reach Center. They assumed that it must be her since she was brought by the sheriff from the court.

Tanya and Michelle, the two "big sisters" reached the car and welcomed her. They introduced themselves and gathered her bags. She walked with defiance and arrogance, and together the three of them moved toward one of the cottages.

The teenagers on the soccer field were "moved" by the newcomer.

"Look at all her shit," Chris said.

"She looks like a frickin' walk-in closet! Look at the way she walks!" Aida commented.

"Dude, it's her entire household! Did you see what she's wearing?!" Mike added. The comments were growing with time.

"Stop judging her. We can't rag on her like that. You all forgot the way we were." Sue said, and the group's comments ceased.

After dropping her bags at the cottage, Karen and the two big sisters returned back to the soccer field.

"Everyone, this is Karen. Introduce yourself and tell Karen why you are here," Michelle suggested.

"Mike. I was at Spofford Prison before I came here. I smashed my teacher's nose for hitting my best friend."

"R-R-R-Rita, a r-r-runaway."

"Chris. I got busted for selling."

"I'm Sue, and over there is Aida." Sue pointed to Aida, who explained herself.

"I tried to do myself in after my pimp rearranged my face…"

"And, of course, I'm Tanya. I ran away from my stepfather and his groping hands."

A few of the other residents lingered in the back, waiting for a response from Karen. She was startled by the residents' stated records. It confirmed the rumors she had heard about the residents that were placed in The Reach Center. She was terrified and even more determined to give them the impression that she was as tough as they were.

Silence Broken

After the introductions were over, Karen said, in what she hoped was a "tough" manner, "Where's the action?"

"What action did you have in mind?" Sheila asked.

"Tell me what you've got for fun around here and I'll tell you which is my pleasure of the week," Karen smirked.

"Hear, hear!" Sima shouted from a nearby playing position. "She just arrived and she's already looking for pleasure."

"Fuck you, bitch!" Karen retorted.

"Twenty-five cents for the first word and another twenty-five cents for the third. Two out of three isn't a good record to start with," Sue counted.

"Now that I see that some of you can count, can somebody tell me what is going on here?" Karen sneered.

"Nothing is going on. *We* don't curse here," Tanya explained.

"What? Are you kidding? They told me about this place!" Karen said, with a know-it-all attitude and tone of voice.

"And what, pray tell, did you learn about us?" taunted Sima, mimicking Karen's tone.

"My PO told me that she sent tough kids here … like me… she obviously lied."

Tanya jumped in, "It's true that we were tough and street-wise, but we have no use for those things here."

"We don't need to be tough," Chris explained.

"My parole officer is going to take me out of here in no time. She promised," Karen sniffed.

"In the meantime, one piece of advice you'll get from us is that you better curb your foul mouth. We are not cursing you, don't curse us," Sue said.

"Cut the act. You're one of us; a few months ago, we were where you are now," Tanya explained.

"Look, you can make it," Chris encouraged.

Karen was shocked. Tanya held her arm as she guided her inside. "It's time to go to the cottages; we have to prepare dinner and today we have a family meeting."

"Family meeting?" Karen smirked.

"Once a week we have a long dinner and we discuss the events of the week, make decisions about special issues, and discuss our recreation program," Chris explained.

"Sounds like fun," Karen responded with clear sarcasm in her voice.

"No need to be so sarcastic," Tanya said. "We look forward to these meetings because we govern ourselves in the family."

* * *

It was dark outside and the cottages were lit. A few of the residents sit around the dining room table. All of a sudden, there was commotion. The residents turned their heads. Karen and Sima were fighting about the telephone outside its glass booth. Two residents and a counselor rushed to separate them.

Karen screamed, "If you ever come at my face again, I'll kill you. That's a promise, not a threat. Believe it."

The counselor stepped between the two.

"What is this all about?"

Sima started, "Could you believe it? She kept knocking on the door to ask me to give her the phone…"

"…After you used it for a long time."

Sima ignored her and continued to explain. "She kept interrupting my conversation…"

"Because you were still holding the phone…" Again, Karen interrupted.

"I explained that there is a schedule…"

"Schedule! I have to call my PO and I can't wait for a fucking schedule!" Karen screeched.

Tanya, the big sister, explained, "Nobody can wait, that's why we have a schedule. We have rules…"

"She could have stopped her call… She could have called later. I would have paid her for the call." Karen interrupted Tanya, impatiently.

"I'm sure that if you had explained yourself…" Tanya said calmly.

"Who had the chance to explain?" Karen screamed. "I came to call and the phone booth was occupied. I waited for a few moments…"

"Could you have called later?" Sue said quietly.

"Later? It had to be done by five o'clock!"

"Now with all this fighting it's too late. Maybe it's for the better. You should give yourself a chance. You might adjust."

"I'll never adjust," Karen said, fighting back tears.

Sue looked at Karen's shining eyes; she knew the feeling.

"I hope you do… I don't have anybody to call today, would you like to use my block of time until the schedule is adjusted?"

"No thanks, it's too late anyway," she said, as she tried to walk away.

"Maybe to somebody else?" Tanya suggested.

"There is nobody I want to talk to. Nobody!" Karen said with an attempted sharp determination, but her voice cracked toward the end of the exclamation.

* * *

Later in the evening, the residents sat around the dining room table doing arts and crafts. Sue was singing in the kitchen, while mixing something she was preparing for the cottage.

Karen sat in the corner of the couch, away from the rest, and went through some papers given to her with her school packets. She looked up, impressed with Sue's voice.

"Ouch! I hurt my finger," Aida screeched in anger toward the kitchen. "If you want to sing, why don't you stay in tune?"

Sue was still singing when she came to the door. She saw what happened and stopped singing. Nobody said anything.

Karen, quite upset from the incident, called to Aida, "Why don't you...?"

All heads turned towards Karen, wondering what was going to happen next.

"You were saying?" Aida turned her chair 180 degrees, waiting for an answer. Karen was about to come forward when Sue came forward.

"It's OK. I don't mind."

"No, it's not OK," Karen said in disbelief. "It's not your fault she hurt her finger."

"I know it and Aida knows it. She didn't mean it," Sue said patiently.

"But that's wrong... and you should not take it."

"It's not right, but that is why we are here."

"If I had a beautiful voice like yours, I would not have stopped."

"I will continue to sing in a few minutes."

"Oh please!" Karen said, looking at Aida disgustedly.

Aida was ready to jump off her seat. Sue approached her chair and attempted to calm Aida.

"Aida," Sue said in a soothing voice, "can I do anything for your finger? It doesn't look good..."

Silence Broken

Karen looked at both of them in disbelief and slowly and sarcastically said, "The victim is defending the offender..."

Sue held Aida back as Sheila got up from the table and slowly approached the couch.

"What are you, a troublemaker?" Sheila glared at Karen. "Do you really want to see a fight for the sake of a fight? You came to the wrong place. This attitude will get you nowhere."

"Another one!" Karen said angrily. "I don't have any use for people who let others step on them. Are all of you afraid of Aida's temper?"

"You really are clueless. It is not a question of fear." Sheila said as she turned away from Karen and walked back to the dining room table.

"We understand that you're new. You will learn! At least, I hope so. Otherwise, I'll agree with Sheila, you came to the wrong place," Tanya said from the table.

There were a few minutes of calmness.

Carol, a counselor, entered from the side door and saw the group was still working on their art projects.

"How's it going? Anybody finished?" Carol turned to the couch. "I have a project for you; come join us Karen. When you finish this, you can decorate your room with it or give it as a gift to you parents next family day!"

"I am giving nothing to my parents. What have they given me?" Karen said sharply in a dismissing tone.

"You don't have to give it to anybody," Carol said.

"You're damn right I don't." Karen said as she walked toward the door.

"You can express yourself, but please, no cursing."

Karen started, "I heard about that... You will take a quarter out of my allowance. You can keep your damn allowance. Nobody is going to tell me what to do or how to speak. Nobody, you hear? I have had enough shit from my so-called parents. I am not taking any more of it." She walked out, deliberately slamming the door.

Aida smiled, "Just a newcomer, she will learn. I did. I still have difficulty controlling my temper, but I am learning."

She looked around for reassurance from the others and they nodded in genuine agreement.

"Anyway," Aida continued, "how could she complain about her parents? Look at the loads of clothes she has. Did you see her stuff when she came in? How could she say 'What have they given me?'" Aida laughed as she imitated Karen.

"I don't think she means *things*. I heard she had a rough life, really rough…" Sue explained.

"So what? Who didn't have a rough life?" Sheila commented.

Everyone nodded in agreement, reflecting privately.

* * *

Later that night Karen stood in front of the mirror. Her hands reached to the back of her neck and she unlocked the clip of her necklace. It was a gold chain with a Star of David charm on it. Every night, just before she headed for the shower, she removed it from her neck and put it in her jewelry box. Every morning, first thing before she left her room, she put it on again. She cherished it, and for years she followed the same ritual.

As she put the chain in her jewelry box that night, she vividly recalled the memories associated with it.

The Burgs used to tease her about it, but she continued to wear it despite their objections. It was like hell until Jim, her adopted brother, intervened on her behalf and the Burgs stopped insisting that she remove it. She never understood the reasons behind their objections. For Karen, it was one more way of showing her that they didn't accept who or what she was. For that same reason, she insisted on wearing it to prove her independence. She had a special attachment to the necklace, even during the years that she did not know the symbolic meaning of the charm.

Silence Broken

The years passed by. Her first emergency placement out of the Burgs' home was to a group home run by the Jewish Board of Guardians. The second day she was there, the residents held a birthday party for a girl named Rosie. The house-parents and residents had chipped in to buy a gift - a Star of David on a chain. Rosie was very happy and had tears in her eyes. Karen was curious about the girl's reaction. Later that evening Karen learned that the Star of David had special meaning for Rosie, who hoped she would get one for her birthday. Karen found out that the girl was Jewish. Up to that point, Karen hadn't had an opportunity to associate with Jewish children her age. Throughout most of the night Rosie told her memories of celebrating the holidays with her relatives. For Rosie, that was long ago, before her parents were killed in a car accident and her life turned upside down. Rosie cried a lot and laughed a lot as she told Karen some of her life stories. Karen warmed up to Rosie and told her about the lady who used to visit her when she was very young and the details of the last time she saw her.

"It was just before Christmas and the lady came with many gifts. My foster parents had a short private chat with the lady and they excused themselves and left me and the lady in the living room. I noticed the changes in the lady's face and I even asked her if she was feeling well. The lady hugged me and gave me the box with the gold necklace. I received many gifts from her that visit, but the gold charm was dearest of them all. In fact, the lady explained that the Jewish people were celebrating Chanukah and that, according to some traditions, parents gave children a gift for each night of the holiday. When the lady was leaving, I thanked her for the Christmas gifts she brought, but my foster mother corrected me and told me that the lady brought me Chanukah gifts."

At the time, Karen didn't comprehend the difference, but, by the time she met Rosie, she understood. Karen hadn't told anybody that she missed the lady and her hugs until she had met Rosie. It was the first and last time she told anyone.

Now, four years later, tears welled as she looked at the charm in the box. She had moved so many times and lost so many people. This place was just one more on a long list. The pain was too strong.

She put on her nightgown and approached the window. She recalled the way her foster parents, Mr. and Mrs. Rocks, used to tuck her in, years before. She felt very lonely and abandoned, wondering how she would survive in this new "home." Tears stung her eyes as she looked up at the sky and the stars. Whenever she was alone and hurting, she looked up to the sky with hope that maybe someone up there was listening to her pleas.

The tears rolled down her cheeks; she couldn't hold them back any more.

"*Dear Lord,*" she slowly started to whisper. The emotions flowed through her, overbearing and endless as she longed for her mother. She decided to call the song she had written *My Prayer*, Karen continued, whispering her song, as she attached her melody to it.

She continued singing, attaching her melody to the words of the song that she had written the night before in the shelter. At that point, her voice became louder. She was singing from the window, in the back of the house, facing the dark back yard and the trees.

Dear Lord, every night without fail

I repeatedly call your name

While the rest of the world is sleeping,

I cannot stop my weeping.

Only my faith in you stops my tears.

You're the only one who can hear my prayer.

Knowing that you are here and near

Helps me cope better with my fear.

I can't wait any longer, it just isn't fair.

What I need is for someone to care.

Help me hold on to my hopes and my dreams

Help me endure my pain and my fears.

Help the one who gave me my first breath

Silence Broken

To find and rescue me from my pain.

For you it is not a big deal.

Make it happen, make it real.

Only my faith in you stops my tears.

You're the only one who can hear my prayer.

Knowing that you are here and near

Helps me cope better with my fear.

She became aware of the sound of a trumpet that accompanied her while she was singing. She stopped singing and leaned forward to look from both sides of her window. The sound of the trumpet stopped. All the other windows were dark.

She shivered and decided to climb into bed, wrapping the sheets tightly around herself, hoping for their comfort. She finally fell asleep with her daily wish that her real mother would come and rescue her.

Rivcka Edelstein

Long Island, New York, September 1990

Chapter 19

"The hearing is over for today," the probation officer explained to the social worker from The Reach Center. "It's very frustrating."

Sophie was angry with Karen. Only five days ago she had brought her to The Reach Center and already she was in violation of her probation. Karen put her case in jeopardy.

She had promised me she'd give it a chance; is this her best effort? Is this assault part of her trying?

Karen seemed to her a very intelligent and sensitive young lady and it seemed inconceivable that she acted as she had. She believed that Karen was "all bark no bite." She talked, yelled, screamed, and threatened, but did not physically act. Nothing in her records indicated that she was violent. What could have provoked her? According to The Reach Center's social worker, there was very little provocation, certainly not enough to bring about an assault. The social worker apologized for the need to place Karen in the shelter and hoped the probation officer understood that it was a necessary procedure. It was important to convey the message to Karen that such behavior would not be tolerated. Sophie knew that physical assault on another resident or a staff member required pressing charges.

Everything went very fast in court and the social worker was confused.

"What was that all about?" she asked Sophie. "What exactly was the problem? I really didn't follow what went on inside the courtroom."

She had rushed to the court that morning, despite the fact that it was her day off. She was told that, if someone from The Reach Center wasn't there, the hearing would be postponed. Karen would be forced to spend another night in the shelter, which they were hoping to avoid.

"It was postponed," Sophie said quietly so as not to disclose her own anger and frustration.

"But why?"

"Because her parents didn't show up!"

"What is going to happen next time? They've already said they are not coming. They said that from now on all her actions are the problem of The Reach Center. How do you intend to solve it?"

"The judge heard that and it was unacceptable to her. I don't think this couple knows who they are dealing with…"

Rivcka Edelstein

Long Island, New York, October 1990

Chapter 20

Two weeks had passed and Karen was having a difficult time adjusting to her new placement. She often broke the rules which she interpreted as limiting her personal freedom. She even objected to the rules and laws drafted by the residents themselves based on the self-governing approach in The Reach Center. She had several serious altercations and conflicts, even physical fights, with the residents and staff. Karen quickly managed to alienate herself from most of the residents and she felt very lonely. The therapeutic team had to act firmly regarding her disruptive behavior and physical outbursts. When punishment in The Center didn't control her behavior, she was placed in the shelter and had to appear before the family court judge.

The team eagerly awaited the return of Dr. Rachel Stone, the Clinical Director of The Reach Center, from her vacation. When she did return, she barely had a chance to sit and go through her accumulating mail before she was asked by the counselors, teachers, and therapists to do something about the new resident, Karen Burg.

Dr. Stone read Karen's personal records and the numerous behavioral reports filed by the staff in the first two weeks of her placement. It seemed clear that there were two basic motivations, often contradicting, which governed Karen's behavior. She fought against any perceived injustice to her or another person while trying to maintain her own street-wise façade to cover her fear of violence and peer pressure. Karen was on guard all the time, fearful that others would recognize her weakness and take advantage of it. In those situations, she acted forcefully.

Dr. Stone felt that those two drives intensified when Karen was placed in a residence such as The Reach Center. Karen perceived the youth there as tough and potentially threatening. It was unfortunate that this same behavior lead to her alienation.

Silence Broken

According to the records, Karen had been placed in the shelter and appeared before Judge Levi three times in her first two weeks.

* * *

There was a knock on the door. After a few seconds, Karen walked in.

Dr. Stone got up and welcomed her to The Reach Center, apologizing for not welcoming her earlier and warmly shaking her hand.

Karen sat in the chair beside the desk and Dr. Stone sat on the couch. After a brief moment, Dr. Stone pointed to the open file on the desk.

"Three visits to the shelter in two weeks?" she said. "That's a new record for us."

"They started with me. The girls here hate me!" Karen retorted.

Time passed and the conversation centered on the trip from the court, the hearings, the room, etc. They slowly moved from light conversation to a more serious discussion.

"Karen, we care about you," Dr. Stone encouraged. "How can we work together?"

"Work together?" Karen asked incredulously. "Why should I? I got my pride. I don't need to change. My parents do."

"I hear you, but is that realistic? Let's try to find ways that you…"

"No way!" Karen cut in. "I've got my pride."

"Karen, what you are doing to yourself doesn't show pride. Pride is an inner feeling that has a time and a place. You are using it in the wrong way."

Karen burst, speaking rapidly and with anger. Her only coherent words were "I have my pride."

Dr. Stone emphasized, "If you really believe in yourself, really believe in yourself, you can accomplish whatever—"

"You mean *Everything is Possible*©*?*" Karen interrupted again. "That stupid therapeutic game you use here? I've stopped believing."

"That's sad."

"It's not sad. It's realistic. I had dreams. Got me nowhere."

"Is this behavior getting you somewhere?" Dr. Stoned questioned.

"Definitely!" Karen scoffed with a dismissive shrug. "It got me out of their home and hopefully out of here."

"Is that what you want? To be rejected by us?" Dr. Stone asked.

"Do I give a damn?"

"Don't you?"

Karen looked at Dr. Stone, fuming.

"Karen, parents sometimes have problems, distorted expectations, and bad reactions to their child's expression of himself or herself. It is their problem and you don't need to make it yours. By changing your attitude about yourself and about your world based on their reactions, you are, in a sense, adopting their problems and making them yours. What might be right for a child and his or her well-being might not be the same as what the parents wish. You took their word that you are not capable and are worthless. Instead of having faith in yourself, you went ahead and fulfilled their predictions. You latched onto their expressions of you and injured yourself in the process." Dr. Stone stopped.

She looked at Karen and added, "You have changed; I read your record from before you came to your adoptive parents and this is not the real you."

Silence Broken

Karen looked up with a pained expression. The mention, in public, of her life before the Burgs brought tears to her eyes.

"I remember happy days," Karen said, "and people who cared for me and had faith in me. I used to sing and dance. I was happy. Then the social system came and took it all away. I had to fight to survive. Now everyone thinks I was born bad."

"People refer to the behavior that got you thrown out of your home," Dr. Stone stated.

"My home?"

"That's the one we've to work with."

"They say I don't deserve them. Guess what. They don't deserve me. Why does no one care about that?" She began to cry.

Dr. Stone reached out and held Karen, who moved to the couch, put her head on Dr. Stone's shoulder, and sobbed.

Amidst her sobbing Karen tried to continue, "You are right. This is not me. Why didn't somebody in the past wonder when and why the real Karen disappeared?"

"This is what we are here for. We would like to help clear the pain on both sides."

Karen didn't react.

"We must work together as partners," Dr. Stone continued.

"Who are 'we'?" Karen asked.

"Us, together as partners. The Reach Center and Karen Burg."

Karen did not say anything.

"We care about you and we feel you deserve a chance. Do you care about you? Do you feel you deserve a chance?"

"Sure, but what exactly do you want from me?"

"What we are asking is that you join us, as a team, to help you. We want you to care about yourself and to show yourself that you *do* matter."

"That's all?"

"Basically, yes. We are looking for a commitment from you."

Karen was not prepared to cooperate that easily; she had been ready to fight them and the proposition from Dr. Stone caught her off guard.

"Don't make an empty commitment. Think about it."

Dr. Stone got up from the couch where she and Karen were seated. She offered her right hand, grasping Karen's, and shook hard.

"Welcome to The Reach Center and good luck," she said warmly.

Silence Broken

Long Island, New York, December 1990

Chapter 21

For the last two hours Karen was pacing back and forth in her room. She hoped that sooner or later she was going to be called to the office, since most of the residents had been called. She knew what she was going to do, but she was scared…

* * *

It all started about a week before, when Dr. Stone was at a conference. Karen had just returned from her *fourth* court appearance in a period of six weeks. On the way back from court, Karen was determined to stay out of trouble. An hour earlier she had heard the judge, who had seen her the three previous times, saying that The Reach Center was graciously willing to give her one more "last chance."

The judge concluded her sermon with, "If I were you, I wouldn't test my luck. Take advantage of this opportunity and don't blow it this time."

Painfully aware of the reasons she got into the last four fights, Karen decided to stop fighting.

As The Reach Center's car pulled into the parking lot, Karen noticed a big commotion. Sue approached and hugged Karen as soon as she stepped out.

"I am so glad they let you come back; I missed you!" Sue rushed her words, excited to see her friend.

"I hope you give your butt a chance to see if it can get used to the good mattress you have in your room. Karen, would you please try!" Sue pleaded, whispering in Karen's ear.

Karen had tears in her eyes, she didn't know anybody cared. She gave Sue a hug in return, but couldn't say a word because of the tears.

Karen came back to reality, noticing the commotion once again.

"What's going on?"

"Man, it's all messed up." Sue shook her head.

"Well? Speak up." Karen gave Sue an imploring look.

"Girl," Sue tried, "you just returned from your fourth court appearance for fighting in yet another one of your justice crusades. Don't push your luck. With a fifth court appearance, you'll get expelled for sure. Stay out of it. The less you know…"

"Sue, spit it."

"While you were gone, somebody stole money. The staff hasn't been able to find out who did it."

"That sucks."

"Even if anyone knows, no one is going to talk."

"That's bullshit. You said that this place was better."

"But it ain't perfect!"

"You said the thief was a lucky bastard, so what's the difference?"

"Dr. Stone just returned. Nothing returns back to normal until the money is found. You're in the clear. They know you weren't here."

Almost immediately the speakers turned on. Karen and Sue listened intently as silence took over the yard and Dr. Stone's voice poured over the crowd.

"I am glad to be back and hearing all the good news. But a disappointing incident occurred this week. When one of us acts against the family, we all are affected. We are going to call you, one by one. For now, all outings are canceled."

There were a few groans from the crowd, but no one seemed surprised.

Silence Broken

Karen turned back to Sue, saying, "I have to finish my homework. I'll see you later."

Sue left and Karen picked a picnic table and started on a school assignment. After a few minutes, Karen looked up and saw Sue run back out toward her.

"Mike, Chris, and Rob made Little Jon take the blame," Sue gasped. "He's expelled."

"No way!" Karen was shocked.

As Sue left again, Karen started to pace. Carol was walking by when she noticed her agitated pacing.

"No dinner tonight?" Carol tried.

"I need to talk to the team."

"You wouldn't be called. Everyone knows you weren't here the night the money was stolen."

Karen hesitated a moment before running toward the conference room.

* * *

Karen burst through the door, seeing Rob on his way out. Slurred words tumbled out as Karen tried to say everything at once . . . Dr. Stone motioned her to slow down. Karen took a deep breath.

"So, why'd you decide to let him go?" Karen was somewhere between asking and accusing the staff before her. "You know he didn't do it."

"It was his decision when he lied," Dr. Stone said calmly.

"Punish him, but don't let him go!" Karen wanted to cry.

"Karen, even though we don't approve of your bursting in here, we thank you for coming forward and caring."

Karen gave up at that point and stormed out of the room. Dr. Stone turned to Karen's therapist.

"Call Carol," She instructed. She turned to the counselor from the Blue Cottage.

"Keep your residents occupied in the cottage. Those involved will try to provoke Karen to fight."

* * *

Karen came out of the building and Rob approached her from the back, pushing and grabbing at her. He tripped Karen, but she got up and kept walking.

Karen wandered in the yard, looking for Little John. Finally, she found him on the grass in the corner of the cottage.

"I was looking all over for you." Karen said, sitting down next to him.

"My parents are on their way to pick me up. They're gonna kill me." Little John looked away, grimacing.

"Tell the team the truth. You got expelled for lying."

"I am afraid to."

Karen put her hand on his shoulder, trying to comfort Little John.

* * *

The furniture had been removed, and the Social Club had been tastefully converted into a dance hall. On the wall, there hung a hand-painted banner reading "THE REACH CENTER WELCOMES THE SAINT PAUL HIGH SCHOOL TO OUR SEMI-ANNUAL DANCE".

Karen stood beside Carol, waiting when she saw Sue enter and walk over.

"Everyone knows you talked to Little John," Sue whispered. "Rob was taken to the shelter. Mike and Chris lost all their privileges. Watch your back."

Silence Broken

Karen and Sue danced next to one another. Karen's eyes were closed.

Mike and Chris entered the club. Mike looked around, located Karen, and then he and Chris began to walk towards her. Halfway there, he motioned for Chris to stop. The room became silent and the music stopped. Karen opened her eyes to find that all eyes were on her. Tanya and Michelle started to edge toward her, but Dr. Stone motioned for them to wait, hoping they wouldn't have to intervene.

"I know you didn't snitch on us," Mike finally broke the silence. "I respect you for what you did. You got guts."

Karen breathed deeply and looked at him.

"I didn't think they would expel Little John," Mike continued. "He told me you bugged him to tell the truth. He decided to tell the truth. I didn't try to stop him… May I have this dance?"

Karen was surprised but agreed. The song *I Am a Believer* by Neil Diamond was playing.

Karen was uncomfortably stumbling while Mike danced surprisingly well. He confidently guided and reassured Karen as she tried to avoid eye contact and followed his lead.

Sue danced with Little John, but her eyes were on Mike and Karen. She smiled.

A slow dance followed and Karen tried to leave the dance floor. Mike pulled her in, looked at her face, smiled, and guided her along the dance floor. Karen still avoided his eyes, instead focusing on his chest where she notices a pendant.

"What's that on your chain?" She asked curiously.

"It's a Jewish symbol. A mezuzah," he replied.

"Are you Jewish?"

"Aren't you? One time I saw you wearing the Star of David. I guess you are Jewish too."

Karen took out her pendant from underneath her shirt.

"You mean this thing?"

"That's a Jewish symbol too," he repeated.

"Oh. I didn't know! I wasn't raised Jewish."

* * *

As the dance came to an end, the guests left and residents followed them. Mike and Chris remained, cleaning and moving chairs. Mike quietly hummed the song that he and Karen had danced to.

Chris looked up for a moment and noted, "I guess stealing that money cost us a lot in the long run. These extra chores suck. Plus, we lost all of our privileges. But seriously dude, you lost a lot more than I did."

"What do you mean?"

"You know. Now you can't be captain of the soccer team anymore."

"Yeah it blows but there's nothing I can do about it now. Who do you think will be the new captain?"

"Definitely not me," Chris smirked and Mike agreed.

"Well, do you think they might give it to a girl?" Chris posed. "How would you feel about taking instructions from a girl captain?"

"If she's good, why not?"

"I don't know. You really would be cool with following a girl?"

"A soccer player," Mike corrected.

"Dude, you are going soft."

Silence Broken

Mike ignored him and continued to hum. Chris looked at his friend, smiled, and nodded his head.

Rivcka Edelstein

Part III: 1991

Silence Broken

Long Island, New York, January 1991

Chapter 22

Another stormy hearing was in progress in Judge Levi's courtroom. It was the fifth in less than two months — each time following a fight involving Karen. This time she spent two nights in the county shelter and her parents were summoned. They were angry both with Karen and with the Juvenile Court for insisting that they be present.

The therapist gave her report about Karen's last fight. Watching Karen, the judge felt sure that below Karen's façade there was fear. She decided to try a different approach: out of the court room she could speak with Karen more freely and hear her view. Judge Levi adjourned the hearing.

The judge called Karen to her chamber and watched as she entered defiantly. Karen stood at the door with her hands in her pockets, testing the judge.

"I asked you to come to my private office so I could speak with you openly — off the record."

"Sure. Go ahead, Judge."

"I really would like to understand you."

"What is there to understand?" Karen challenged.

Judge Levi ignored the provocation and continued, "Why do you keep doing these things? Why do you fight with everyone?"

"How would you like to have been adopted, not even having a clue as to why you were given up by your own parents?"

"Don't use that as an excuse," interrupted the judge. "Thousands of children are adopted every year, and they don't all end up in juvenile court."

"I don't need excuses. I don't need to explain myself. For a moment, I thought you were human. You talked to me nicely, so I told you what was bugging me. Forget it! Just forget it! Do anything you want to me."

"You've misinterpreted what I said. I do wish to understand you, but your attitude will only hurt you. This is the fifth time you've appeared before me in the last two months. What do you expect me to do? Is the shelter what you want? You don't belong in a lockup."

"Why don't you tell my *parents* to take me home. That could solve some problems."

"I don't think so. Your behavior at home is what got you here in the first place."

"That's because my father was never pleased with me. He was too strict…"

Judge Levi noticed Karen's hesitation and prompted her gently, "Too strict?"

"They never should have adopted me. They wanted a genius."

"Your father and mother wanted you; they chose you."

"Not him, he never cared for me… And now I am not sure about her either."

"I'm sure the adoption agency did a thorough check. People who do not like children do not adopt, especially if they have one child already."

"They only adopted me because she wanted a girl."

"Your father seems to really care about you. It is because he cares that he is disappointed with your behavior."

"Do you think they threw me out of their house out of concern for me? You don't know what you're talking about . . ."

Karen was beginning to lose her temper.

Silence Broken

"Did anybody ask why my behavior is so 'unacceptable,' to quote the professionals? The best thing for me is to find my own mother. I would like to know my roots."

"You know that is impossible."

"Don't ever say 'impossible;' everything is possible if you want it bad enough."

"For seventeen years old, you really…"

"I'm not seventeen yet; I'll be seventeen next February. As a matter of fact, February 14th. You can send me a gift at whatever institution I'm in at the time…'"

"Hey! I'm just kidding," she added when she noticed the judge beginning to write down the date.

"Why don't you try to work with the staff at The Reach Center and get the therapy you need so you can go home? You don't belong in a shelter," implored the judge.

"Who said I wanted to go home? I cared in the beginning, but during the last two years I've come to realize that I am not wanted there and I've accepted it."

"Are you telling me you really don't wish to return home?"

"Yes. You've got it now! I'm a human being and they can't play games like this with me. Now they want me, now they don't. You see, a real mother would not have thrown me out just because 'he' said so."

"Your real mother did give you up for adoption."

"You don't know what made her do it." Karen had become very agitated and was already screaming at Judge Levi.

"Don't you dare judge my mother - she is not in your court."

"I am not judging her and I would like you to stop judging your adoptive parents."

"Can I give you some advice?" fumed Karen. "Have somebody investigate them. You'll be surprised at what they'd discover. Sure, I'm not an easy person — maybe even a brat, but I'm not that bad. I only wanted them to accept me, the real me, and not the little girl they imagined that they were getting . . . Is that too much to ask?"

"I don't think that is necessarily the case."

"I've been labeled as emotionally disturbed, and if you grant them their wish of reversing the adoption, they would be thrilled. They feel I've brought shame and dishonor to the family name. All I did was react to years of abuse and disregard for my feelings. Mother made some effort to be warm and caring, but Father didn't even pretend. Almost from the day I arrived he said that I'm not what they wanted and I'm no good. It hurts the first time you hear it and every time after that, but then you start hurting them right back.

"One time when he told me that I was not what he wanted, I told him that he was not what I wanted either. He slapped me across the face so hard that I lost my balance. All Mother said was, 'You hurt your father.' I, a ten-year-old kid, hurt him, a 39-year-old man. What about my pain? I guess he believed that children should be seen and not heard. Anyway, from then on, things went downhill."

After a long pause, Judge Levi made up her mind. "I'm sending you back to The Reach Center. It will be up to them to decide whether or not to transfer you, and where to. What do you think can be done to foster your adjustment?"

"Find my mother; I bet she would want me."

"Do you truly believe that finding your mother would solve all of your difficulties?"

"I'm not sure, but it can't be any worse. Maybe she would love me for who I am."

Karen burst into tears and Judge Levi let her cry. Karen took a deep breath, wiped her eyes, and said apologetically, "I don't usually let myself cry... I'm glad we spoke. I know that you didn't have to give me a chance to talk — you could have just sent me to the shelter again."

"Is that what you want?" Karen shook her head and the judge continued, "I didn't think so... You remind me of someone I once knew..."

Karen was silent.

"Anyway, Karen, good luck. I hope I will not need to see you here for violations of your probation. Just give it a try. Do it for yourself, not for your parents. Look at who you are hurting. Who is unhappy and who has lost so much?"

Karen was listening intently and when the judge stopped she said very slowly, "I will try. And again, thank you."

Karen walked toward the door, hesitated for a moment, and then turned back toward Judge Levi.

"Please try to help me find my mother. My parents are very serious about rescinding the adoption; please don't try to convince them otherwise. I know I'm asking a lot, but think of it as saving a soul — mine — for what it's worth. I just hope I didn't miss my chance at The Reach Center. "

"I hope so too. Good luck."

"Thanks. The girls in the shelter and in The Reach Center were right about you — you're O.K."

Those last words were ringing in Judge Levi's ears as she smiled and reached out her hand to Karen.

"So, you aren't planning to come here again?" Judge Levi joked.

"I think I'll try a field trip to places other than the court building. I agree with you, I come here too often."

After Karen closed the door, Judge Levi sat at her desk and began making phone calls.

The first call was to the Burgs. She informed them about Karen's decision to give The Reach Center a real chance. Judge Levi sensed their indifference; they'd heard that story before. She suggested that maybe they would like to be more involved with The Reach Center, but the Burgs gave her weak excuses about being too busy and not being able to take more days away from work. They told her that they had requested their lawyer to proceed with rescinding the adoption. What surprised Judge Levi most were the antagonistic comments made by Mrs. Burg. The conversation ended when Judge Levi said, "Well, I just thought you might want to hear that Karen is really going to try."

"Thank you for making the effort, but we really don't care what she does," Mr. Burg responded courteously

* * *

On the ride back to The Reach Center, Karen was very quiet in the car. She was worried: she had been given another chance by the judge but she was not sure if The Reach Center was going to keep her or try to transfer her to another facility. She violated probation several times. Actually, she may have set a new record. The Reach Center tried to help those who reached out to grasp the new chance, not those who abused it.

By the time her therapist dropped her off, it was late afternoon. She was asked to wait in the Social Services Building until she was called to the staff meeting.

Silence Broken

Long Island, New York, January 1991

Chapter 23

Judge Sharon Levi sat in her chambers, exhausted. It was not the first time she had noticed the familiar features, but today when she heard Karen's voice she was stunned. She finally realized who Karen had reminded her of. Her face, voice, everything... Her mind wandered — 23... 24... 25 years ago... She closed her eyes and reminisced.

* * *

Coaxing her mind back to the present, she thought about her implied promise to Karen to help her find her mother if the Burgs were indeed serious about rescinding the adoption. She would have to review the regulations on such a procedure.

In the meantime, she decided to wait and see if Karen would really make an effort to adjust at The Reach Center and whether or not the Burgs would change their mind. She pulled out her memo pad and made two notes: "Karen's birthday — February 14th," and "follow Karen's progress." Absentmindedly, she added a star to the first.

Judge Levi knew that despite the firmness with which the therapist presented her case, The Reach Center staff wanted Karen back. Some of the other judges felt that The Reach Center was taking advantage of the court as a disciplinary route and they wanted it stopped. She felt differently; if this technique helped the teenagers to shape up, why not be a strong part of it?

From her bench, she saw that it was an effective approach with many of the residents.

Rivcka Edelstein

Long Island, New York, January 1991

Chapter 24

An emergency staff meeting was in session at the Social Services Building. The issue: Karen. So far, she'd had five violent outbursts which ended by sending her to the county shelter. Each incident was serious enough to result in her expulsion from the program. The staff expressed their concern that keeping her in The Reach Center would jeopardize the therapeutic accomplishments of the other residents. The clinical director, Dr. Stone, was reluctant to dismiss her; she believed Karen was reachable.

Despite Karen's recent behavior, no one on the team wanted to see her hurt. Gina, Karen's therapist, mentioned this to the judge before the hearing began.

Once Gina returned from court, the meeting progressed more smoothly. She reported the judge's decision following her private meeting with Karen. "She said, 'I don't think another night in the shelter is necessary. The Reach Center should decide how to proceed from here.'"

Aside from Gina, Carol and Dr. Stone, the entire staff seemed to be in favor of a quick dismissal.

"Isn't the point of our program is to help adolescents exactly like Karen?" Dr. Stone glared at her staff.

"What else can we do?" The science teacher said, exasperated.

Dr. Stone scanned the faces of each of her staff. "What is the common element in all of the incidents?"

"She was fighting for justice!" Carol exclaimed, her face brightening.

"Yes, and in each case, if you recall, she didn't start the fight. Each report stated she was physically and verbally provoked by

Silence Broken

others after she interfered on behalf of the perceived injustice," continued Dr. Stone.

"Are you saying that if someone is provoked it gives them the right to physically attack another person?" The math teacher was furious.

"G-d forbid, no!" Dr. Stone instantly clarified, "What I'm saying is that our rejection and dismissal of her would not be the ideal solution. We need to work with her. Rejection is too easy and she has received plenty of it in her life. How about firmness and acceptance instead? We can proceed in such a way that our disapproval is clear, but we can still work with her."

The staff members were agitated.

"Have you considered the message this gives to the other residents?" one of the therapists asked.

"My suggestion is that we begin looking for another placement for her, but take our time in doing so. We must give ourselves enough time to work with her even more intensively. This way we could give Karen another chance without jeopardizing the program. We have used this approach successfully in the past."

"How much more intensive? We are already working with her twice as much as the original treatment plan provides," Gina pointed out.

"First, we will call her and ask her if she would like us to facilitate her transfer by making an emergency placement. We can see how serious she was all those times she screamed she wanted to 'get the hell out of here.' Second, we must be sure to occupy her constructively. If she is active in a positive way, the other residents may see her from another perspective and stop provoking her. What about her skills? What is she especially good at?" Dr. Stone asked.

The staff members looked at one another in complete silence.

"Come on, everybody is good at something," Dr. Stone pleaded.

"Well," the music teacher started reluctantly, "Once in choir the students took turns with solo parts. Though she hesitated, she had a pleasant voice. I was very impressed."

Everyone looked up in surprise. It was hard to believe that Karen's often harsh and scratchy tone of voice could have a pleasant singing quality.

"I heard her singing once in the shower. She has a beautiful voice," Carol agreed. "When I told her that I heard her singing, she was very embarrassed and apologized. It was odd."

"OK, aside from encouraging her singing, how else could we approach her?" Dr. Stone asked.

"I remember reading a story which she wrote during one of her stays at the shelter," Laura, the English teacher, added. "Karen had left the paper folded inside her assignment book. The next day, when I returned the workbook to her, I told her that I had found it, but reassured her that I hadn't read it. She seemed relieved, but a moment later she came back to me and asked if I would read it. It was a very creative and touching story about a mother searching for her lost daughter. It described a great deal of pain she had apparently experienced in her own life."

The room was quiet again.

"Good. She sings nicely and she writes creatively," Dr. Stone summarized. "I am sure that with these two skills we can get Karen involved in more constructive endeavors. What about a column in The Reach Center magazine or a solo at our Easter Dinner?"

"How do you expect to get her to agree and to cooperate?"

"I can try," volunteered Mrs. Darcey. All eyes turned toward the gym teacher. She never felt she had anything to contribute, so she usually kept to herself. She dreaded the decision to dismiss Karen; she liked her and saw a side of her that apparently no one else did.

"You have a suggestion, Mrs. Darcey?"

"I think that Karen lets her guard down during athletic activities in gym. She really tries her best and she's quite good. She plays best at soccer. I could see her being voted captain of the team in no time. I think the residents would see her natural ability if not for their anger with her attitude. She listens to me and pays attention to my suggestions. One of the rainy days when we had dancing in the recreation center, she developed some creative moves. She made sure that nobody was watching. I feel she can be worked with, and I think she, like all the residents, is worthy of our extra effort. She has a lot to offer." She said it forcefully, surprising herself as much as she surprised her colleagues.

"I agree," said the English teacher as the others nodded.

Dr. Stone was pleased. "If we help Karen shine in a positive way she won't need to resort to negative behavior. The residents might then realize that she is worth giving a chance. Each of us needs to consider how we can incorporate her skills in our work with her. Start slowly, build her confidence in these areas, and move as far as we can to actualize whatever potential she has. Maybe when her parents hear how well she is doing they might give her a chance, too."

"Don't count on her parents changing their minds," Gina interjected.

"What do you mean?" asked the Clinical Director.

"They are going ahead with rescinding the adoption. They all but begged the judge to free them from their responsibilities for Karen."

"Well! I guess we are all she's got, if she'll have us."

"She is waiting outside," Gina reminded them.

"It would be better to let her think about it for a while."

* * *

Sheila walked into the student bathroom. As she washed her hands she overheard a conversation from the teachers' bathroom coming through the vents:

"The optimist, Dr. Stone, and her three pigeons think they can change the untamed Karen? Good luck."

"I can't believe Carol joined them. She's the one who takes Karen back and forth to court."

"Quiet. Someone may hear you."

"Nobody is here. Anyhow . . ."

Sheila waited in the bathroom until she heard them in the hall walking away.

Silence Broken

Long Island, New York, January 1991

Chapter 25

That afternoon, the residents in Karen's cottage called an informal house meeting. There was a great deal of commotion and excitement and many angry comments were said.

"Enough is enough," Sima sighed.

"How much more abuse are we supposed to take from her?" Aida managed through clenched teeth.

"Let her go someplace else," Sima agreed

"I suggest we vote on it," Michelle, one of the Big Sisters, chimed in.

"It is not an issue that should be voted on; not yet, anyway," Tanya said calmly and assertively. "The Team put her in our cottage because we've been here longer and have already adjusted. They hoped we could help her."

"What do you mean? It's our home. She's not happy here and she's just making it worse for the rest of us. We did our best and…"

"Did we?" Tanya interrupted.

"Wait a minute. Are you suggesting that we didn't try our best for the last few weeks? Didn't we try?" Sima challenged, standing up and facing Tanya.

"We did try, that's for sure. But did we really do our best?" She looked around — everyone was quiet.

"I didn't even try," Aida admitted. "I didn't like her from the start. But you have to admit that she provoked me and… well, as you all know, it doesn't take much to provoke me."

Each of the girls in the room nodded.

"Well, that's exactly what I mean," Tanya continued. "If we all try to figure out our feelings and reactions, most of us will find that Karen stirred something in each of us. It's up to us how we react. We might have initially tried to help, but we stopped. Did we give her a fair chance? Try to remember what we were like a year ago."

"You have to admit, we weren't like her," Sima said to Tanya.

"Weren't we?" Sue asked. "Maybe you've forgotten. I think Tanya is right. It is difficult for us to see it because the conditions were different six or nine months ago. We didn't give each other a lot of trouble because we were a collective mess, but we sure did give the staff a run for their money."

The room filled with laughter.

"And how many chances did we get?" Sue continued. "Plenty! I remember all the times I was called into Team meetings and made promises which I didn't even make an effort to keep. It wasn't until I was put on 'guest status' and I had a choice to shape up or leave, that I really tried. I made the effort because I didn't want to leave."

"That's what they should do with Karen," Michelle thought out loud. "Why don't they call her?"

"Maybe they will call her to a general meeting." Sue offered.

"I believe that there is more than meets the eye. I mean, they know things about her that we don't." Tanya added.

"We all know each resident is treated uniquely. Besides, you have to admit that aside from her filthy mouth and outbursts, she's OK. She cares for others and gets into trouble for it," Michelle said.

"You forgot she was sent to the shelter five times for attacking people!" Aida reminded the rest.

"Let others have their chance at helping her. How do we get her out of here?" Sima felt impatient with the others.

Silence Broken

"Do we want her out?" Sue asked quietly.

"Do you have any doubts?!?" Aida glared at Sue.

Tanya spoke up again. "If we are honest about it, I think that most of us have some doubts. To be fair, we should discuss it, after dinner, with Karen present, and see how she feels about it."

The girls nodded. Sima looked at her watch.

"Wow, dinner time! No wonder my stomach is grumbling." Sima laughed as she began setting the table.

Karen appeared in the door, still dressed in her court outfit. She quietly said hello to everyone as she closed the front door behind her.

"How was your court hearing?" Tanya asked.

"It could have been better." Karen replied, but after a short pause she added, "It could have been worse."

"Which judge did you get?"

"Judge Levi. She's OK. I've met her before."

"She is more than OK, she's good and she's fair. She gives it to you straight. You're very lucky."

"Yeah, I guess so. She called me to her chambers and there she gave it to me good. She probably felt it was better not to scold me in front of my parents; there had been enough of that in the court room. She pointed out the good things about The Reach Center and how it could help me if I gave it a real chance. Judge Levi seems to know a lot about the program here."

"I guess she sees enough of us," Aida smiled.

"And she really cares," Tanya added.

Karen went upstairs to change out of her court clothes and wash up before dinner.

Downstairs, Sheila ran in, out of breath.

"You won't believe what I heard!" She gasped.

Everyone gathered around as Sheila recounted what she'd overheard about the staff meeting and the teachers' reaction.

* * *

After dinner, Karen told Sue and Tanya about the events from court that day. "My parents were delighted to hear the details about my behavior here. 'Now, your honor, maybe you can understand why we want to rescind her adoption,'" Karen imitated the way her parents carried on in court.

"They demanded that I be sent to a more restricted institution. My talk with Judge Levi really got to me, though. She said, 'Do it for yourself, not for your parents. Look at who you are hurting.' Well, all of that made me think. Suddenly I saw how much I'm being offered here. I was afraid of losing this place. I feel ashamed for what I did to you, my only real family." She pointed to everyone in the room. She barely finished when tears came to her eyes. Sue, Tanya, and the others in the room waited attentively in silence.

"When I was placed here, I felt that if I behaved tough, I would make it. I didn't expect your kindness... I was not ready to accept it. Now I know I can use all of the help I can get." She fell silent.

Tanya looked around. Some of the girls' faces expressed sincere regret for words and feelings previously expressed.

"We were not as patient as you think we were. I'm sure it's going to work, Karen."

Karen nodded and the girls seemed relieved. There would be no need for the unpleasant meeting.

Carol's voice came booming from behind them, "I'm glad to see you're back, Karen. How was your court hearing?"

"OK," she responded quickly, with a glance at her "family." The girls smiled warmly back. "You're going to see an all-new me, I hope."

Silence Broken

"What do you mean?"

"You will see a new leaf, that is, if I am given another chance at the general meeting."

"Sounds good to me," Carol answered, trying to hide her curiosity. Looking at her reflection in the mirror as she walked toward her room. *Thank God it's not too late.*

* * *

After her meeting with Dr. Stone, Karen met up with Sue and Aida for lunch. She was bursting with excitement, impatient to tell Sue the news.

"How was the meeting with Dr. Stone and the committee?" Sue asked.

"I promised to try harder and they agreed to give me another chance." Karen smiled.

"You should thank Dr. Stone. She fought for you in the meeting." Aida chimed in.

"How would you know that? I thought those meetings are confidential," demanded Karen, crestfallen.

Sue whispers to her what Sheila had overheard.

"They call her 'an optimist'? They make fun of her faith in me? I'll show them all. For the last eight years of my life I've felt like hell on wheels. Nobody cared for me or had any faith in me; even my therapist didn't like me! I'll show them all!"

"Good for you!" Sue said, trying to ease Karen's frustration.

Karen nodded and then walked away, hiding the falling tears, repeating "I'll show them!" over and over again to herself.

Rivcka Edelstein

Long Island, New York, April 1991

Chapter 26

Easter dinner was an extraordinary success. Most of the parents were present and almost all of the residents participated.

Dr. Stone leaned against the back door, admiring the dance performance. It was beautiful to see the result of endless rehearsal hours. She was still amazed at the changes Karen had made since her last court appearance. The stream of negative reports had dwindled and then finally stopped altogether. Karen had become more and more involved in the dance rehearsals, and it had proved to be an unexpected opportunity for her to use and display her talents and get recognition for what she did best.

Karen danced creatively, and the others deferred to her leadership in the choreography. Favorable reactions from her peers had motivated her to further improve her skills. She had also been invited to join The Reach Center's choir and was eventually given an opportunity to sing solo. Dr. Stone smiled. She recalled Karen's surprise.

"You must be kidding! My parents always said my voice was a nuisance and that it was only good for the shower where nobody could hear it," She said, her eyes wide. "I always loved singing! It makes me feel better."

Now she was on stage singing. Her voice carried beautifully through the hall and there was neither a whisper nor a movement in the audience. As her last note still rang clear in the air, the room erupted into enthusiastic clapping.

"Who is she? ... She is so talented."

The clapping continued as the residents began to chant: "Karen — Karen — Karen." She was stunned, and her eyes were filled with tears. She looked across the room and for a moment wished her parents were there, if only to hear the crowd.

Silence Broken

Her father had informed the staff they had a prior engagement and could not attend. She knew better; they wouldn't be caught dead in the same room with the rest of "those people." He constantly reminded her that it wasn't their fault she'd turned out to be a loser; she wasn't even their real daughter.

The clinical director was thrilled. Maybe Karen's obvious success tonight would help to erode her negative feelings about herself.

Dr. Stone glanced around the room, happy to see that most of the parents were present. A few parents still resisted the community family events. Karen's parents were a prime example of this, but the staff was not ready to give up.

The entertainment program was over and the residents ran to the welcoming arms of their parents and relatives.

Karen came down from the stage, but didn't look for anybody in the audience. Dr. Stone approached her and hugged her. She was baffled and kept asking, "Were we really O.K.?"

Dr. Stone nodded. "Karen, you have a beautiful voice and it's wonderful to hear you use it."

Rivcka Edelstein

Long Island, New York, April 1991

Chapter 27

Tanya, Sue, Mike, Chris, Aida, and Karen sat on the floor of the big living room playing *Everything is Possible*©, a therapeutic board game. Some of the cards had already been discarded and the residents were deeply involved in the game. It had proven to be very beneficial even when the residents played on their own. In fact, the residents welcomed the opportunity to share their feelings.

"'Share a secret with the person on your left,'" Sue read the next *Relate* card aloud. She thought for a moment and then bent down toward Tanya and whispered something in her ear.

"No! What did you do about it?"

"Nothing!" said Sue. "Who could I tell without causing trouble?"

"I would have died if it happened to me. So, you never told?" Tanya was still in disbelief.

"Never!" Sue said, distressed. "Anyway, my mother would never have believed me. She would have blamed me." Tears came to her eyes and Tanya leaned over to give her a hug.

After a minute, Sue reached to pick a *Move* card, but then hesitated. "Anybody else want to respond to this card?" Nobody volunteered, so she read the *Move* card and moved her game piece.

Tanya took the next *Relate* card and read it aloud, "'I got angry with my teacher when...'" She didn't need long to answer.

"I got angry with my teacher when . . . this one time, I saw a 'good student' steal money from his friend. The teacher asked the boy who had been robbed who had been standing near him when it happened, and he mentioned three names including mine. The teacher asked who took the money. No one said anythin'. So, she freakin' assumed that it was me and dragged me to the principal, yelling, 'Once a liar always a liar!'"

"What happened in the principal's office?" Chris asked.

"He gave me a lecture on how he was tired of my stealing and denying it. I got mad and said, 'Just because I'm poor doesn't make me a thief or a liar.'" Tanya took a few deep breaths.

"Good for you, girl. And he said?" Karen asked.

Tanya mimicked him, "Interesting. Every time you're involved, you don't say who did it!' I said 'I'm no thief or snitch!'"

"Good!" Mike smiled. "What did he say to that?"

"He said, 'Figures!' My mother came, and I got suspended for lying, stealing, and having a big mouth."

"What? He suspended you for something you didn't do? What did your parents say?" Sue was incredulous.

"If they are like mine, they'd convince you, 'If the principal said you stole and lied, you better believe you did it,'" said Karen.

"Exactly! My mother was annoyed. 'You're just like your Uncle George. You'll amount to nothing, just like him,'" Tanya finished, imitating her mother's tone of voice.

Karen looked up at her, gently finding her eyes. "Be proud of yourself. If we wait for our parents and others to be proud of us, we might wait forever."

"I accepted my mother's constant criticism. I was never good enough. I was too young to know better. But never again. Now I know that I can be proud of myself. I won't let anyone shake my confidence in me," Tanya's confidence grew with each word.

"The system sucks!" Aida agreed. "I hope we believe our children, instead of repeating the things our parents did."

Tanya finally moved her piece on the board.

Aida picked up the next *Relate* card: "I am happy when…"

The group was in the middle of discussing Aida's card when Sheila burst into the cottage, excited and short of breath.

"There's going to be a contest. The winner gets an award and the entire cottage receives a prize."

"What kind of contest? How did you hear about it?"

"Some kind of a creative contest, writing a story, or a play…"

"Great! We can win it if we work together," Michelle suggested.

"What can we write about?" asked Sue.

"We can write about what we know best," Tanya said, decidedly.

"I don't know anything." Sue responded.

"Stop it! Do you enjoy degrading yourself?" Michelle asked her.

"No, I don't enjoy it; I'm just used to it," Sue said quietly.

"Well, stop it," Tanya told her firmly.

"If you're not going to respect yourself, nobody else will. You set the tone for how others react to you," Michelle added.

Karen was impressed with this exchange. She could see why the staff had chosen Michelle and Tanya as Big Sisters. Karen knew the Big Sisters had extensive training before they were nominated for positions in the cottage. She also heard that when Tanya came to The Reach Center, she was worse than Karen herself had been a few months ago. But not Michelle; none of the residents in the cottage actually knew why she had been placed at The Reach Center.

"So, are we gonna do something for the contest?" asked Tanya.

"I say we write about what we know best," said Sheila.

"Like what?" asked Aida.

"Ourselves. Why don't we write about us?" Karen suggested.

The girls enthusiastically accepted Karen's idea. The cottage residents were brainstorming when Carol entered from the staff meeting.

She confirmed the 'rumor' about the contest, saying, "The idea is to put on an original play."

That night Karen began to put her ideas on paper, furiously writing notes and outlines late into the night.

* * *

During one of her meetings with Dr. Stone later that week, Karen recounted watching a TV program on child sexual abuse when she lived at home. There had been nobody she could speak to or ask questions about sex.

"Why?" asked Dr. Stone.

"He was the type who hollered if the word 'sex' was even used. He kept referring back to the 'good old days' when women and children, especially daughters, were obedient and subservient. He believed that was what nature intended…that women had to be put in their place and shouldn't pretend to be equal to men. It was ridiculous to him for us to talk about equality of the sexes when men were clearly superior."

"What about your mother?"

"She told me to ignore him, that he really didn't mean it."

"Do you think he meant it?"

"I sure do. He meant it in his words, he meant it in his voice, and he did everything possible to convince me he meant it through his actions. Once I asked my mother what my father had against women."

"What did she say?"

"Well, she...," Karen trailed off, but then continued. "She said she wasn't a psychologist, and how would she know."

"What else?" Dr. Stone asked patiently.

"I just remembered an argument I overheard between them. He was yelling 'You're just like all the other women!' She replied 'Just because some of the girls picked on you in high school...'" He was furious and shouted, 'Shut up! I told you never to mention those sluts in my presence.'"

"Maybe your father was humiliated when he was young. It may explain why he's so bitter about so many things."

"It didn't give him the right to take his anger out on me."

"True, it is not an excuse for his behavior, but it may be an explanation for you to think about."

"He should have sought help. He always said that I was the sick one and the troublemaker. His life had been peaceful before I came along."

"But you know better, don't you?"

"I guess so."

Silence Broken

Long Island, New York, April 1991

Chapter 28

Dr. Rachel Stone heard some sounds.

Where am I? Is it over? Did it begin? She thought to herself before she drifted off again.

Time passed. The voices were still around her.

Are they still preparing me?

She recalled the nurses strapping her arms and inserting the needle... She tried to concentrate on the voices; they seemed so far away...

Is it over?

She didn't feel any pain; as a matter of fact, she didn't feel anything. It was as though her blurred mind was now functioning on its own, not attached to the rest of her body. The voices were more audible, but she drifted again...

"Mr. Bryer," she heard a soft voice near to the bed. "This is Ms. Robinoff. Everything is O.K."

Ms. Robinoff? Mr. Bryer? The woman's voice was very familiar. With great effort, she opened her eyes slightly. The room seemed bigger and there was motion around her.

This is not the operating room. It must be over. I'm back. I'm alive. I made it once again.

Rachel Stone was thrilled, remembering the horrible feelings she was having as they prepped her for the operating room. She didn't believe she would make it this time and was afraid to say so. Everything had gone well and she was happy. She drifted again...

"It's still very low."

She heard a voice close by. She opened her eyes slightly and saw a nurse beside her. "I guess we should wait," the nurse reported to someone as she detached an instrument from Rachel's arm. Rachel started to drift again.

Hold on. Think about something. Don't drift. What did my son say before I came to the hospital...?

Like you always say, mom – "Think positive. I have faith in you." You'll find something good about the operation.

They both laughed.

She decided to concentrate on the mysterious purpose of her current ordeal. She never accepted the view that there was a purpose behind pain and suffering. A conversation near the next bed interrupted her thoughts.

"Mr. Bryer, welcome back. Everything went well. The tumor was benign and you're doing fine. The surgeon is pleased and your wife is waiting to see you."

"Thank you, Ms. Robinoff. You are wonderful human being." He spoke slowly and with considerable effort. "I don't know what we would have done without your help and support."

"It's my pleasure; I'm here anyway," she said very shyly, obviously embarrassed by his compliments.

"I know how much pain you are in since your accident. You are quite a lady." Mr. Bryer sounded very weak.

"I'm a youth lawyer. I care about my clients — and their families," Ms. Robinoff said as she touched his shoulder affectionately.

The woman's voice was very familiar to Rachel. Did she know a Ms. Robinoff? Not to her recollection. But that voice, she was sure she'd heard it before, maybe even recently.

"May I have my glasses?" Rachel asked. She felt that if she could see, she would be less likely to drift off again.

A nurse popped in from the other side of the curtain and asked, "How do you feel? Any pain?"

Silence Broken

"No. Did you get my glasses?"

"Sure." She put the glasses on Rachel's face.

That's better.

Now Rachel had a chance to see the faces associated with the voices she'd heard earlier. She could see Ms. Robinoff through the curtain. From the way she moved and held her left hand on her lower back, Rachel could tell she was in pain.

"Do you have any pain?" Ms. Robinoff asked Mr. Bryer.

"Not bad. Tell me, Ms. Robinoff - are you married? Do you have any family?"

Ms. Robinoff paused and shifted from one foot to the other, supporting her back with her hand. "I am not married and I don't have any children." There was a short silence. Then she turned to leave the room.

Rachel felt a strange sensation in her stomach as she suddenly realized why Ms. Robinoff looked and sounded so familiar.

"Excuse me, Miss, can I speak with you for a minute?"

Ms. Robinoff turned, startled, as though awakened from deep thought.

"Oh! Excuse me, sorry. I didn't realize you were talking to me. Is there something I can do for you?"

"No, I'm fine. I'm just wondering how to get in touch with you," Rachel's voice trailed off as she gazed at Beth intently. Her eyes scanned the room and beyond for a nurse's assistance as she cleared her throat. As Beth spoke, Rachel returned her attention to Beth as she leaned closer to Rachel to answer her question.

"I'm in the phone book. I practice and live in New York."

"Are there other Robinoffs in the book?"

"Many, yes. Sorry. My name is Beth Robinoff and I'm a juvenile attorney."

Rivcka Edelstein

Long Island, New York, May 1, 1991

Chapter 29

Two weeks later, Dr. Rachel Stone returned to work ready to tackle the problems she feared may have arisen during her absence. She had barely taken off her jacket when the phone rang.

"Welcome back. How do you feel?" asked the familiar voice of Mr. Roth, the Administrative Director of the Reach Center.

"Good, thanks. I'm glad to be back at work."

"That sounds like you. Not to start your day with old problems, but I need to speak with you. Do you want me to come to your office or you can come here?"

"Can't we do it on the phone?"

"Sure! We had a couple of incidents…," he began in despair.

"Go on."

"We've discussed it before, but we really need to find a replacement lawyer immediately."

"So far we've only received negative responses. It's difficult to find a lawyer willing to work with our tough population for the small fees we're able to offer."

"You're telling me!" Mr. Roth sighed.

"Nonetheless, I have someone in mind. I'll call her."

"Doc, you made my day. I'll let you get back to work."

"By the way, thank you very much for the call and the flowers. It was very thoughtful."

"You're very welcome. We're all glad to have you back."

Dr. Stone leaned back in her chair. She asked her secretary to locate Ms. Robinoff and make an appointment for them to meet as soon as possible. Immediately, she changed her mind and she decided to call and speak to the lawyer directly. Ms. Robinoff apologized that she was especially busy and preparing to leave for back treatment in two days, but that she would try to schedule some time if Dr. Stone could come to her office.

Once that was arranged, Dr. Stone turned to the files on her desk. Most of the residents were on a field trip, giving Dr. Stone the opportunity to attend to the accumulated work. She remained in her office for the rest of the day. Late in the afternoon, the phone rang.

It was Carol. She informed Dr. Stone about the ferry incident and suggested immediate action.

Dr. Stone turned on her TV. She continued to work till she heard the BNN TV station's anchorwoman announce the "The Mysterious Rescuer." Mesmerized, she focused on the screen.

It started with the view of The Statue of Liberty and a beautiful sunset in the distance. In the background, there were sounds of people yelling excitedly. The sounds gradually increased in volume as the camera turned in the direction of the commotion. Ten male and female youths and a class of first graders and their teacher rallied around the ferry railing. They screamed and pointed at the water. A young boy in the water struggled to stay afloat. Karen, a slim and tall white female, took her sneakers off, threw her jacket on the floor, and climbed onto the railing. The other youths tried to stop her. She jumped into the water. The ferry's alarm sounded. Karen surfaced for air. She circled around, searching for the boy. She didn't see him. The crowd screamed and pointed. The boy's head appeared and then disappeared. She dived again. The boat gradually came to a halt. Some people threw life preservers into the water. Karen resurfaced as she held the boy with one arm and swam toward the life preservers. She lifted his head above the life preserver and put her arms around him. Two ferry employees jumped into the water and rushed toward Karen. One diver held the child and quickly climbed the ladder; the other diver helped Karen. Surrounded by a teacher and classmates, a doctor urgently attended to the child who showed signs of life. There were cheers and clapping. Karen's friends and on-lookers hugged her. She clutched herself and shivered and walked toward the revived young boy. "Good job! What is your name?" a male voice behind the camcorder asked Karen.

Rivcka Edelstein

"No pictures, please," Carol, the counselor, put her hand in front of the camera to block the picture."

"What is your name? The parents might want to reward you."

From Carol, she understood that it was shot by a tourist with a camcorder and later the BNN crew joined in.

At the end of the clip, Dr. Stone picked up the phone and dialed the producer of the BNN news and the newspaper editor who had arrived on the ferry.

Silence Broken

Tel Aviv, Israel, May 1, 1991

Chapter 30

Jeremy sat in his office after a long and tedious day. It was almost midnight. The closer it came to his wedding day, the more irritable and moody Jeremy became and the more he felt the need to be alone. Busy with meetings and phone calls, he had not had a minute to himself all day.

Days like today made him wonder if he had chosen the right profession. Lately he found himself dealing with too much red tape and very little with the cases themselves. Everybody told him that it came with the territory and that he would get used to it. Unfortunately, after all these years, he still didn't like it. Now he doubted that he ever would.

As his colleague, Ben, poked his head inside Jeremy's office, Jeremy's phone rang. The unexpected ringing startled Jeremy and he didn't notice his visitor right away. His mother was on the line; her calls had become more frequent since his engagement to Danielle.

"Yes, Mom… I'm at work. I'm fine… No, Mom. I don't have time to think about my engagement party. I'll talk to you tomorrow. Love you," he said in Hebrew.

"Why don't you and Danielle go on a vacation? I'm sure you both could use some relaxation," Ben suggested cheerily.

"We'll see," Jeremy sighed, unmoved. Ben just shook his head and popped back out of the office.

Jeremy turned to face the window. He loved this view of the Mediterranean Sea and Old Jaffa; looking at the water always calmed him.

Over the radio, Jeremy heard Yehoram Gaon's voice and those words that had such special meaning for him: *"Ah, ah, od lo ahavti dai"* — *"Oh, I have not yet loved enough."*

Rivcka Edelstein

How true, when had anyone had enough when it came to love?

He turned, reached for the TV remote and leaned back in his recliner. He enjoyed watching the BNN news at that time of the night; it was after five o'clock New York time. A news segment was just beginning; at first, he was unsure as to what he was watching.

On the screen, there was a view of the sunset over the Statue of Liberty. The view changed to the deck of a ferry as the background noise gradually increased, ringing clearly of human voices. There were children screaming and pointing to the water. The camera moved in the direction of the commotion. Ten boys and girls, a class of first graders, and their teachers rallied at the ferry railing, screaming and pointing toward the water below. The camera followed the water — a young boy struggled to stay afloat. Back on the deck, a slim, tall, white female teenager quickly took her sneakers off, threw her jacket on the floor, and climbed onto the railing. The others tried to stop her, but she jumped into the water. The ferry's alarm turned on. She surfaced for air and circled around, searching for him. The crowd screamed and pointed in the direction of the boy as his head quickly surfaced, then disappeared. She dove again.

The boat gradually came to a halt and a few life-preservers were thrown into the water. A few seconds passed, great tension grew on the deck and then cheers broke out as the teenager resurfaced, holding the boy with one arm and swimming toward the life-preservers. She lifted his head above the life-preserver and put her arms around him. Two ferry employees jumped into the water and rushed toward them. One diver held the boy and quickly climbed the ladder; the other diver helped the girl.

Surrounded by a teacher and classmates, a doctor urgently tended to the boy who showed signs of life. People cheered and clapped. The girl's friends and on-lookers hugged her. She clutched herself, shivered, and walked toward the revived young boy.

A voice from behind exclaimed, "Good job! What's your name?"

Before the girl could answer, a woman, about 25, put one hand on the girl's shoulder while using the other to swat away any photographers.

"No pictures, please," she demanded sternly.

Silence Broken

The voice from behind emerged again, asking: "What is your name? The parents might want to reward you!"

The woman pulled the girl away as the ferry stopped. The picture changed to a screen shot of the young woman and child. Jeremy heard the BNN's anchor continue:

"This clip was taken by a tourist on the ferry. The young woman was told that the child's parents would want to reward her. She reportedly responded, "I jumped into the water because it was the right thing to do and not because of a reward." Little is known about this courageous youth. The parents of the young boy, who was on a school trip, want to reward 'The Mysterious Rescuer,' who was part of a group of teens. If anybody knows the young woman's identity please call 1-800-555-3636.

"Why not reveal her name?" Jeremy wondered. She had been part of a group. Does she attend some exclusive school which prohibits publicity? He looked at the picture more closely: a wet skinny girl with long straight hair stood beside a small shivering child who tightly held her hand.

The TV camera zoomed in and focused on the youth's face. Jeremy focused more closely as well... Her face looked familiar...

Jeremy turned his recliner once again, and from the 27th floor of his office he saw the antiquity of Old Jaffa blend in beautifully with the sea. He tried to relax, but couldn't. He felt a strange uneasiness. He knew what had triggered it. The picture on TV had reminded him of Beth. Scenes flooded back from the winter of 1970 ...the summer of 1973...

The ringing telephone jarred him back to the present. He tried to ignore the persistent sound. After a few moments, he reluctantly answered.

"I was just about to give up! What took you so long?"

The voice came through remarkably clearly, as though the caller was speaking from the next room.

"I wasn't sure I'd reach you," she continued.

"Sharon!"

"It's late, even for you. What are you doing at the office in the middle of the night? Afraid to go home?"

"This is refreshing. I think it's the first time you've called me while I was still awake," Jeremy joked. As always, her voice was like a fresh breeze.

"Guess what! I'm planning ahead and I need to know if you'll be free," Sharon said.

"That is definitely refreshing! Free for what? Are you coming to visit us?"

"You're quick as usual. My flight leaves in two days; I'm scheduled to land the day after tomorrow, at 1 p.m. your time."

"I'm glad you're coming, and yes, I'm free. Are you ever going to let me know more than a few days in advance?"

"Sorry, I just cleared a vacation which was overdue to me and I decided to spend it in Israel. I need good rest, good food, and good company. Where else can I find all three?"

"I see what you mean! Ben is pushing me to take a vacation as well."

"Maybe you can return with me."

"To the U.S.? Sorry, it's too far. Besides, I've never known the United States to be a place of rest…"

"We can talk more about it when I get there. I'll see you the day after tomorrow. Remember, it's a secret."

"Sure, have a safe flight, Shalom."

He replaced the receiver. He was happy Sharon was coming; they always had a good time together. Maybe they would have a chance to talk about some serious things too. Jeremy made some notes for his schedule the next two days, turned off the office light and walked out.

Silence Broken

Long Island, New York, May 1, 1991

Chapter 31

Karen and the rest of the group finally arrived back at The Reach Center.

Early in the evening Dr. Stone made her rounds through the cottages before heading home. These visits gave residents the opportunity to chat with her and show off their cooking, homework and other projects. That evening she saved Karen's cottage for last.

As she entered, she heard the residents talking excitedly about the incident on the ferry. The TV was on in the background. The girls were laughing at how the reporter pushed her way toward the front when the ferry docked and the photographer clicked away with the camera.

The girls recounted the story to Dr. Stone and told her about the clip that they'd seen earlier. It was clear to them that someone had radioed to the TV station and the newspaper from the ferry.

Dr. Stone nodded as her eyes searched the room for Karen. She was not in the living area.

Dr. Stone found Karen in her room. She lingered in the doorway for a few seconds as Karen wrote at her desk.

Dr. Stone looked at Karen with a smile. She really had come a long way during the last few weeks. Karen often said that she saw both the individual and the group therapy sessions as a total waste of time. Yet, despite her apparent resistance, Karen seemed to be relieved when called into a session and she was always an active participant.

"How do you feel, Karen?"

"You know Doc," Karen went on, excitedly, "I really feel great. I almost never feel this way. Of course, it's seldom that I do something that makes others proud of me, or for that matter, that make me proud of myself." She paused for a moment.

"I think you're right. You said that the pleasure of giving is greater than the pleasure of receiving. Now I understand! When I jumped in, I didn't think about what I would need to do, only that he needed help." She paused again.

"You know, when I was swimming back to the ferry, holding the kid above the water, I wasn't sure I could make it. I thought the ferry would never stop, but I had to hang on for the kid's sake. I felt responsible for saving him and it gave me the strength to keep going. Dr. Stone, you were right, pride is a feeling from inside…"

"I am very proud of you, Karen. You are certainly the center of attention this evening."

"Doc, wait a minute, anyone would have done what I did."

"But nobody else did — you did," Dr. Stone said.

"I beat them to it, that's all." Karen shrugged her shoulders.

Dr. Stone looked at her affectionately.

"All this attention makes me feel uncomfortable."

Dr. Stone understood. "The parents of the little boy want to thank you and give you a big reward."

"Please tell them I don't want a reward." She turned to pick a shirt from the floor. Under her breath she added, "No reward can be a substitute for my real wish."

"Which is?"

"You know what I want." Karen said with her teary eyes looking at the floor.

"I know. I hope you don't mind, but I asked the producer at BNN and the editors of the newspaper to make sure your name is never mentioned."

Silence Broken

Karen nodded and Dr. Stone continued speaking with her for a few minutes longer. She noticed that Karen had no pictures of people in her room — no relatives, no favorite stars. Her room was neat, but there was something different since the last time she had seen it.

"Where is your makeup? You used to have so much."

"I gave them away. I don't need them. I decided I like my face without all of that gook," Karen said shyly.

"You have beautiful clear skin and long, dark eyelashes. You really don't need it. Good night, young lady."

As she approached the door, she turned and added, "I hope you like the clip on BNN. You look very good."

"What clip? I thought you said you talked to the producer and the editor?!"

"They promised not to print your name, but they insisted on publishing the story and a picture. They feel that the public should hear of courageous acts when they happen."

"Great! My parents will see it," Karen said nervously.

"That's good. It will give them proof of your good nature."

"You don't know them. They'll find something to criticize."

"I don't see how."

"You'd be surprised . . ."

* * *

And surprised she was. The next morning, not long after she read the newspaper article about "The Mysterious Rescuer," she received a call from Mr. Burg.

"It wasn't courage and bravery; it was stupidity and was typical of Karen. She's impulsive and doesn't think before she acts," he barked as soon as she was on the line.

Dr. Stone put down the receiver after half an hour of futile conversation. Karen was right; they did find something to criticize. "Well, you can't win them all," she said out loud in dismay.

Silence Broken

New York, New York, May 3, 1991

Chapter 32

"We're looking for a good, caring lawyer who specializes in juvenile population and charges modestly. Of course, it has to be the right person."

"You aren't asking much, but why me?" inquired Beth Robinoff.

Dr. Stone hesitated, "You have been highly recommended."

"You're staring at me."

"I'm sorry, I don't mean to stare. But you remind me so much of someone I know at the center; same voice, facial features, movements. The resemblance is uncanny." Beth stood up, put her hands through her hair, and appeared slightly uncomfortable.

"As I started to say…" Dr. Stone changed the subject, "it's a center for emotionally disturbed youths. Our lawyer retired and we are having a hard time replacing him. Our current residents are mostly victims of sexual abuse."

She paused, surprised, as she saw Ms. Robinoff shudder. *As a youth lawyer, surely she is aware of child sexual abuse.* She continued, "Usually they've been abused by a male perpetrator. Our staff thought that a female lawyer may be better able to gain the girls' trust. We are looking for a good, caring, patient, compassionate, tolerant person; but, we can't pay very much."

"You aren't asking for much!" Ms. Robinoff said, smiling.

"I know it's quite a list," Dr. Stone conceded, "but we have a serious problem since we need all of these good qualities, but we cannot afford to pay." She paused and then added, "I know it's not fair of me to ask others to contribute simply because I feel like giving but, we desperately need someone whose first priority is protecting the legal rights of our residents."

"Why me?" asked Ms. Robinoff, her voice shaking.

'Why is she so nervous?' Dr. Stone wondered.

"To be honest, I decided to approach you on a hunch. I noticed the way you handled Mr. Bryer in the recovery room. We need someone just like you," she stopped as she noticed Dr. Robinoff's expression.

"Believe me, you would not be the first, second, or even tenth person to say 'no'."

"Why don't you tell me more," Ms. Robinoff backpedaled, feeling guilty as she realized her face had betrayed her hesitance.

"Well, the next step depends on your answer."

"Do you know anything about me?"

"Not more than your educational background and specialization. Simply put, I am going on a hunch thinking you're the right person, and that money is not the motivating force."

"Is that a hunch or a psychological diagnosis?" Ms. Robinoff said, laughing.

"Even your laughter is similar."

"Tell me about her - the person I remind you of."

"I cannot tell you much; all our material is confidential. You want to know? Come and work for us, then you can have access to information on all our boys and girls," Dr. Stone ventured, hoping it was perceived as a joke and not a bribe.

"They say we all have a twin somewhere," Ms. Robinoff's said. Her voice was shaking again. She could barely cover her fear. Once again, her right hand combed through her hair.

"She's not your twin. She's maybe twenty years younger than you."

"Don't make me that old. How old is she?"

"She turned seventeen last February."

"You remember the birthdays of each of the sixty residents?" Ms. Robinoff said, changing the subject, buying herself time to control her reaction to this revelation.

"No, how could I?" Dr. Stone laughed, "It's just that her birthday was celebrated at the Valentine's Day party and a special event happened that day."

By now Dr. Robinoff was numb, her thoughts racing.

"What are you thinking?" Dr. Stone asked, noticing Ms. Robinoff was lost in thought.

"I'm considering your offer," she lied.

"Take your time, but please do give it serious consideration. We could use someone like you."

"Give me two weeks," Dr. Robinoff tried to recover her composure.

"Why don't you come and visit us? It might be beneficial for you and it might affect your decision or at least I hope so . . ."

"I might do that, but first I have to consider the offer. Anyways, even if I could I cannot do anything before my trip to California; I need to receive treatment for my back injury. I have a full schedule until I leave."

"I will wait for your response. Only an affirmative response will be welcome," Dr. Stone said half-jokingly as she reached for her briefcase. "I brought some materials which outline our therapeutic program. Our physicians become members of the therapeutic team." As she removed the descriptive material, she noticed the newspaper article she had been reading earlier in the morning. Ms. Robinoff stood up as Dr. Stone handed her the Reach Residential Treatment Center's brochure and the article. Dr. Stone added, "Here is the picture of the girl that sounds and looks like you. As of yesterday, she is a hero. We are very proud of her."

Ms. Robinoff took all of the materials and placed them on her desk after a quick glance. "I'll read it after I finish today's appointments. Thanks!" The familiarity of the face in the newspaper picture registered in her mind and she looked at the picture a second time. Dr. Stone noticed her reaction. Being aware that she was being observed, Dr. Robinoff quickly added, "You're right . . ."

"By any chance, is she a long lost relative of yours?" Dr. Stone asked lightly.

"What do you mean?" her voice was clearly shaky. She wondered if the Clinical Director knew about her past.

"I was just joking; you would have known her if she was." After a brief pause she added, "On the other hand, in this case you might not have. You see, she was adopted."

Dr. Robinoff' turn pale and fell into her chair. The girl in the photo reminded her of her own high school picture when she won the swimming tournament.

"Are you OK?"

"Sure, I just stood up too fast . . . my back . . ." She made an extreme effort to say a few words.

It was obvious to Dr. Stone that she was in an agony. Dr. Stone proceeded toward the door. "I'll see myself to the door, Ms. Robinoff. Please give my offer serious consideration. I'll call in two weeks."

"Two weeks then," she managed to mumble.

Dr. Stone reached the door and turned back. "Good luck with the treatment in California." The door closed behind her.

Ms. Robinoff's head was covered with cold sweat and her body became weightless. For a second, she saw the room turning around and everything in her proximity became dark, disappeared. She passed out...

The intercom buzzed and Ms. Robinoff answered in a slow, disoriented voice.

Silence Broken

"Are you OK, MS. Robinoff? Is it your back again? . . . The waiting room is full . . ."

"I am fine. Give me a minute." Many questions came to her mind but they all seemed remote; she couldn't even grasp the idea that the teenager in the picture might be her child.

Dr. Stone waited for the elevators. She had never interviewed a professional in this manner before. Even though there were moments when Ms. Robinoff acted strangely, she felt the meeting went well. She believed Ms. Robinoff would respond positively.

Once she got off the elevator, she called Mr. Roth and relayed to him the conversation with the young lawyer.

She concluded the conversation, "At least she didn't reject the offer outright as the other lawyers did. Nevertheless, we still have to wait two weeks."

Rivcka Edelstein

Tel Aviv, Israel, May 3, 1991

Chapter 33

"Jeremy!" Sharon exclaimed, as she came out of customs."

"Shalom!"

They hugged each other. She looked very tired.

"My dear cousin, smile! You are on vacation, remember? Is being a judge too hard on you?" Jeremy joked. "Have you heard from Rami recently? How is he doing on his project? I really miss both of you."

"Questions, questions, questions!" Sharon joked, noticing a hint of sadness in Jeremy's tone.

"I'll drop you at your parents' home first, and then I'll come over after dinner. We can go out and talk."

"You see me awake now, but don't bet on it later. I haven't slept in 36 hours. I had a tremendous amount of business to finish before I left; the excitement is keeping me awake now."

He suggested they sit in the café before they go to his car; they ordered some coffee.

"I'm glad you came! So, what's new in the world?" He said after their order. "Is the big city still there?"

"Nothing new: corruption, murders, rapes, muggings, drugs… Forget it. How free are you in the next three weeks?"

"I have some vacation time coming up. I'll talk to Ben. Your visit will somewhat help to break my routine."

"A young guy like yourself, recently engaged, speaking about routine?!"

Sharon noticed that he didn't answer, so she decided to continue.

"So, when do I meet the lucky lady? I heard all I care to hear, and now I want to see for myself."

"Soon, I guess."

"Anybody who finally succeeded in capturing the heart of the last available, great bachelor of our generation must be very special."

"Special she is…." Jeremy answered mindlessly, wandering in and out of his own private thoughts. He had yet to share these specific sentiments.

"My mother does not stop praising Danielle in her letters," Sharon smiled. "I guess everyone is anxious to see you married and starting a family. I'm glad they didn't resort to the antiquated tradition of arranged marriages."

Jeremy didn't respond.

"Tell me about her. Feed my curiosity."

"She is special. She is talented. She is successful. She sets goals and achieves them…" He stopped again, his mind wandering. He really should talk about it. On second thought, maybe not.

"Is she as beautiful as they say?"

"I'll say she is definitely attractive."

Sharon noticed sadness in Jeremy's face.

"Why are you so sad? Why do I have the feeling you are about to say 'but…?'"

When he didn't respond, Sharon wondered whether he had heard her last comment. She decided not to repeat the question.

"Let me make a few phone calls before we head out of the airport. Do you mind?" Sharon asked.

He nodded, "It's fine."

She left her luggage cart with her suitcases beside him. There was a newspaper, which she brought with her from New York, atop the suitcases.

He picked up the newspaper and went through the headlines, skimming the pages.

His eyes lingered on a picture under the headline, "The Mysterious Rescuer" and proceeded to read the article.

Judge Sharon Levy smiled when she returned from her phone call. She looked at how he focused on the picture. He caught Sharon's smile and he said, "Last night I watched the BNN segment."

"The segment is about Karen," Sharon explained.

"Do you know her?" He asked, excitedly.

"Do I know her?!" She said jokingly. "Are you kidding? She is a frequent visitor...I even had a chat with her in my chamber."

Something about her..." She was searching for the words.

"... reminds you of someone you knew?"

"Yes," she replied, surprised, "that's right. The similarity in the picture is nothing. You have to hear this girl talk. You would feel as though . . ." A silence followed the pause.

He asked, "Anyway, why?"

"Why didn't they put her name in the article?"

Jeremy began to lose interest in the topic. He started to move the luggage cart.

"About Karen, she is really very bitter about her parents and they are completely rejecting her. I think her problem is her parents and that is why I wanted your advice."

"What about her parents?" Jeremy tried to refocus.

"Actually, they are her adoptive parents." Sharon mumbled the last few words, as though talking to herself.

Silence Broken

Jeremy was about to enter the parking lot when he heard the last two words.

"You said adoptive parents?" he asked, turning the lights on his car and looking at Sharon. There was something in those words that had triggered his interest.

"Yes, why?" she asked, surprised by his sudden renewed interest.

"I was just wondering to myself," he said in an effort to compensate for his sharp reaction.

"Not so much to yourself. You have something in mind? Speak up." Sharon was intrigued. She was amazed at the change in the conversation and at Jeremy's physical reaction. She looked straight at him, waiting for an explanation.

"When I saw the segment on the TV something stirred in me. I can't explain it. Memories from the past came to me." He stopped. It was clear he was uncomfortable and he paused to collect his thoughts.

"Memories?" Sharon prompted him to continue.

"I was thinking about…the girl I knew years ago."

"Was her name . . ." she said, wondering if that would help in her own questions about Karen.

"Beth Robinoff," he whispered slowly.

"Sure, you met her the year you visited us in the States. She was a regular visitor at our house those days. She liked Rami a lot, but they were 'just good friends' to quote his overused expression."

"Did you know her well? Weren't you in college during that time?"

Sharon nodded. "I was in college, but I met her before I left …and I also saw her since then."

"What happened to her?"

"Our families were very close until a few months before she left for Israel back in 1973. Just before she left, she visited us to get some information and addresses and to tell us about her research project. My parents and Rami greatly encouraged her; they knew she was nervous. She wasn't the same Beth we had known years before."

Sharon noticed that she had captured Jeremy's attention and his facial expression encouraged her to proceed with the long-forgotten memories and details. "After she returned from Israel, she simply disappeared. She was home for a few weeks and then she was 'shipped off to college in the middle of the year, a semester ahead of her classmates. It's all coming back to me now. Beth stopped by two days after her return from Israel and Rami had just left for two weeks on a special winter science program. Beth told my mother about the days of the war. She was very excited about Israel . . . I remember that she talked about the kibbutz where you were and her wonderful memories . . ."

"My mother asked her if she was there when the exchange of prisoners took place and she said she had just called the kibbutz and she heard that you had returned from the prison in Egypt. We were so relieved and at that time we didn't know about your injury and operation." Sharon stopped. She then added, as an afterthought, "Funny, from the way she spoke, Beth gave us the definite impression that she was going back to Israel quite soon. You can imagine our surprise when Rami returned from science camp and told us he heard that Beth had gone to college. There was a mystery about the whole thing. Rami couldn't get her address, even though he tried a number of times. Her mother used to say, 'I will tell Beth you called. She will call you back,' but she never did. Rami was surprised too, especially when one of his messages through her mother was that it was urgent that he talk to Beth. Nothing came of it though and consequently our families became estranged. After a few months, both my mother and brother gave up trying to figure it out. Soon afterwards, we heard that their house was sold and that they moved. As I said, Beth disappeared for a couple of years."

"A couple of years?"

Silence Broken

"Yes. I saw her a number of times later, but every time I mentioned my family's efforts to see her family and Rami's efforts to make contact with her, she seemed to .... She made efforts to avoid questions about her own parents... How long did she stay at the kibbutz? Did you get to know her well that summer?"

"She stayed from June until the end of November, and you might say we were close."

"I might or I should?" Sharon asked curiously.

Jeremy didn't answer and avoided eye contact with Sharon.

"Secrets, secrets, secrets! I thought you didn't like her the year you visited us in the States. You gave Rami a hard time about her."

"I wasn't wrong about my impression of her, but I never said I didn't like her. I didn't like her attitude back in 1970. Besides, the Beth I met in the summer of '73 was very different."

"Interesting! All of these years I didn't know that you were close. You never cease to amaze me."

"Well, it happened so quickly. I fell in love with her that summer, and just as fast, I lost her . . ." After a short pause, he continued. "So, where is she now?"

"You know, a few things are starting to make sense now. I saw her about fourteen years ago when she was in college and I was in law school. At that time, she did mention that you had met in the kibbutz. Since then, our paths have crossed a couple of times and the last time I saw her she in a law conference. It's funny, every time we met she asked some questions about different members of my family, but she always seemed most interested in you — your school, your work; she seemed pleased, almost relieved, when I told her that you were not married. The truth is, at the time I did not read much into it. I thought that it was just curiosity. I'll be damned; now it makes sense . . . So, you two were close," she said slowly savoring the idea. "What happened to the closeness?"

"You might say circumstances . . . life events."

"I might say many things. I would like to know what you have to say. I seem to recall that when you were in the hospital, you sent a letter to Rami to find her address. That's why Rami made such an effort to reach her. He exploded after each phone call to Mrs. Robinoff. He used to say, 'What is the mystery? Why wouldn't she give me Beth's address? What's going on?' Poor Rami. Well, Jeremy, I have a feeling that you are the clue to the mystery. Speak up."

"I wish I could, but I cannot."

"You cannot or will not?"

"I really cannot. I don't know much."

"Start with the little you do know."

"Not now. How about later tonight?"

Jeremy was glad the topic of the conversation had changed for the time being. *I am not ready to talk about Beth. I need time to pull myself together before I can continue.* His mind kept wandering back and forth from the youngster's picture in the TV segment and the picture in the newspaper to the memories it triggered about Beth and back to the information Sharon had provided about the girl in the picture. He wanted to find out more about her and he decided to bring it up again, later, during their outing after dinner.

* * *

After dinner in his mother's house, he and Sharon left for a café where they talked.

Sharon was touched by Jeremy's pain as he talked about the events in 1973. She came up with the unexpected suggestion that even surprised her as she made it.

"Come to NY and find Beth and get some answers. You deserve closure. It's clear to me that that chapter of your life has not been closed."

Jeremy was quiet.

Silence Broken

"What have you got to lose? You can deal with more than one mission." She paused when she saw Jeremy's questioning expression.

"If you come, you can find Beth and get some answers, and you can help my client and..." she was about to continue when Jeremy interrupted her.

"What do you mean help your client?"

"Karen, the one in the picture...I sort of promised to try to locate her mother. My hands are tied. You, however, through your affiliate firm in New York, can pursue it. If her mother can be located, and if she will be able and wants to be involved, it might help Karen. I really don't have a choice, since..."

"What's going on? How did you get to promise?"

"It's a long story."

"Start now."

She told him about her meeting with Karen and her shock at the resemblance . . . about Karen's adoptive parents and that they were actively seeking to rescind the adoption. She concluded with Karen's plea to Sharon to help locate her real mother.

The dinner conversation with Sharon and his lack of peace of mind for the last seventeen years were enough for him to make a fast decision.

"After all these years, I still ache for Beth. You are right, I need closure. I am coming to New York to find Beth."

He knew Ben wouldn't have any problem with his impulsive decision to go to the States. Actually, Ben was the one that encouraged him to take time off.

"Good decision!" Sharon exclaimed.

"My passport is in order. I can leave when you leave..."

"What about Danielle? Your fiancé?"

Jeremy knew that it was time for him to finally confront his nagging doubts about their future together.

"I don't know. All I know is that I have to do this first. I'll talk to Danielle tomorrow. I can't think about marrying Danielle before I close that chapter…"

From his point of view, there was no need for any delays. His passport was current. The only thing he dreaded was breaking the news to his family and Danielle.

She calmly accepted his decision and told him she was aware of his unhappiness and had anticipated this. His mother was not as understanding. Her line of questioning was more thorough and she was clearly disappointed. She was afraid he was going to get hurt. "Why reopen the wounds?" she asked. She couldn't forget the months of torment he went through after his return from the Egyptian prison in 1973. The constant questioning whether a letter had come from Beth, the endless searching and attempted contacts through Rami. All had been in vain; she had vanished. In the end, realizing he was not about to change his mind, Mrs. Offir conceded, 'I guess you have to do it. Good luck.'

Ten days later, he was on the plane with Sharon. She was right, what did he have to lose? On the contrary, he might gain some peace of mind. He knew that "The Beth Chapter" of his life needed an ending. One way or another, he had to find some answers and move on.

Silence Broken

New York, New York, May 1991

Chapter 34

Beth Robinoff gave her paralegal some last-minute instructions regarding her clients before heading to the airport. She was the last to board the plane to California. Pleased with having obtained an aisle seat, Beth settled in for the long flight. Throughout the first part of the flight the pain in her back increased and she regretted her decision to fly alone.

Her orthopedic-surgeons had recommended surgery. They did not understand why she even considered the unconventional back treatments used at that clinic in California. Beth made her decision to go to California based on the overwhelmingly positive reports she had received. She viewed surgery as a last resort.

She looked at her watch and was disappointed to find out that only half-an-hour had passed since she took her pain killers.

Beth remembered the article Dr. Stone had left with her. She opened her folder and looked at the photograph once again. She tried to concentrate on the article about the "Mysterious Rescuer," while her eyes constantly wandered back to the picture. *Indeed, she really resembles me when I was about 16 or 17, but that doesn't mean anything.* She read and reread the article. *What a story. So many unanswered questions.*

She became curious about the girl in the picture. The intensified pain and the remorse, that she felt all those years, fully resurfaced. *I wonder if Dr. Stone knows about my past?* A second later she dismissed the thought, *No, how could she?*

Beth decided not to confuse the issue of being the lawyer for the residential treatment center with her curiosity about the girl in the newspaper picture. *It might be a rewarding experience to protect the rights of these youth. What makes these teens act out? School? Home? Both?* She thought about the job offer and knew she would be able to find the time. *I wonder if I might be right for the population described by Dr.*

Rivcka Edelstein

Stone. A visit to The Reach Center might be a good idea. Besides, I will have enough time to think during the next two weeks.

Silence Broken

Long Island, New York, May 1991

Chapter 35

"Thirty minutes to landing," the captain's voice came over the loud-speaker. Jeremy looked from the window to see the Statue of Liberty. His heart started to race. He swallowed deeply, fighting the waves of excitement and anxiety about the challenges he was about to face. He recalled a song sang by Yehoram Ga'on, "Vehulyi Otah Shtika" (And Maybe That Silence). It was about a person searching for answers after a long silence and he wondered whether that silence would be broken. If he would find what he was looking for, or the silence would continue and he would return empty handed.

Jeremy had tears in his eyes. He hoped for answers and closure. Events from the past flooded his memory... events from more than twenty years ago . . . his first flight to the United States — his landing in New York. Sharon held his hand as the plane touched the ground. She understood.

Jeremy and Sharon were the last off the plane and by the time they reached the baggage claim area, their suitcases had already arrived and they proceeded through customs without delay.

* * *

"OK, tell me what I have to do?" Jeremy said impatiently after listening quietly as Dr. Stone, the Clinical Director, had listed the rules he had to follow before permission could be granted for a resident to leave with anyone other than a parent or staff member.

"With all of these procedures, by the time I get permission the summer will be over." He tried to control his agitation. He always had difficulty dealing with bureaucracy.

"We really aren't trying to make your life difficult, but you have to understand, we are responsible for our residents and we can't just let anybody come and take them out. We owe it to the residents themselves. I'm sorry."

"I wish Judge Levi had told me all of this ahead of time. She thought that a letter of introduction would help facilitate the process."

"Sorry, but the judge doesn't make the rules here," the Clinical Director snapped quite sharply. She had enough of these judges and their sense of omnipotence; they inappropriately interfered so many times in the course of treatment.

Immediately, she regretted her unprofessional response. Upon reflection, she remembered the reports from the social workers stating that Judge Levi was an exception to the rule. She had cooperated with The Reach Center, had given the youth a stern speech to reinforce The Reach Center's efforts, and then gave them another chance. Still, she wondered, *Who was this person in her office and why would he want to see Karen?*

"Personally, I am in favor of Karen having a visitor." Dr. Stone tried to smooth the atmosphere. "Her adoptive parents made it clear that they did not want to be contacted anymore. I am well aware of their efforts to rescind the adoption. The situation had become a real mess. To avoid embarrassment that she had no place to go, every time her scheduled home visit drew near, Karen managed to get herself in trouble. This provoked restriction provided her with the best excuse for not going home." She paused. For a few seconds, she weighed the possible choices she had, given the program's policy.

"For Karen's sake, I would like to help you," she added. She was aware of the special interest the judge had taken in Karen. She was impressed and encouraged by the fact that Judge Levi had engaged Mr. Offir to help Karen, *but why?*

"I need to know more about you and the interests you and Judge Levi have in Karen's case." She continued by asking her questions with a preface that her job was to protect Karen's welfare; she begged his pardon for her probing.

Jeremy was surprised at how easily he was able to open up to Dr. Stone. He felt comfortable speaking with her.

"I am an Israeli lawyer with a license to practice in New York. I am Judge Levi's cousin."

With Judge Levi's permission, he told Dr. Stone about the promise that the Judge made to Karen.

"She'll help her find her biological mother if, and only if, it was within the limits and regulations of the law. Also, only if it would clearly be advisable, desirable, and beneficial for both mother and daughter."

He explained that since he was coming to the United States on business, Judge Sharon Levi asked him to assist in Karen's case through his affiliate firm in New York City.

"All of these proceedings can take place only because the adoptive parents are in the process of rescinding the adoption. If her parents succeed, Karen might end up becoming a ward of the state. Judge Levi hopes to avoid that if the mother is a possible option. Also, she felt the child could use a friend rather than added disapproval." Jeremy concluded.

"That still does not explain yours and Judge Levi's personal involvement. Is there anything else?"

Jeremy sensed that Dr. Stone could be of help if she understood the picture as a whole. He explained how the BNN TV clip and the picture of the "Mysterious Rescuer" in the newspaper article evoked old memories about a person he used to know well.

"How did you and Judge Levi come to discuss Karen?"

"Sharon, that is, Judge Levi, was recently in Israel and saw my reaction to the picture in the newspaper she brought with her. She commented that when she had met Karen a few weeks earlier, there were similarities to a girl we knew when we were young."

"How interesting . . . almost amazing . . . could it be?" Dr. Stone said to herself, but her words were audible.

"What?" Jeremy wondered seeing her excitement.

"There is something I can share with you. It is not a question of confidentiality since it happened to me." She proceeded to describe her meeting with the lawyer who came to visit her client's father in the hospital. "It really was amazing; her voice and face truly reminded me of Karen."

"Are you OK? You look sick. . ." She noticed Jeremy turned quite pale as he rested his head on the back of the couch.

"Yes, I am fine." Jeremy was beside himself. He hardly could believe his luck. He was almost afraid to speak. He tried to disguise his emotional turmoil. Finally, he asked, "What was the lawyer's name?"

"Ms. Robinoff. I must say she looked extremely young …"

"Did you happen to know the name of the law firm?"

"Why are you asking?"

Jeremy didn't know if he should tell her. He remained quiet.

When Dr. Stone realized he wasn't about to answer, she reached for her briefcase, removed a folder, copied the address and handed it to him. She didn't mention her conversation with Ms. Robinoff.

"Look Mr. Offir, I would like to help; your cause is our cause. We can facilitate the process of your visitations if we consider you to be her lawyer along with the New York firm.

"Thank you! It is important, however, that Karen doesn't develop expectations about my efforts on her behalf. There are so many 'ifs' about the process as a whole. It's best if I could see Karen as a lawyer and a friend of Judge Levi, who is trying to help her in the legal matters regarding her adoption and her parents." Dr. Stone nodded in agreement.

"Can I take her off grounds?"

"Not yet. I'll let you know more once we talk about it at the staff conference. Thank you, Mr. Offir, for caring."

"Thank you!"

"Please return tomorrow afternoon, if you can, and in the meantime, we will prepare Karen for your visit. Make sure to tell Judge Levi that we appreciate her efforts on Karen's behalf."

Jeremy got up, shook hands with Dr. Stone and thanked her again. He dreaded the many hours he would have to wait until tomorrow.

Rivcka Edelstein

Long Island, New York, May 1991

Chapter 36

The next day, Jeremy sat in the main office at The Reach Center. Nellie, Dr. Stone's secretary, was sizing him up. She was curious about his repeated visit. She knew that today he was coming to visit Karen and that his request to see her was approved without the usual, formal procedures.

The door opened and Karen strolled in.

Jeremy raised his head when Karen entered and he was stunned. There was no need for anyone to tell him who she was — her resemblance was even greater than the newspaper photo had suggested. Now he understood Sharon's reaction when she saw Karen in the court room for the first time. Karen looked like the exact image of Beth when he last saw her in 1973. He felt a strange sensation throughout his body.

"Dr. Stone called for me. What did I do now?"

"It's funny you asked, I was just wondering the same thing." Nellie realized Karen's concern and added in a whisper, "I didn't see any 'blue behavior report' on you."

Karen sat beside Jeremy and he moved a little to give her more space. Nellie dialed Dr. Stone's number and announced Karen's arrival and then motioned for both Karen and Jeremy to go in.

Dr. Stone greeted them both and said, "Karen, this is Mr. Offir. He is the lawyer I told you about." She then turned to Jeremy and said, "Mr. Offir, this is Karen."

Jeremy extended his right hand and said, "It's nice to meet you, Karen. I've heard a great deal about you from my friend, Judge Levi."

"So, how can I help you?" Karen enthusiastically shook his hand. She was willing to trust anybody sent by Judge Levi. Karen asked jokingly, but with a shaky voice. Jeremy was stunned by her voice which sounded just like his memory of Beth. He never saw such a resemblance between two people.

Dr. Stone suggested that Jeremy and Karen walk outside so they could talk while Karen showed him the grounds.

They walked slowly, greeted by several residents who asked Karen who he was. She was happy with the way the residents acted towards her now that she had changed. Every once in a while, she used to wish they would forget her behavior from the first few months.

After a few social pleasantries, they settled down in the shade and Jeremy began. "Since your adoptive parents requesting to rescind your adoption, Judge Levi asked me to help her in finding your biological mother. However, I don't want you to have false expectations about it. It is neither legally nor administratively simple. Even if we find your mother, it doesn't mean she will be able or willing to be involved. However, both the Judge and I would like to try and help, and we'll do our best, as long as you understand there are no guarantees, O.K.?"

"O.K."

"Can you tell me a little about yourself?" Jeremy asked. Although he had heard some things about the Burgs from Sharon, he was going to read the files once he had obtained a written consent from Karen and the Burgs. He was completely unprepared for what Karen was about to tell him. Once she started, he didn't interrupt her.

"When I lived in the foster home, I prayed for my own mother to appear. Don't misunderstand, I had very caring foster parents, but they were not mine. I now believe they loved me, but in those days, I kept wishing for my own mom and dad. Whenever my foster mother hugged or kissed her own daughter, I craved for the same warmth and affection, daydreaming that my own mother was kissing me. At night, I always asked, 'Why me, God, what did I do to deserve this?' As I got older, I added another part, 'It is still not too late to fix the injustice done to me. Let my mother come and take me.'

"I was not a great believer but I was so desperate. Sometimes I even bargained with God - I used to promise that 'If my mother came to me before my next birthday, I would start believing; that I would start practicing whatever faith, just bring my mother back.' Nothing happened.

"As the years passed, my desire to have my own mother became stronger than ever. As I grew up, I understood it was impossible. First, she must have given me up because she could not keep me. Then I feared that even if she had regretted her decision, she wouldn't be able to find me." Karen noticed that Jeremy looked puzzled.

"You see, I was placed in a foster home in one community, but when I was nine, I was adopted by a family that lived somewhere else. Sometimes I believed that she hesitated and that's why I wasn't adopted until I was nine. Other times, I remember that nobody I knew actually ever saw her."

"When I was adopted, I was told by Adela to call her 'Mother.' That was easier said than done. How could I erase years of dreams and hopes? I really tried. In the beginning, she, too, really tried, but I could not bring myself to betray my own mother. Maybe it was partly my fault that the relationship between the Burgs and I went badly. They had their own dreams and expectations of me, their 'carefully selected daughter'. She never stopped telling me how they had chosen me out of dozens of children. I had mixed feelings toward 'Father' and 'Mother.' I was glad to have been chosen, but I blamed them for squashing my hopes and stopping the search for my own mother. Even so, I was determined to be a good and grateful daughter.

"Regardless of what Adela believed I had said or done, I did try. She made the effort to accept me and to give me a physical affection, but it didn't feel right. Maybe it was the lectures and speeches that preceded it. Maybe it was the way she did it. It was ironic how I had yearned for affection all of those years, and then when it was finally given to me, it wasn't what I dreamed it would be like." Karen's voice shook as she said these last few words.

Jeremy noticed that she was fighting back tears. She looked blankly into space, as if searching for something in the distance. Her eyes were shining. Jeremy didn't interrupt her, nor did he urge her to continue. It was very painful for Karen.

"The problems started the day my last report card of fifth grade arrived in the mail." She continued after a long pause, "It was the first report card I received since I moved to live with them. My marks were not as good as 'Mother's' niece. "Father" kept saying that he had given me everything, even more than my cousin got, and look at what I gave **him** in return. He saw my school work as a sign that I was not grateful for the **'golden opportunity'** he had given me." Karen emphasized the last few words with disgust. "I was nine and a half years old and their words have echoed in my ears nonstop ever since.

"Later that night, I woke up from a nightmare and I got up to go to the bathroom. I heard them discussing my report card again. He pointed out how 'disappointed' he was and that 'I' was not the daughter he had hoped for. He said I probably had bad genes and the adoption agency probably lied about my earlier report cards. "Mother" did not show any sign of disagreement. On the contrary, she kept saying 'Yes, I know, I know what you mean, I know how you feel.' I stood there paralyzed. Although I knew he was not crazy about me, I thought she liked me.

"He said, 'I blame myself for giving in to you when you selected her, even though we did not know much about her real parents.'

"She said, 'We just need to have more patience, you'll see.' This was as far as her confidence in me went." Her voice cracked and Karen was fighting back tears.

"At that point Father said in disgust, 'Optimist! Naive! I don't know how or why I let you coerce me into **this mess.'** These words cut into me." Karen gave in, letting the tears roll down her cheeks.

"This conversation was just the beginning of a pattern that repeated itself when almost every report card came. Future conversations about my lack of meeting father's standards were done in front of me."

Jeremy wanted to put his arm on her shoulder, but he stopped himself. He wanted her to know he understood. Her silent sobs turned into intense crying and Jeremy could only watch helplessly. After a few deep breaths, Karen went on reluctantly.

"One time I heard 'Father" say, 'if she was so great, how come she wasn't adopted sooner?'

"To this mother answered, 'You know all of the facts as well as I do. Until the old lady died, she was not available for adoption.'

"Then he would say, 'Sure, that's what they told us. They wanted to get her off their hands.' I felt like damaged merchandise. He often said they would not have been in this mess if he had followed his gut feelings. When he said 'this mess,' he pointed at me or looked in my direction!

"'Mother' used to take his side when she was talking to me. 'You are not really trying', she used to say to me. She strongly believed it was in my power to make him happy. She would often send me to apologize or try to appease him for things I had not done.

"My marks continued to decline no matter how hard I tried. From then on, things became progressively worse. He used to be very impatient with me, punishing me severely for every little thing: sending me to my room without dinner, cutting my involvement with relatives and friends, etc. In front of me, he told everyone that he had made a mistake by adopting me. He said he was ashamed I used their family name, that it reflected badly on his family's honor. I had nightmares, and at night, I would cry to be rescued. My life was miserable and there was no way out.

"Eventually, I started to respond back. When they couldn't take it anymore, they placed me out of their house. The rest is history, fully described in all of my records," she said in a deep sigh.

She looked at Jeremy and then continued, "How do you like it so far? Now you can understand why I don't want to go back."

Jeremy nodded. He also noticed through the entire story that Karen did not refer to the Burgs as 'my father and my mother', but rather expressed the words 'mother' and 'father' with indifference.

"This place, which I objected to bitterly in the beginning, proved itself to be very good for me. I am working hard on improving my behavior. The only thing I want now is to **find my real mother**." Karen finally stopped and wiped her tears.

Karen fumbled through some papers in her wallet before taking out a folded Polaroid photograph.

"Here is something I have from before I was adopted. It could be a start." Karen placed the picture in front of Jeremy.

"This picture was taken on Christmas when I was almost nine years old; my foster parents took it. The lady was not pleased about it, but my foster parents said it would be nice for me to have a 'souvenir.'"

"Who is she?"

"Don't really know. I used to see her regularly before then, but this was the last time I ever saw her. At that visit, she kept hugging me and saying good-bye. From some of the comments among the adults, I have the feeling that we were related."

Jeremy looked at the picture more closely. The face of the lady was familiar...very familiar. Based on what Karen said, the picture was taken around 1982 and the lady could have been in her late forties."

"Well, what do you think?" Karen asked eagerly.

"You looked cute when you were nine, not that you aren't very pretty now."

"Thanks, but I was asking about the lady."

"Well, it could be a start. What happened to her after that Christmas?"

"I don't know. I think she was sick during the last few visits. Maybe she expected something bad to happen. My foster parents seemed sad at the time and the lady hugged me and said these hugs had to last me for a long time."

"Did you ever ask your foster parents about her?"

"No, but soon after that I was placed for adoption. My adoptive parents might be able to give you better answers. I know they searched for a while because they wanted a 'perfect' girl. I'll lend the picture to you if you think it might be useful. If there is nothing you can do, send the picture to me at The Reach Center."

* * *

"What do you like to do for recreation?" Jeremy asked her during one of his subsequent visits.

"What do I like to do or what do I do?"

"Isn't it the same?"

"No! Not in my case."

"So, answer both questions," Jeremy smiled. He expected it was going to be a challenging conversation.

Karen seemed to be quick in her responses, having both implicit and explicit answers. He was impressed with her acute knowledge of right and wrong, even though she didn't necessarily agree with or practice it. She had great insight for her behavior.

"First, I've to explain that my whole life was about survival."

"What do you mean?" he asked.

She went on explaining, "To survive, I had to do what was expected of me. I learned to be a show-off amongst my parents' friends and relatives and then a know-it-all amongst my middle-class peers in school. At The Reach Center, I was yet again pretending, this time to be a street-wise, experienced delinquent.

Sometimes my acting was so convincing, that I really had difficulty remembering who the real Karen was. It seemed as if my life was all an act and lacked reality. Though I did it well, it took a great deal of energy. I wanted my real feelings, thoughts, and behaviors to be accepted, the real me sought warmth, honestly cared for others, and wanted to share my feelings. Those behaviors were criticized and dumped upon in both my middle-class home and my street life." She stopped and looked at him.

"It is different with you; you encouraged the expression of the real me." She smiled. "Now I will answer your question. Ready?" She looked around and continued.

"I like to sing, dance, and play soccer. At home, I mean with my adoptive parents, I was not allowed to do any of that. I was told my voice was irritating, the dancing I liked was forbidden, and according to my adoptive parents, soccer was a male sport and not very ladylike. Here I am allowed to do all these things."

"I heard from Dr. Stone that during the Easter Dinner, you sang very beautifully."

"Oh, well," she tried to dismiss the compliment and shrugged her shoulders.

"How are you at playing soccer?"

"I try my best." Karen said modestly. "By default, I became the Captain of the team."

"Whoa!" He exclaimed, "I used to be quite good. I can give you some pointers," Jeremy offered and saw the shine in Karen's eyes.

"Now?" Karen said pleadingly.

"As a matter of fact, I have gym clothes in the trunk of the car."

Karen was excited. "Wonderful! I'll go change and I'll meet you on the field. It's beside the Social Services parking lot."

Despite his leg injury, Jeremy was able to run and play ball quite well. He showed her some ways to improve her kicking, they joked around, and she learned how to hit the ball with her head. They weren't on the playing field very long before Mike, Chris, Little, John, and Aida joined them. The boys and the girls played together and Jeremy found the environment very refreshing. He was impressed with how well they played and they were all eager to try out the tips he gave.

After a while, Karen noticed Jeremy's limp. She suggested they stop.

"What is with the limping?" she asked, pointing to his leg.

"It's an old injury," he said without elaborating.

Driving back to Sharon's house, he found himself singing. He felt good; he felt young again. He noticed how relaxed he was and that he had not felt this way for a very long time.

Silence Broken

Long Island, New York, May 1991

Chapter 37

On Friday evening, Jeremy came to visit Karen. It was the first visit that he did not initiate. It was suggested at the last minute, by The Reach Center's staff. Dr. Stone wanted to reward Karen's positive changes. Karen was the only resident who did not have guests visiting her on weekends. Jeremy was pleased that they had called him, even more so when he was informed of the team's approval to take her off the Reach Center's grounds.

Karen was sitting on the floor of her room, leaning against her bed, busily writing. She had been so absorbed that she didn't even hear the approaching footsteps and Jeremy's knock on the open door. Jeremy was impressed with the zeal with which she worked. He stood watching her for a short while and then quietly, so as not to startle her, said, "Hi, Karen." She raised her head and grinned at the sight of her visitor.

"Jeremy," she jumped up toward him, "I am glad you are here. Do you know we received permission to get off the grounds?" she asked happily.

"Yes! I know, they told me." He smiled. "Would you like to go out for a walk?" he asked, pointing to the piles on the floor.

Karen pushed the papers aside and grabbed her keys. As they walked in the quiet evening, Karen asked about the progress he was making concerning her case. Jeremy told her that Judge Levi was trying to facilitate the process.

"I know Judge Levi cares about me, but I don't know why."

"Must she have a reason? Couldn't it be simply because she likes you?"

"Did you know she sent me a gift for my birthday? On February 14th, I got a pink rose and a necklace and a card that said 'Because you are special.' It meant so much to me. I wrote her a note that evening to thank her. I told her that she was special to me, too."

Jeremy made a mental note to remember Karen's birthday.

"What kind of trouble did you get into when you were restricted?"

"Last time, I was caught smoking pot with two other residents."

"I get the impression that they are very strict about it. I am surprised that they didn't dismiss you."

"Dr. Stone feels that it's possible to control drugs. The fact that the schools and parents on the outside fail to supervise their children does not make it right. All the counselors and residents had to attend lectures. At first Dr. Stone had a difficult time with some of the staff's smoking habits. Obviously, they had to stop before they could enforce any rules over the residents. We're kept busy with various activities, so that we don't have to search for 'personal entertainment'." She said it all proudly.

"Can you believe that the residents themselves are cooperating in preventing pot smoking? I like pot; it's hard for me to resist it. When a new resident offers me a smoke, I usually join in."

He was amused in the way she went on about the topic. "Are you telling me that you are happy here?"

"Hell yeah! I hate to admit it, but I shiver when I think that they might have transferred me. I care more about being expelled from here than about being disinherited by my adoptive parents."

"How do you explain it?"

"A few months ago, I had a physical fight with someone in a high position here and I was afraid I would be transferred. I really wanted another chance; I practically begged Dr. Stone and my therapist. Some of the staff was pulling for me, even the person I hurt. I was determined to try even harder. Dr. Stone had faith in me; even more than I had in myself. At the beginning, I tried hard

Silence Broken

for her, but Dr. Stone and my therapist said, 'Don't do it for us, do it for you.' Did you know that I was a terror? Of course you did, you probably read my file. I heard that everything goes on our records. I wonder how thick it is." She was fishing. She really hoped he hadn't read her file even though she gave written consent to allow him to read her records. She wanted him to know the real Karen, not the one she pretended to be. "Anyway, didn't you get the impression, from my file, that I am a certified delinquent'?"

"I don't think you are. I think you've been hurt. You are a fair and honest person. By the way, I didn't read your file . . .."

"You should read it..."

"I also heard from Dr. Stone that they believe you have great potential and abilities."

"Did they tell you about my fighting?"

"No, but knowing you, I'm sure you are going to enlighten me."

"I better tell you in small doses. If you heard it all at once you might not come again. Heaven knows, I don't get many visitors."

He smiled.

"You know, you look handsome when you smile. Why don't you do it more often?"

"I don't get many occasions to meet people like you. Being with you relaxes me."

"I guess it's mutual. You treat me as an equal; you don't talk down to me."

"How would you like to go for brunch and a play tomorrow?"

"Wow! Sounds great! Are there any musicals?"

"I will check."

"It sounds very exciting."

"How early do you want me to come pick you up?"

"If you come early, we can have more time . . . Everyone must be back by six in the evening. I don't want to be late on my first outing . . . the earlier, the better. I am an early riser, so . . ."

"I'm not, but I will make a special effort to be here by 8:30."

Jeremy asked her as they approached the cottage, "What were you working on when he arrived?"

"I'll tell you, but it's a surprise."

"What kind of surprise?"

"The Reach Center announced a contest for a creative work; I am writing a play."

"What kind of play?"

"I'd like it to be a musical, but I am still working on the script. If we win, then the play would be performed at the Grand Opening of the new Cultural Complex."

"That sounds very exciting. What is it about?"

"It's about us . . .the life here in The Reach Center. My title is *Everything Is Possible*. I am a living example of it."

He smiled. Their time together passed quickly and soon it was time to say good-bye. "Shalom," he said.

"Sha-a-lom," she replied happily, imitating his pronunciation of the Hebrew word.

When she went to bed that night, she made some modification in her nightly prayer to God. This time she added, "God, you have provided me with a good friend; can you now help him find my mother?" She closed her eyes and took a deep breath.

Silence Broken

Long Island, New York, May 1991

Chapter 38

Early Saturday morning, Jeremy drove his rental car through the gates of The Reach Center. He was half an hour early.

As he pulled up in front of Karen's cottage, Carol, the counselor came running out of the cottage. She seemed quite distraught and didn't notice him. She unlocked the school car and was ready to get in, when he called out to her.

"Good morning! Is Karen ready?"

She turned and saw him.

"Oh, here you are. I asked Gina to call you, but they told us you'd left already. You're quite early."

"Why did you try to reach me?"

"They called from the hospital emergency room..."

"Hospital?" he repeated.

"I really don't know the details, but she lost a lot of blood... There was a bad accident on their way back..."

"Accident?" He was alarmed. "When, how?" He felt light headed.

"I don't know exactly... I'm going there now."

"Can I take you?" It was the first thing he could think of saying. He wanted to be there for Karen... he had to get to her.

"Do you mind? I'm so shaky, I am not sure how I could drive."

The counselor was crying and trying to explain what she knew about the accident. From her disjointed comments, Jeremy understood that Karen and two other residents went running together in preparation for an upcoming mini-marathon. During their run, Karen was hit. The car did not even stop. The other girls stopped a passing car that drove Karen, Aida and Tanya to the hospital. . . . from the hospital they called the cottage, but could not explain exactly what had happened to Karen and what was her condition.

As they reached the hospital, Jeremy's mind was racing. Should he try to reach Beth? What if she had nothing to do with Karen?

He followed the counselor into the emergency room. They heard that Karen needed an immediate blood transfusion and the family had been called for compatible blood. Carol informed the doctor that Karen had been adopted and he seemed concerned. "Well, it is going to be hard. We are better off with fresh blood, both because of the amount we need and because she is in shock. We don't have her exact type in supply, but we've already called a nearby hospital blood bank."

Carol, Tanya, and Jeremy interrupted, and said in unison, "I'll donate."

Carol pointed out that Tanya is a minor and she would not be allowed to donate. The doctor asked, "Who are you?"

"I am Karen's counselor."

The doctor turned to Jeremy and asked, "Who are you?"

"A friend of hers."

"When did you donate blood last?"

"Six months ago . . . I will give whatever you need," Jeremy replied.

"Fine. Both of you go next door for a blood test and typing." The doctor was in a big hurry and pushed Jeremy and Carol along.

After the technician took the blood sample, Carol and Jeremy waited for the doctor's decision. Carol, who seemed speechless,

Silence Broken

approached Jeremy and whispered, "Thank goodness you came with me. I did not realize how serious it was."

Jeremy called Sharon and informed her about the events of the morning.

The doctor approached Jeremy and said, "You will do."

Jeremy was not surprised. He knew he was a universal donor. He didn't say a word, but just nodded. How could he explain his feelings and thoughts at that moment?

He was led to another room where he lay down and prepared for the procedure. As the needle was put in his arm, he watched his blood fill the plastic bag. Jeremy felt it was going too slowly. He was worried and found himself resorting to prayer. *Oh God, give her a chance. Please God! I will do all I can to help her.*

He heard the doctor instructing the technician to stop the transfusion. "He's done and now it is our turn to try to do the rest. At least now her chances are better."

Jeremy felt weakness throughout his body . . . a loss of feeling and a sense of floating . . . things in the room became unclear . . . The room had become darker and darker and he felt as though he were drowning . . . sinking . . . down . . . down . . . deeper . . . He was out.

He opened his eyes slowly and closed them again. At first, he was not sure where he was and what had happened to him. He heard a voice, but not words. He opened his eyes again, recognizing some of the faces, the words becoming clearer. Dr. Stone, Gina, Carol and Mary were all there. He did not know how much time had passed.

"Mr. Offir, you passed out. Did you eat breakfast?" Dr. Stone asked him. For a second, he felt like a small child.

"How is Karen?" he asked weakly.

"She is still in shock. We can only wait. You need to rest."

But Jeremy didn't have the patience to do so. He vowed to himself to speed up his efforts in locating Beth. If there was no connection between Karen and Beth, he would look in a different direction. Now that Karen had his blood, he felt that she was a part of him, regardless.

In the corner of the room the Clinical Director was talking to Mr. and Mrs. Burg on the phone. From the look on her face, she was quite angry. They were called early in the morning and told about the need for a blood donation . . . It sounded from the part of the conversation which Jeremy could hear that Mr. Burg had complaints about Karen and her actions.

"I can't believe it. Mr. Offir is a stranger and he is willing to donate blood for your daughter. You . . ." Dr. Stone said, irritated.

Jeremy was surprised to see the anger and rage which Dr. Stone expressed at that point. At the end, she moved the telephone close to Jeremy.

"He wants to speak to you." She could barely keep herself from screaming.

"Thank you for donating the blood. You probably have heard that neither one of us has the suitable blood type that she needed. I hope she wasn't too much of an inconvenience to you," Mr. Burg said. "If she minded her own business, it would never have happened." Mr. Burg was referring to Karen's forthcoming participation in the marathon, against their explicit wish.

"You are welcome," Jeremy managed to say, slowly. He wanted to continue, but he held back. There was a short pause.

"Anyway, it's not your problem and, with God's help, soon it might not be our problem either." Mr. Burg added.

Jeremy gathered his strength and said, with added energy, "What do you mean?"

"Well, we've applied for the court to rescind the adoption; the sooner we get out of it . . ."

"I'm sorry to hear that. If you don't mind, I'd like to stay close. . ."

"Be my guest! Though I couldn't imagine why you would want to . . . she will use you the way she used us; she is **Trouble**, with a capital 'T.'"

Jeremy hung up. He ignored the food that had been placed beside him.

Dr. Stone thanked him and invited him to rest at The Reach Center until he felt better. The doctor approached the group and reported a slight improvement in Karen's condition. He turned to Jeremy, concerned about his condition, and offered to keep him in the hospital to rest.

"She would probably want to thank you," the doctor added.

He started walking away and suddenly stopped -- he had finally figured out what had been puzzling him since Karen had been brought in. He pulled Dr. Stone aside.

"Isn't she the 'Mysterious Rescuer'?" he asked.

"Yes, she is."

"God bless her!"

"Please don't say anything about her here, we do try to protect our children from unwanted publicity," Dr. Stone explained.

"My lips are sealed," he reassured her.

Jeremy laughed, recalling that it was the picture of the 'Mysterious Rescuer' that had brought him into this escapade.

Jeremy accepted the doctor's offer to stay. The Clinical Director approached him again and said, "I am sorry you were subjected unknowingly to Mr. Burg. I could guess his attitude from your facial expression and your responses."

"In a sense, I am glad he did say what he had said. I finally had the chance to understand what Karen was trying to tell me and what I was not completely able to believe. I'm sure you were not spared his anger either," he said smiling.

She looked at him, but did not respond. How could she tell him how she felt about Karen's father? If she expressed her true feelings, they would not sound professional. She had choice words to describe such creeps.

Instead she said, "Listen, you need rest. We are relying on your help and support. She really likes you. Even better, she trusts you; that's a big change for her."

"I will try. Mr. Burg said that I am welcome to do what I want . . ." He paused and leaned against the door feeling weak again.

"Please, go rest. I understand that because of the emergency they took an unusually large amount of blood from you. From what I understood from the doctor, they were very grateful you were available and willing to donate."

They discussed how to take turns sitting beside Karen's bed so someone would be there when she woke up.

As the counselor left the room, Sharon entered. She approached Jeremy and hugged him. "I was upstairs, talking to the doctor. I understand there is a slight change and that Karen is going to pull through . . ." She tried to sound optimistic. Then she recalled something and added, "Oh, Jeremy, I am sorry you have to go through all of these again . . . it probably very hard for you. . . I imagine it takes you back to the 1973 war, the time you were captured after you were wounded . . . all the tortures you went through . . . and to top all of that all the surgeries you had to go through after you had returned home." She stopped as she became aware that there was a woman sitting in the other corner.

"Oh, I am sorry. I didn't see you. I am Sharon Levi, Jeremy's cousin. I met Karen in my court room, several times, and I was concerned . . ." Dr. Stone introduced herself. She was glad to finally meet the residents' infamous judge.

Silence Broken

As Jeremy and Sharon stepped outside, Dr. Stone had a chance to go back to the information Sharon just had shared. In the past few weeks, she had individual talks with Jeremy and with Karen. She heard about the war and about his injuries. Now, from his facial expression. she wondered if he ever got help for his traumas. She concluded, "He probably didn't!"

Rivcka Edelstein

Long Island, New York, May 1991

Chapter 39

Karen was moved from the recovery room to the pediatric ward once her vital signs had stabilized. She lay pale and motionless for hours, connected to a number of monitors.

The doctor told them it was important that she sees familiar faces when she wakes up. The Reach Center didn't allow the residents to cut school. Dr. Stone took turns with the counselors sitting by Karen's side. Jeremy, however, didn't leave. He saw her lying on the bed motionless with the medical equipment attached to her body. This brought back distant, but not forgotten, memories. How could he forget his endless ordeal in the hospital at Tel Ha-Shomer, more than 17 years ago?

He sat there until she finally opened her eyes, 48 hours later.

"Hey! How do you feel?" Jeremy asked quietly.

Karen's eyes opened for a second. "I don't know," Karen managed weakly, closing her eyes. "I guess it wasn't a dream . . . from the pain I guess I'm still alive."

"Do you remember what happened?" Jeremy asked her as he moved closer to hold her hand.

"I'm not sure . . . we were jogging, Tanya, Aida, and I were practicing for the marathon . . . all of a sudden I heard Tanya scream." Karen closed her eyes again and took a few deep breaths. "She screamed; I looked back and . . ." She paused. "Are they OK? I'll never forgive myself if something happened to them . . ."

Tears came to her eyes and Jeremy held back his own; she was lying there, barely alive, worrying about her friends.

"Tanya sustained minor bruises and she is OK; likewise, Aida is fine." He stopped and looked at her. "They are really worried about you."

Silence Broken

"Thank God they're OK," she said and closed her eyes. Tears flowed freely down her cheeks.

"I hurt all over. I can't move any part of my body. What's wrong with me?" she asked weakly.

Jeremy held her hand gently and smiled. "As you said, pain is a sign that you are alive. I'll let the doctor know you are awake -- he'll be able to better explain the situation. In the meantime, you must get some rest."

At that point, the nurse entered quietly. "I thought I heard voices." She looked at Karen with a smile. "Sleeping Beauty is finally awake; let me call the doctor . . ." She left as quietly as she came in. The doctor arrived a few minutes later and motioned Jeremy to excuse them. Jeremy left the room.

The doctor examined Karen and spoke to her about the accident, the surgery, and her luck that Jeremy walked in when he did. Karen took some time to understand, especially the part about the blood types. After she grasped what the doctor said, she shivered when she thought about what could have happened if Jeremy had not arrived. She fell asleep. When she woke up, Jeremy was again sitting beside her bed.

Rivcka Edelstein

San Francisco, California, June 1991

Chapter 40

Three weeks after Ms. Beth Robinoff had left for California, her personal secretary and paralegal, Ms. Sylvia Block, was leaving the office with a copy of the telephone number left for her in case of an emergency. Keeping in mind the time difference between New York and California, she decided to call at 8 PM New York time.

Since she left for the West Coast, Ms. Robinoff had called several times and reported to Ms. Block about the technique in the clinic and how they are hanging her from her ankles using the Gravity Guidance System and that it really worked. She also said she was able to do exercises which she had thought she would never be able to do again.

Ms. Block dialed the California number. Earlier that morning, she called Dr. Stone and delivered verbatim the message given to her by Ms. Robinoff that she "was interested in the idea and wanted to come to visit The Reach Center." She had the impression that Dr. Stone had expected those exact words. Ms. Robinoff worked too hard already and she did not need any extra work. *It couldn't be the money*, since most of her clients couldn't pay and she made little effort to collect. *What was so different about this particular offer?*

The call went through and she asked if Ms. Robinoff could be paged. After a pause, the clinic receptionist laughed, "You mean Beth, why didn't you say so?" Funny, she knew Ms. Robinoff for years and never called her Beth. Ms. Robinoff would have been happy if she did use her first name, but Ms. Block refused; it seemed disrespectful to her.

"Hello, hello . . . hello?" Ms. Block wondered how long Ms. Robinoff was on the line while she was daydreaming.

"Hi, it's me. It took them time to find you."

Silence Broken

"I was being "stretched." Sorry, what's up?!"

"I gave Dr. Stone your message. She said to tell you that she is happy to hear that you agreed to consider their offer. She seemed anxious for your quick return . . ."

"What do you mean?"

"She said something to the effect that 'we sure could have used her now. I hope we aren't going to miss the boat.' I don't think I was supposed to hear that because when I asked her what she meant, she quickly replied, 'Never mind' and then asked about your treatment. What kind of doctor is she? It sounded as if she really knew something about back injuries."

"She's a psychologist. Maybe she knows people who have back problems. Or maybe . . ." She didn't want to elaborate about Dr. Stone. Anyway, thanks for getting the message to her."

The paralegal paused for a few seconds and then said, "By the way, a pleasant-sounding man called a few times asking for you."

"Did he leave a name? A message?"

"No, but he said it was a personal call, not business. He was very polite, if you ask me, and he did not sound like any of your friends or any of the voices I've heard before."

"Is that so..."

"It wasn't only his accent, but also his clear pronunciation and refined language. He sounded French or maybe Israeli. Anyway, he asked when you would be in. I didn't want to give him any information and just said he should call next week." After a short pause, she asked, "Did I mention that he called a number of times?"

"Yes." Beth was starting to feel anxious. "What else did he say?"

"He called before, but I didn't want to bother you with every call to the office. When he called again today, however, he sounded very worried, especially when I said that I didn't have an exact date for your return. Is he a 'new friend'?"

"How should I know who he is, you're the one who spoke to him." Beth replied curtly. Then she added lightly, "No, I don't have any 'new friends' — stop marrying me off. I can hear from your voice that you are starting again."

"Don't just hear it from my voice, hear it from my heart. It's about time, Ms. Robinoff."

"Yes, Madam."

"When are you coming back anyway?"

"What's the rush? I'm having a good time here."

"No rush. In my opinion, you should stay until they decide you are done and not a day earlier, but I know you better than that."

"You'd be surprised!"

"So? When are you coming back?"

"Maybe one of these mornings, I will wake up and it will be my day to be free of pain. I will call you soon . . . If that man calls again, ask him to leave a name and numbers, so I can return his call. Thanks again."

Beth was preoccupied with the conversation that just ended. She found herself worrying about what "missing the boat" might mean. She hadn't felt there was any urgency about the position, especially now that she said she would consider the offer. Something must have happened since their meeting a few weeks ago.

She recalled her dream on Saturday, early in the morning. The details of it terrified and haunted her; the dream was about her daughter, that she was hurt and calling for her. This was not unusual for Beth, for years she used to dream that she heard her daughter calling her . . . but she couldn't find where the voice was coming from. In her dream, she would go from town to town and

Silence Broken

house to house searching for the voice. But she couldn't find her and she didn't even know what she looked like. Since the time Dr. Stone showed her the photo in the newspaper, the dreams were more frequent and the person for whom she was searching had distinct features. It was so painful for Beth that she always woke up before she was able to find out if her daughter was O.K.

Her dream that Saturday morning was different; it began as usual, with her daughter calling her, but this time Beth found her and she was unable to move.

She didn't see any connection between the fear and agitation she felt at the moment and the news Ms. Block gave her. She was only aware that since she met Dr. Stone in May her dormant feelings of regret for giving her daughter up for adoption had surfaced and become increasingly frequent and forceful. Despite her conclusion two weeks earlier, that the girl in the newspaper picture could not be hers, in her mind, she paired Dr. Stone with her daughter. Dr. Stone had commented on the resemblance - the youngster in the photo did look the way Beth had eighteen years before, but that didn't mean anything. Over and over she tried to convince herself that she agreed to consider being The Reach Center's young lawyer because they needed somebody and not for any other reason.

"Anything the matter, Beth?" The physical therapist had come up behind her. "Was it a bad call?

She nodded her head and quietly said, "I don't know what to make of it."

"Well, if you feel I can help you, let me know; I'll be downstairs in the treatment room."

"Thanks . . . how long do you think it will be before I am ready to leave?" she heard herself asking.

"I am not making any promises, but your progress, so far, has been good. Let me talk to the doctor and see what can be done to speed it up . . ."

"Thanks, see you tomorrow."

Rivcka Edelstein

The walk back to the hotel took forever. Beth went over the conversation she had with Ms. Block. As she reached the hotel, she dragged herself upstairs to her room with the intention of eating in and going to sleep early. She fell asleep quickly, despite the heat and noise, but woke up with a sudden scream, sweating and shaking. She realized immediately what had awakened her; she had another terrifying dream. She could still feel its impact. Although similar to her other dreams, this one had a slight variation: by the time she arrived to get her daughter, she was told, 'It is too late. You missed the boat. Seventeen years is a long time, don't you think mister?' *Mister? Who was that man with her?* He held her with reassurance and promised to help her find the girl while the people were screaming at her, 'You missed the boat.' He was young and resembled . . . Jeremy. Not the Jeremy she left behind seventeen years ago, but an older one. He appeared to be exhausted and sad. *Why was he sad? Why did he appear in her dream? What's he got to do with her daughter?* She then realized that Dr. Stone was not in her dream; she was not among the people who accused her.

Beth didn't know what to make of it. Usually her dreams had some connection to events which took place in her life. She tried to figure out why it was all combined in one dream. She assumed that in her dream, the caller Ms. Block told her about was Jeremy. *How odd. Why would he be in the States now? Why would he call me after she hadn't heard from him all these years?*

She got out of bed and headed toward the shower to clear her head and get some relief from the dreadful heat. When she got out of the shower and dried herself off, she noticed something was odd - she had forgotten about her back, there was no pain. Today was her day to be pain free and Beth couldn't help but laugh for a while. Then she suddenly burst into an uncontrollable cry. She felt very much alone. She had nobody to share the good news with.

* * *

The next day passed quickly. She completed her exercises with ease, compared to earlier days, and the therapy was both helpful and relieving. The meeting scheduled between the physical therapist, the physician, and her took place late in the afternoon and all three agreed that her progress was very promising. With continued exercise at home, she should be able to maintain her progress with only occasional physical therapy. They told Beth that she should take it easy for the next few days, and hopefully by the end of the week she could leave.

She left the meeting crying in disbelief. She was finally on the right path. She called Ms. Block to tell her that she would be at the office Monday morning.

The week flew by and on Friday afternoon, she said good-bye, offering her best wishes to those remaining for more treatment. There was an exchange of addresses, the bill was settled, and the last *Thank You* was said.

The trip back to the airport seemed faster than when she had arrived and she was certainly more comfortable. The physical therapist had warned her that there might be some set-backs, but they could be overcome with persistent exercise and minimal treatment. When they said good-bye, they agreed they would stay in touch. She felt as if she had left her "new family" behind. These people were closer to her in the last three weeks than anybody had been in the last seventeen years. Once again, she felt sad and alone.

Her flight was called and the boarding cards were collected. She could not believe her luck at having empty seats beside her. She lay down throughout the entire flight trying to figure out her life. She summed it up with one sentence, "The only thing I've got is a career." Tears flowed down her face. She didn't bother to wipe them. She fell asleep.

The stewardess woke her up to prepare for landing. The dreaded trip was over and she was back home. Seth, a firm colleague, was going to meet her at the airport; he had insisted, despite the early hour.

"Welcome home, Ms. Robinoff!" he cheered as she passed the gate.

"Shhh. Don't tell the whole world I am back; nobody is supposed to know — it's a secret."

"Are you sure you were in California?"

"What do you mean?"

"Tan! No tan! Didn't you see the sun? The beach?"

"Who are you kidding? I didn't see my own reflection in the mirror, never mind the sun. I was busy. I'll tell you all about it after you safely deposit me at home."

"One thing I'll say, you are walking better than you did before you left. How do you feel, kid?"

"One hundred percent. I returned because I felt I was doing better and the rest is up to me."

"Suntan or no suntan — welcome home." He hugged her affectionately and they moved toward the baggage claim.

Essex County, New Jersey, June 1991

Chapter 41

Jeremy drove to the meeting with Adela and Max Burg. He felt irritable and confused. He didn't care for the hostility he sensed when he tried to schedule the date and time.

What bothered him the most, however, was the "why?" The Burgs didn't see any point in discussing the matter and were disappointed when Jeremy said he was asked by Judge Levi to unofficially help facilitate the matter, if it was still the Burgs' intention to rescind the adoption.

Jeremy understood from the phone conversation with them that they were disappointed. They had believed that once they rescinded the adoption, Karen would be left as a ward of the court. They hoped it would teach her a lesson for all of her actions. They didn't understand why a person like Jeremy would come to her aid. Why would a New York firm provide the legal work for her?

Their lawyer, whom they had been pressuring for more than six months, barely moved to take action and now Karen was being represented. They seemed worried that now that she has a legal firm representing her, someone might listen to all the "inexcusable" lies that she had told about HIM. But since Karen didn't talk about these things, Jeremy wondered what they were afraid of.

Jeremy was quite impressed with the Burgs' house and the beautiful grounds. He believed Karen must have had serious reasons if she was so determined to give it all up. She was vehemently persistent in her request to rid herself of these adoptive parents, even though she knew very well that she might become a ward of the court. He wondered if the dysfunctional relationship Karen described to him was also between the Burgs or just toward Karen.

Mrs. Burg greeted him at the door and directed him toward the study without a word. Mr. Burg raised his head from his work and rearranged some of the books scattered on the table. He pointed down to the research article which he had been preparing for an upcoming dental conference.

"As you can see, Mr. Offir, life goes on here without her. We weren't going to let her stop our lives, despite the hell she has put us through." Mr. Burg took his time before offering his hand to Jeremy. He motioned for him to sit down, keeping the desk between them as a physical barrier. Mrs. Burg sat on the couch at the opposite end of the room, careful not to divert Jeremy's attention from her husband.

After a short and uncomfortable silence, Jeremy decided to begin the conversation, realizing it was not going to be easy.

"As I told you on the phone, Judge Levi is taking your request to rescind Karen's adoption very seriously. I am here, on Judge Levi's behalf to ask you, once again, if you are still as determined to follow through with that request."

"Absolutely!" Mr. Burg answered arrogantly. "We are absolutely determined to get her out of our lives."

"Well, then, we can proceed. The New York branch of Reim International Legal Services is going to take on Karen's case."

"Why? Who is going to pay for it, the state? Why isn't she represented by Legal Aid? Isn't it a waste of public money?" Mr. Burg went on, hoping to change Mr. Offir's opinion. "After all," as Mr. Burg put it to Jeremy, "you are a reasonable and intelligent person, despite the fact that you are concerned with a person like Karen."

Jeremy tried hard to control his anger. They were silent for a couple of moments.

"If it is a simple question of rescinding the adoption," Mr. Burg continued, "why does she need a firm to represent her?" Mr. Burg questioned.

Jeremy took a deep breath, slowly formulating the right words. He needed the Burgs' cooperation and he could not afford to antagonize them.

Silence Broken

"As your lawyer has probably informed you, rescinding an adoption is not a common procedure, especially when we are talking about a minor without a home . . ."

"She brought it upon herself. We served her, gave her, did for her . . . You might ask what she's done for us and the answer is nothing but cause us heartache and embarrassment."

"What did you expect when you chose to adopt her?"

"Respect and obedience. We expected that she would contribute to family pride, just like you expect from any normal child, the way our parents expected us to give to them and we did," Mr. Burg barked at Jeremy.

"What do you feel might be the cause for her poor adjustment?"

"Funny you should ask. If you read her records, you'd know that she's rotten to the core! Look at her past escapades; they'll sum her up — rotten to the core," Mr. Burg appeared quite pleased with his choice of words.

"What did she do, specifically, that made you so determined to follow through with rescinding the adoption?"

"Why dig into the past? Look at her recent actions, how she acted purposely to hurt us."

"What for example?"

"Her refusal to take the reward money offered to her."

"What reward money?" Jeremy asked naively.

"I don't know if you heard about her recent stupid, irresponsible, asinine adventures. Those can show you how little this kid is using her small brain."

"Are you talking about the accident?" Jeremy asked in amazement. He wondered if they found the car that hit her.

"That and her previous adventures."

"Which ones?" Jeremy persisted in his questions. He was not aware of any "stupid, irresponsible, asinine adventures."

"The one where she jumped into the water — she jumped without thinking that she could have been killed. As they say, 'God protects children and idiots'; she was saved on the second account."

"But that was praised as a heroic action."

"Heroic my foot. If she drowned. they would have labeled it accurately as an 'idiotic response.' To make matters worse, she had the nerve to refuse the money."

"You mean the money offered by the parents of the rescued child?" He just remembered reading about it on the plane coming over to the States.

"Yes. Can you believe the ungrateful bitch refused to identify herself so we could not get the money?"

"From what I understood, she didn't refuse to identify herself. The Reach Center was protecting her because she is a minor. Anyhow, how does that affect you?"

"The 'grateful parents' were offering to reward her, through us, with a large sum of money. The Reach Center told us she refused to take any money because she did it to save a life and not to be recognized as a hero."

"Well, didn't she have a right to say that?" Jeremy asked.

"Give me a break! All her life, she's been seeking attention - negative attention. Now these people try to give her something that could have helped to pay some of her bills and the extra expenses she incurred on our budget and what does she do? — She refuses to take it. I don't know why those people even accepted her decision instead of our preference as her parents. Can you believe that those people, knowing that she is a juvenile delinquent and in need of supervision, still decided to honor her request?!?"

"How did they find out that she was in an institution?"

"We told them. After we heard that she refused the reward, we found their address. We called and told them about her. We hoped they would follow through with us rather than listen to her. I can't believe she gave it up!" he ended angrily.

"So, that's what caused you to follow through with the rescinding?"

"Absolutely not, no. We decided months before they placed her in The Reach Center; we told Judge Levi hoping that she would leave us alone. Yet every time they placed Karen in the shelter, the court subpoenaed us to attend the court hearing. We lost so many days of work and we couldn't afford it. We had to get a lawyer to facilitate the process before we went broke. We should have hired you, you seem to work fast," he said sarcastically. "If we had any doubt before, the incident with 'the reward' reinforced our position that we made the right move in deciding to get rid of her. The only one who doesn't agree with us is my sister. In her own blind way, she doesn't see the damage that Karen incurred upon the family. She worries about what is going to happen to Karen. Can you believe that?!"

"Before we proceed into her background and discuss alternatives for Karen, it might be advisable if you take time to reconsider, in case you plan to change your mind," Jeremy suggested.

"As I told you before, absolutely not! We are moving ahead and if you move fast it will also be beneficial to our lawyer and may reduce the time he spends on the case. I guess, after all, we should be grateful to Judge Levi's efficiency." He was pleased; he just realized how they could benefit from Jeremy's work.

"Well, if you are determined, we should proceed. We need some information about Karen's life before the adoption." Jeremy opened his notebook ready to write.

"Why do you need all of that? It's been so long."

"We might try to see whether the foster parents could be an available resource for her. We are also considering trying to locate her mother," Jeremy answered politely.

"If the lady didn't want her daughter seventeen years ago, what makes you think she will want her now that everybody knows she's a juvenile delinquent?"

"You keep saying she's a juvenile delinquent — I didn't see JD charges on her record," Jeremy countered.

"Just because they are protecting minors by not labeling them, it doesn't mean she isn't a delinquent. They go out of their way to protect these kids instead of being firm with them and teaching them a lesson. That is why there is no law and order in this country, no respect for parents, and no obedience. Children do what they want to do and you can't even touch them."

"Did she perform or participate in any delinquent acts?"

"What do you call all of her actions? It was certainly not normal. Not by my book. Not by our values. Yet, she is protected and we are believed to be the criminals."

"Nobody called you a criminal."

"No? . . ." he said wondering and then added, "Because maybe some of them have the sense not to believe all of her outrageous, contemptible lies."

"What lies?" Jeremy asked innocently.

Mr. Burg caught himself in time before he aroused Jeremy's curiosity in an area that was better left untouched. "Never mind, what's the sense of rehashing adolescent fantasies?" He tried to divert Jeremy's attention, "How do you plan to locate the mother? Not that it would do you any good."

"I hope to obtain as much information as you can offer and proceed from there. We don't know if we can locate the mother, and if we do, what her reaction would be. We have to try for Karen's sake."

"Why is everybody concerned about Karen rather than about us and the poor woman who wants that part of her life to be forgotten?" Mr. Burg asked angrily.

"I must remind you, she is a minor. The court must seek alternate placement for her, if possible, before making her a ward of the court. She is too young to be on her own." Jeremy paused and then went on. "Anyhow, we do not plan on causing trouble, the investigation will be confidential."

The rest of the meeting proceeded with greater efficiency, cooperation, and less belligerence. Mr. Burg took out a file of documents covering the correspondence with the adoption agency, and answered Jeremy's questions about the foster parents and as well as some other facts. He was now acting like a reasonable person. Mr. Burg even suggested that his wife bring some coffee and refreshments. It was late in the evening by the time they finished.

Jeremy, pleased with the information he obtained, asked his question again. "I realize I might sound redundant, are you sure you want to remove Karen from your life? Does the reminiscing about what you went through for the adoption make you want to reconsider your decision before I start approaching all of those people?"

Mr. Burg smiled. "If that was the purpose of all the questions, nice try. Thanks, but no thanks. We are sure. I appreciate your effort on her behalf."

"Actually, it was on your behalf. I am trying to make sure that you wouldn't have any doubts or regrets later."

"No chance. Believe me, no chance!" Mr. Burg said confidently. "I want to add, my initial impression of you has not changed, either — you are a very nice person and apparently, a thorough and efficient lawyer. Good luck with your search."

"If you are determined, I need you to sign some release forms for . . ."

"My pleasure," Mr. Burg said before Jeremy could complete his sentence.

"I suggest you date them as of next Tuesday. That will give you time to reconsider, and unless I hear from you otherwise, I will use them to proceed in gathering the information I need," Jeremy finished.

Mr. Burg removed an elegant fountain pen from its stand and signed the forms. "This pen is for special occasions and, you must admit, these are the start of a good thing," Mr. Burg said pointing to the papers he had just signed.

"If you have any, even the slightest qualms, please call me before next Tuesday." Jeremy gave Mr. Burg the number of the New York office.

He drove out of the neighborhood slowly. In the dark, he couldn't see the street signs, but he was in no rush. He was pleased with himself for not losing his temper during the meeting. He decided he was right not to mention to the Burgs that Karen was actually more eager for the rescinding of the adoption than they were.

Now he had to wait until Tuesday in case either the Burgs or Karen changed their minds, although he doubted they would.

Silence Broken

New York, New York, June 1991

Chapter 42

The moment Beth Robinoff stepped into her office, Ms. Block buzzed her.

"Before you start your heavy schedule, you should know that The Reach Center called again. If your schedule permits, they would like you to come for an on-site visit as soon as possible; they have a lot of pressure."

"I'm afraid to ask, but how my schedule between is now and Friday."

"You have good reason to be afraid. All of those clients who needed to see you while you were away are coming this week."

"What?" Beth said, shocked. "I had asked them to schedule a light client load. I cannot believe it." She was extremely angry. "I have no respect. I don't even have control in my own office."

"We didn't have a choice."

"How am I going to manage? Call each of the clients and see who is willing to reschedule instead of sitting here for hours."

"What about the Reach Center?"

"I guess I'll call them directly. Give me five minutes to catch my breath."

Beth sat down and dialed the Center. Nellie answered. Dr. Stone was not there. She was in the hospital visiting one of the residents. Beth described her time constraints and suggested visiting in the evening. "Yes, evening will be fine. No, it would not be inconvenient for Dr. Stone, she often stays until late hours." Nellie added that Beth should speak to Dr. Stone directly about choosing which evening.

Later that afternoon Nellie called. The on-site visit was arranged for Wednesday evening and she gave Beth directions to the center.

Minutes after she finished scheduling the meeting, Beth received another call.

"May I speak to Ms. Beth Robinoff?" Jeremy's heart was pounding.

"Speaking!"

"Beth? . . . This is Jeremy . . . Jeremy Offir."

"Jeremy? Is it really you?" Her voice cracked in disbelief.

"Me, in person," he said, trying to overcome his excitement at hearing her voice after having dreamed this moment so many times. "I arrived in New York a few weeks ago and tried to locate you since; you're a hard person to track down."

"I just returned from the West Coast. What are you doing here?"

"Combining business with pleasure."

"Which business and what kind of pleasure?" she asked, trying to gain control over her shaky voice. She continued, "Where are you staying?"

"At my cousin's house. You remember her, my cousin Sharon?"

"I haven't seen her for years. How is she doing?"

"She's fine and would love to see you."

"I would love to see her, too. Is that why you are calling?"

"Beth, Beth . . . No. I am calling because I want to see you."

"After all of those years that I didn't hear from you, I…"

"Did you expect me to keep writing after you sent back all of my letters unopened?"

Silence Broken

"What???"

"Beth, can we meet?"

"Wait a minute. What do you mean your letters were returned unopened? I waited for news from you after I returned to the States. I had hoped that those months we spent together had meant something to you, but I heard nothing and I didn't get any letters from you. I assumed you were not interested."

"Beth, I don't understand," Jeremy protested. "I sent you dozens of letters. I kept sending letter after letter and they were all sent back. I kept hoping that you might open the next one, but ... You didn't return Rami's calls on my behalf, either."

"I don't believe what I am hearing," she sighed heavily.

"Beth, can we meet and talk? I really must see you."

There was no answer from Beth. He decided to take a chance. "Does this have something to do with the time between your leaving that letter for me and my finding it?"

"What time? What are you talking about?"

"Beth, I'd rather not do this on the phone; can't we meet? Don't you want to see me?"

"It depends ... I'm not sure ... I was hurt and ... well, I don't see any sense in reliving the past." She was uncomfortable. The old pain was triggered by the mere mention of the past. Yet, she didn't want to close the door on this unexpected opportunity to understand what happened in 1973.

"We can meet like old friends and find out what happened to us since the last time we said good-bye. Is that wrong?"

"It could be."

"Beth, what are you afraid of?"

"I am settled into my life. I'm content. I've overcome my feelings of ... rejection ... feeling unloved."

"All my letters were about my love for you, Beth. You feel that you've been hurt and up to this moment, I felt that I was the one who was hurt. There must be a good explanation."

"What is the sense of opening healed wounds?"

"Beth, our wounds aren't healed; at least I know mine aren't. If yours were, you wouldn't be hesitating to meet. Beth, it is important for us to meet and clear up this misunderstanding; the way things are now, we don't have a complete picture of why things ended up the way they did. No matter what life you made for yourself, how could a dinner and friendly conversation hurt?"

"Maybe you are right, but don't expect much besides a 36 year old woman."

"No expectations; just a good dinner and friendly chat. Where shall we meet?"

"Well, I am off Thursday evening."

"Thursday evening — you are talking about three days from now," he sounded very disappointed.

"You don't understand. It's difficult for me to be free for an evening without planning ahead."

"O.K., Thursday it is. Where?"

"We can meet at Grand Central Station under the big Kodak picture. How is 5:30 PM?"

"OK, 5:30 then, under the big Kodak picture."

"Good-bye." After a short pause he added, "Just for the record, I did look for you years ago, both during and after my active duty with the Army, and after your mother sold the house and moved."

He raised his head, exhausted, and saw Sharon standing there. He had not noticed her when she came in. He caught her reaction to his last comment and added, "We can discuss it on Thursday. See you then."

Silence Broken

"My, that was a long conversation to set up a date," Sharon said after Jeremy replaced the receiver.

"She didn't really want to meet me. There must be a good explanation. I don't understand, but I think she really sees herself as the injured party," he said to her, choosing his words carefully.

"I have confidence that you will find some answers. Just do me a favor, Jeremy, if you were wrong about her, don't be too reluctant to admit it."

The conversation didn't go the way he planned it. He didn't expect the reaction he got from Beth. He felt his knots in his stomach and he couldn't get rid of the lump in his throat. *How am I going to make it until Thursday? I shouldn't build up too much hope about the meeting and about the questions it is supposed to clear up.*

Beth was shaking. She was very confused. She went over and over Jeremy's words, trying to make sense of them. *Could I have been wrong all this time? Did I cause all this mess?* She became aware of the nuts in her stomach. She shook her head. *No, he is not going to put the blame on me. He rejected me.* She felt being pulled in opposite directions: she wanted to see him right away, but she felt that she was not ready to re-aggravate the unhealed wounds. She wondered if she had done the right thing by postponing the meeting.

Rivcka Edelstein

Long Island, New York, June 1991

Chapter 43

Beth was impressed with the program as it was outlined to her by Dr. Stone. She found herself very motivated to become a part of The Team's effort to help the residents, and agreed to make herself available as the new lawyer. During the entire meeting, she wanted to ask if she could meet her "twin sister," but she held back.

Beth still had an ongoing dilemma. Did she want to find out that the girl was indeed her daughter? Would she rather find out that this look-alike girl wasn't related to her? As much as she wanted to find her daughter, she also wanted to hold to her well-established belief that her daughter was adopted by nice people who loved her and that she was happy. More than anything, Beth wanted to believe that she made the right choice by unselfishly giving her child up for adoption.

"Well, since you don't have any further questions, why don't we start the tour," she heard Dr. Stone saying as she stood.

Beth followed, realizing that she missed part of the conversation. She couldn't remember the answer Dr. Stone gave to her last question and decided to ask her the remaining questions during their walk.

"I hope you aren't in a rush. I am combining this tour with my evening rounds." Beth nodded. She was in no rush and she was eager to walk since the extended sitting was hard on her back.

Their progress around the grounds was slow. In each cottage, the residents were very sociable and eager to show Dr. Stone various new items, papers, and modifications of their private rooms. Dr. Stone introduced Beth as "Ms. Robinoff, our new lawyer." The residents shook her hand, commented about how young she looked, her stylish suit, the nice necklace she wore, and so on. Beth was impressed with Dr. Stone's attention to the quiet ones who sat separately and weren't involved.

"I noticed in each cottage you met new residents," Beth commented.

"We accept more new residents during this time of the year. Between the end of the academic year and the end of the summer, our graduates and those whom we place in less restrictive settings leave. As residents leave, we accept new ones. We have a waiting list, though, since unfortunately, there are more applications than there are beds."

"What happens to those who cannot be accepted immediately?"

"They stay in diagnostic centers. Unfortunately, it delays the onset of treatment."

They finally arrived at the last cottage. Beth had been looking closely at the faces of the female residents whom she met. So far, she didn't see anyone who even remotely resembled her.

"I didn't see my 'twin sister,' was she among the ones that graduated or transferred?"

"Oh, no! She's in the hospital. She had a terrible accident and is actually quite lucky to be alive."

"When did it happen?" Beth could barely breathe.

"While you were in California."

"How is she?" Beth sounded anxious.

"She is OK, now, thank God. The doctor felt that she recovered miraculously, partly because of her strong will and partly due to the great support she had received."

"I'm glad she's improving." Beth was definitely relieved. "When did it happen?" She tried to sound calm.

"Saturday morning two weeks ago . . . It was very early, around six in the morning. She was injured by a hit and run car when she and her friends were practicing for the mini-marathon run . . ."

"Saturday morning? At six in the morning?" Beth asked. She was barely audible.

"Yes, I'll never forget that day. . . "

Beth was no longer listening. She was sweating. She remembered waking up from a nightmare that Saturday.

"She'll be back in time for summer session; you can meet her then. You'll like her."

"I'm sure."

"When can you start working here?" Dr. Stone asked.

"It will take me at least two weeks to see all the cases that were backlogged. Then I'll be able to clear a day to come here once a week to start."

"It sounds good to me. We are glad that you agreed to join our program"

"Well, I hope I can be of use."

"I'm sorry you didn't meet the therapeutic staff; we'll have a special meeting to introduce you on the morning of your first day. It would be helpful for you to meet them before you start."

"Thanks. Also, thank you for seeing me in the evening."

"I am looking forward to your joining us in two weeks," Dr. Stone said, standing beside the car as Beth got in and put on her seat belt.

"I really like her," Beth said out loud as she started to drive the car. She was excited about her forthcoming involvement in the program. She forced herself to block any intruding thoughts about the look-alike youth. She wondered if she should go to the hospital to have a look at the girl, but decided against it. She knew it would be professionally inappropriate.

Her mind wandered to her upcoming date. Tomorrow she was meeting Jeremy. She still questioned some of the statements

Jeremy had made; they confused and haunted her. Too many things were happening at the same time.

Rivcka Edelstein

Long Island, New York, June 1991

Chapter 44

The meeting with the Rocks, Karen's foster parents, was scheduled after another phone conversation between Jeremy and the Burgs. Since he didn't hear from them by Tuesday, he called, just in case. Mr. Burg was terse. Yes, he did understand that Jeremy wanted them to call if they changed their mind, but they hadn't and wouldn't. No, there was no need to talk to Mrs. Burg, she was as eager to get it over with as he was.

Jeremy wasn't sure what to expect from the Rocks, but after his conversations with the Burgs, nothing could surprise him. The initial phone call was pleasant. The Rocks said they would be very pleased to hear news about Karen. They told him that they had begged the Burgs to keep them posted on Karen's adjustment, but the Burgs felt it would be a bad idea. Jeremy arranged to see them the following day. They said they weren't busy people and he could come at his convenience.

The ride out to their home was very relaxing. It reminded him of things he did and places he visited twenty years before, on his first trip to the US. The community in which the foster parents lived was about twenty miles east from where Beth and her family and Jeremy's aunt and uncle had lived. Jeremy was impressed with the intensive development since he had last visited that part of Long Island. With the few landmarks that Sharon had given him, he was able to reach the Rocks' home in less time than he had originally estimated.

The neighborhood presented a different image from the Burg's community. Jeremy parked on the street and approached the front door. He was ready to ring the bell when the door was opened. The Rocks welcomed him at the door with eager smiles and outreached hands.

Silence Broken

"Come in, come in!" they said warmly. "We figured you'd probably be thirsty from this horrible heat so we prepared some lemonade for you," Mrs. Rock said as she pointed the way to the family room. Jeremy and Mr. Rock followed a few steps behind her.

"My wife was so excited yesterday that she didn't stop talking about your visit. She called everyone that knew Karen and told them that she was about to hear something about her," Mr. Rock whispered to Jeremy. "From all the excitement, it didn't occur to us to ask why you are involved and whether something happened with Karen . . . it's been so long . . ."

Jeremy was overwhelmed with their warmth and he tried to get a word or two in before he was bombarded with more questions.

"I hope that by the time I finish explaining the nature of my visit, all of your questions will be answered." He opened his briefcase and removed a pile of papers, which he placed on the coffee table in front of them. He went through the pile and selected two specific items he needed at that point.

Turning to the couple, he said, "For various legal reasons, I have to show you both of these before I can begin to discuss Karen with you. The first is a consent form signed by the Burgs, and the second is a court document affirming that my firm is representing Karen." As he passed the documents to the Rocks, he noticed a look of fear in Mrs. Rock's eyes.

"What does all of this mean? Did something happen to Karen? Why does she need a legal firm to represent her? She couldn't have done anything bad...she is a wonderful little girl." Mrs. Rock looked anxiously at Jeremy.

Mr. Rock tried to comfort his wife while at the same time seeking answers. "Whatever it is, I am sure Karen didn't do anything wrong. She always sought justice, she's such a compassionate person..."

Jeremy began by telling the Rocks of the ongoing conflicts between Karen and her adoptive parents and that she was currently placed by the court in a residential treatment center for adolescents. The Burgs were rescinding the adoption.

"Rescinding the adoption?" they exclaimed. "Why? When Karen was with us there were no conflicts, she was such a helpful little girl. We never had to punish her or scold her like we did the others."

"I don't know how the whole thing started, but the papers to the court indicated that Karen was disobedient, running away from home, and associating with bad company. The court placed her in The Reach Residential Treatment Center for Emotionally Disturbed Adolescents."

"Karen isn't emotionally disturbed." Mrs. Rock interrupted. "If you ask me, they are emotionally disturbed. She was such a well-behaved child…so cheerful… so friendly… always loved to sing and dance…they did it to her."

She paused to take a breath. She seemed too distressed to continue. "Did you talk to her? She would tell you she isn't disturbed. I knew we should have adopted her despite the objection."

She turned to her husband and said, "I told you we should have fought them; we gave up too easily…"

"Mr. Offir, you need to talk to Karen, she will tell you the truth. Whatever she tells you, believe it. Don't listen to all those words that are in the court papers. We've had many foster children under our care in the last twenty-five years. Karen wasn't the type to become involved with bad company. She was such a bright little child…a lot of talent. We always felt she would be an artist, a writer, or with the right education even a doctor or a lawyer …" She stopped and looked at her husband who nodded in agreement.

"My wife and I were just talking about it last night. We remembered some of the things Karen said and did. We used to call her 'The Judge.'"

Silence Broken

Mrs. Rock started to laugh wildly. "When I told my next-door neighbors you were coming to visit to give us some news about Karen, they said 'Karen, the little judge.' After all these years, this is how they remember her. I don't believe she deteriorated to whatever…It must be a mistake…No! Not Karen!" She wiped her tears.

She paused and then continued, "I've got to say only one thing — we should not have let them take her away from us." She shook her head and looked toward Jeremy for validation.

"I don't know the details of Karen's adoption or why they didn't let you adopt her, but…"

"Why? I'll tell you why," Mr. Rock interrupted, "They said we were too old. Ridiculous! We were fine as foster parents, but too old to adopt her? Eight years later, we are still alive and healthy and Karen is being rejected by those rich, icy people. How could they do that?"

It was clear to Jeremy that neither one of the Rocks could perceive any possible wrong-doing on Karen's part. Every comment he made drew more responses of disbelief and defense of Karen. He made one more attempt. "I met Karen, I agree with you that she is a lovely girl. I heard from The Reach Center that she is very intelligent… "

"Figures!" She interrupted him. "I told you, they didn't take her to love her, they took her because the Mrs. wanted to have a daughter, especially a smart one." Mrs. Rock paused, obviously frustrated. "Did you talk to Karen about the conflicts…I bet you there were good reasons for her disagreement with them…What did she tell you?"

"Karen feels that they don't love her. She…"

Once again, he wasn't allowed to finish the sentence.

"They never loved her. They only cared about her report cards." Mr. Rock added, "they were quite satisfied when they heard that in addition to the fact that Karen entered school early she skipped a grade."

"They were so cold to her even during Karen's first visit to their home. Karen kept saying she didn't want to go to their house because it was big and cold. That child was very perceptive for her age. What bothered us was why the adoption agency didn't see through them." Mrs. Rock wondered aloud. "What can we do to help Karen? If you came to us, you probably have a plan in mind." Mr. Rock asked as he rolled back his sleeves.

"I basically just need some information from you. First let me tell you that Karen speaks very fondly of you. The positive memories she has about the past are of the two of you — the picnics, the family games..." Jeremy took the photo, which Karen had given to him, out of his briefcase. He gave it to Mrs. Rock and asked, "Do you remember when this picture was taken?"

Their faces saddened at once. The swift change could not have been missed. "Sure I remember. That was the end of Karen's life as a child and the beginning of her life as an object," Mrs. Rock said bitterly. "Please forgive me, Mr. Offir, but I cannot forgive them..."

"When was the picture taken and who are the two people?"

"The picture was taken in December 1982, when Karen was almost nine."

"Is the lady related to Karen?" Jeremy asked again, hoping that he might get the answer to his question which they were still avoiding.

Mr. and Mrs. Rock looked at each other and then at Jeremy, obviously not prepared to answer. "Maybe the adoption agency can tell you that," Mrs. Rock said, avoiding Jeremy's gaze.

"I have the feeling you know."

"We can't tell you," Mr. Rock said.

"You can't or won't?" Jeremy asked. He was hoping to avoid having to go to the adoption agency.

"We want to help you, but we promised," Mr. Rock said apologetically.

Silence Broken

"To whom did you promise?"

"To the lady," Mrs. Rock said. "She wanted Karen to be adopted and get used to her adopted family. She felt it would be best for Karen. We didn't agree with her. We felt it might be useful for Karen to know her roots, but we promised." Mrs. Rock was tormented. She looked at her husband for guidance and he nodded in agreement.

"Maybe it would help you to know that Karen asked the court to find her mother. She gave me this picture as a starting clue. Karen hoped you could help with the information."

"The lady didn't want Karen to know who she was. She wanted Karen's mother to be able to start her life again without being handicapped by a child out of wedlock," Mrs. Rock said.

"Karen is going to try until she finds her mother, with or without our help. What if her mother regretted giving the child up for adoption?" Jeremy posed the question to the Rocks.

"The mother is probably married. This was all settled over seventeen years ago."

"What do you mean seventeen years ago? I understood that Karen was in foster care until she was nine." Jeremy realized that this new information could make the difference. "I understood from the Burgs that she wasn't freed for adoption until then," he went on to clarify his previous statement.

"That is only partially true," Mrs. Rock explained. "Karen's mother signed the papers for adoption just after the child was born. During her pregnancy, she refused to give the child for adoption, despite her parents' objection. But as soon as the child was born, she changed her mind. Unfortunately, adoptive parents were not available immediately after Karen was born. It was never clear what caused the mother to change her mind — she didn't even look at the child. The social worker gave Karen for temporary placement till suitable adoptive parents would be selected. However, given the fact the mother already signed the adoption paper, the lady chose to keep Karen in the foster care system for the time being. This enabled her to keep in touch with Karen and to see what might develop with Karen's mother. Karen's mother continued her studying, but she was so depressed that there was no way of telling her and expecting her to make a sound decision. Things went on this way for a number of years," Mrs. Rock summarized tearfully. She could not continue her explanation.

Mr. Rock took over as he looked sadly at his wife. "The lady came to visit Karen every weekend and brought gifts. We suspected for a long time that something was wrong with her. She looked thinner and thinner from one visit to the next. In December 1982, she told us that it would be her last visit and that she gave the adoption agency the papers that were signed by Karen's mother nine years prior. The celebration we had in mind for that day turned to be the saddest ever. During all of those years we had become so close to her, she was like a member of our family. When the lady was ready to leave, we cried. I remember Karen asked why we were all crying and the lady said to us, 'Please, put on your happy smile.' We took the picture of Karen and the lady."

"Weeks later, Karen kept asking about the lady; she missed her visits and the outings they had together. Finally, around her birthday Karen told us to be sure to invite the lady. We told her that the lady wasn't going to visit us anymore. Soon after her birthday, she was adopted. It was heartbreaking. First she lost the lady, then us and the other children who had been like brothers and sisters for her all those years. We did try to fight the decision to remove her. They said we were too old." Mrs. Rock took a quick breath. "Well...that's the story in a nut shell."

Jeremy felt tears stinging his eyes, but he wasn't about to let them flow. The story fit perfectly with Beth's history. He decided to try one last approach. "So, when did you find out that Mrs. Robinoff died?" he asked, looking them straight in the eyes. Their reaction affirmed his hunch. "Don't feel as though you broke your promise, you didn't tell me."

"But how did you know? Please don't use that information, it may ruin Karen's mother's life."

Silence Broken

"I'll promise you. We will investigate the situation very responsibly," he assured them.

"More than that we cannot ask. Otherwise, all the sacrifices that Karen, her mother, and the lady made all of those years, living apart from each other, were for nothing."

Jeremy took the newspaper clipping and showed it to the Rocks. "The Mysterious Rescuer is Karen," he explained.

"God bless her. That's more like her." Mr. Rock said.

"I told you!" Mrs. Rock added, "She needed different parents, not an institution."

"From her records, I wasn't aware she skipped a grade..."

"Two, actually...Once when she was in the beginning of kindergarten. Karen was a self-taught child. Between the TV and the other children, she picked up a lot...and fast. The teacher felt that she was so advanced that she would be better off in the first grade and she later skipped second grade."

It was wonderful to listen and watch the Rocks. They were so proud of Karen and happy together.

They walked with Jeremy to his car. They thanked him for the visit, and invited him to come again.

"With pleasure," Jeremy responded waiving from the car window. "On my next visit, maybe I can bring Karen to visit with you...Or, even a better idea, you might want to visit her in The Reach Center. I am sure she would love to see you."

"Could we?" They both asked it together.

"I will try to arrange it with the director of the program," Jeremy spoke slowly as he pondered the possibilities. He regarded them with warmth as he knew how pleased Karen would be about them coming to visit.

Jeremy was pleased with the information. He knew details that had been hidden from Karen's mother. He wondered if Karen could be a relative of Beth or…could she be …?

He tried not to jump to conclusion. Yet, he was excited.

Silence Broken

New York, New York, June 1991

Chapter 45

On Thursday afternoon Rami, Jeremy's cousin, called Jeremy at Sharon's house. He wanted to hear what was going on since their last talk. Jeremy told him about the disappointing and confusing phone conversation with Beth, and that they were meeting for dinner. Rami didn't know whether this would be a happy ending, but it was certainly overdue.

"Good luck, Jeremy. Heaven knows it's about time."

"Thanks!"

From the moment he met Jeremy at Kennedy Airport a few weeks ago, Rami had mixed feelings about Jeremy's search for Beth. He felt that Beth had wanted to cut her ties with the past and he believed that her wishes should be respected. Yet it was apparent that Jeremy never moved past his strong feelings for her.

Although Rami knew most of the details about the relationship between Jeremy and Beth, he suspected there was more that he hadn't been told. Beth's complete disappearance after returning from Israel disappointed him, but he wasn't surprised. Beth had begun to distance herself from her friends since they were fifteen. He missed their close friendship and her lively laugh. He had been observer to the painful changes she went through in her school involvement and social life; she wasn't the same Beth after that. She no longer looked directly at him or made eye contact when they spoke. The spark had disappeared from her eyes, she seemed lonely and unhappy.

When she had told him about her forthcoming research project in Israel, he had been very happy and supportive of her. Rami knew that, despite Beth's trust in him, she was not going to disclose the reasons for the changes in her life.

"Whatever is wrong, remember, I am your friend and I am here for you," he once told her. Beth hugged him and said, "I know, but I can't tell you." He had noticed tears in her eyes.

Beth visited his family before she left to say good-bye and to get some addresses and tips from his mother. She had been so eager and excited. When Beth returned, Rami was away on a school trip. He was thrilled when he heard from his parents about her trip, but soon confusion grew. He would call her home and be unable to get through; he began getting urgent messages from Jeremy to locate her, but he never could. He became frustrated and disappointed.

For a whole year, he attempted to locate Beth. Her mother would merely say, "If she wants to hear from you, she will let you know," and she never did. He assumed that she got his messages. By the following summer, he finally gave up. He didn't understand what happened. *After all, Beth knows where I live and she could get in touch with me if she wanted.*

Over the years, he did receive a few letters and New Year's cards, but none had a return address. In one of his talks with Jeremy the following summer, he expressed his frustration at knowing something was wrong in Beth's life, but not being able to help. "It seems as though she is afraid," he had told Jeremy.

Rami and Jeremy hadn't discussed Beth for years, but he had sensed that Jeremy had never really gotten over her. Rami remembered Jeremy's lack of enthusiasm when he called congratulate him on his engagement to Danielle. *Maybe Jeremy should have taken this trip years ago.*

Rami waited for Jeremy's next call. He had promised to call as soon as he returned from his meeting with Beth.

Silence Broken

New York, New York, June 1991

Chapter 46

Jeremy arrived at Grand Central Station a few minutes early. He stood under the Kodak picture as was planned. He wondered if he would recognize Beth when she arrived. *'God knows what she looks like today.'*

The words and melody of *V'ulai Ota Shtika* (And Maybe That Silence) sung by Yehoram Gaon echoed in his ears. He felt as though the song had been written especially for him, to describe his feelings and fears at that moment as well as a summary of his yearnings in the last seventeen years.

He looked over the crowd, but didn't see anyone even remotely familiar. He turned around and backed up a few steps to look at the Kodak picture which covered most of the east wall of the waiting room and tried to figure out where the picture had been taken. By now the pain in his leg intensified the restlessness, progressively turning into severe anxiety since his last conversation with Beth.

"Beautiful, isn't it," said a female voice from beside him.

He had no desire to chit-chat with strangers. He had to calm himself before Beth arrived. On second thought, he noticed that there was something very familiar in the voice. He turned around and saw a tall and beautiful woman, well groomed, with a smart hairdo, and an elegant dress. He stared in disbelief.

"Say something," she said in a voice now familiar to him.

"Beth?" he finally uttered, surprised, excited, but also questioning. He wasn't sure.

"That suggests you did not recognize me."

Her hair was gathered and folded around to the back, emphasizing more of her face and long neck. She looked more beautiful than he had remembered.

"You are so beautiful!" he managed.

"I tried to look my best for the occasion. I detect a note of surprise."

"You were always cute, but I guess with age you . . ." he was stumbling, trying to find the words.

"Never mind age," she interrupted, laughing. "You simply forgot how gorgeous I used to be . . . but you are still the most handsome man I ever met."

"Is that how you recognized me so quickly?" he tried to cover his nervousness.

"No. I just looked around for the tallest person in the crowd; I was sure that did not change, in spite of the years."

Jeremy and Beth both paused, looking at each other, unsure of what was to follow. It was noisy around them and the small talk could not hide the nervousness they both felt inside.

Beth took his hand gently and, pulling him behind her, led him through the crowd. It was magnetic. Waves of warmth passed through her and he felt it, too. As they approached an even more crowded area, Beth was pushed against him; he cradled her back with his hand and could feel her shaking.

He was confused. Her touch was warm, but her words were cool. He had expected her greeting to be far different. And yet, her response to his touch, her trembling and closeness to him, betrayed her words. *Is she as confused as I am?*

Her head brushed against his shoulder as she was pushed against him again. She turned a little to say something to him, but he was not listening. He felt overwhelmed by his desire to touch her and his craving to re-experience those old sensations. He wanted to hug her, but he wasn't sure how she would respond: she was the one who had left and never answered his letters. She was the one who had hesitated to make this meeting.

She turned to him again, trying to catch his attention, but she was not successful. The closeness overwhelmed him. He put his arms around her and a warm feeling flowed through her. It felt good to be in his arms, but she could not meet his eyes. She felt embarrassed and hid her face in his chest.

His arms tightened around her, drawing her closer to him. When she raised her face to speak he lowered his eyes and his lips came down to hers. It was a gentle and tender kiss. She was trembling as their lips met. He held her more tightly and her tremors stopped. Drawing her close, he kissed her again, with urgency, more demand, and more passion.

It took her completely by surprise. Powerful sensations ran through her like lightening. It seemed to burn its way through her entire body. Her heart was pounding. It was impossible to think about what was happening. She completely dismissed her prior decision not to let her feelings show at the meeting. The sensations that he aroused in her were the only feeling that counted. Her body responded and she did not resist. Instead she passionately returned his kiss. She felt alive. Every inch of her body was tingling. It was something she had missed for so many years. The endless dreams of being in his arms became reality at that very moment.

Jeremy happily raised his head. Her responses to his kisses told him all he needed to know. She cared. She remembered. She hadn't changed. Now that he had met and kissed her, he felt that whatever had happened in the past must have been with good reason. He did not know whether she was married or was dating someone and even if she was, at the moment he did not care. He made a vow to himself to try to work things out, if possible. He knew that he should take things slowly and not rush her. He held her close to him, her head resting on his chest.

Beth was happy, happier than she had felt in years. When she looked up at him, she saw the same emotion radiating from his face. Her face tilted further up towards his. She parted her lips slightly and he bent his head to kiss her again. Their kiss was long and sweet and she wished that it would never end. They stood there for a while, not wanting to break the spell. Then, slowly, they became more in tune with their surroundings, the noise, and the crowd.

"We shouldn't block traffic here," he said gently.

Beth reluctantly agreed.

He placed a loving hand on her shoulder and took the lead on getting them out of the crowded hall. They walked close to each other, not saying a word, until they finally got out to the street.

"Shall we go to the restaurant? I already made a reservation" he asked.

"I'd rather we went some place where we could talk privately, but I guess a restaurant is fine. I didn't eat all day and you are probably hungry, too."

He didn't answer. He was sure that what he was starving for was not served in any restaurant. He raised his hand to hail a cab, but it took some time.

"Welcome to New York City, Jeremy," she said jokingly.

At that point, a cab stopped. They entered and Beth told the driver the address of the restaurant. Jeremy sat back and put his arm on her shoulder, pulling her towards him. They did not notice that the cab had stopped. They did not hear the driver commenting upon their arrival. He had to knock loudly on the window separating the driver's compartment from the passenger's. "We're here!" he said.

Jeremy ended the long kiss and responded apologetically, "Oh, yes. Sorry. How much money do I owe you?"

"Four seventy-five."

Jeremy pulled his wallet out to pay the driver, while Beth pulled her clothes together and straightened her hair. Getting out of the cab she said shyly, "I don't do this often, neither on the street nor on the first date."

"Neither do I," he assured her. After a quiet moment, he added, "Beth, we do not have to apologize for our feelings."

Silence Broken

"No! But we do have to talk. When we set up this date I decided not to let my feelings show. I rehearsed being cool and calm and it did me no good. I had not planned it this way, but I am glad it happened," Beth said shyly.

"We only took a shortcut. I am glad you did not stay 'cool and calm'. I don't up know how long I could have tolerated our awkward conversation at Grand Central. Yes, we do have to talk and understand what has kept us apart for almost eighteen years. Please Beth let's not hide what we feel. Let's not play games about our emotions. We do feel something for each other. I know I did and I do, and I think you do, too. OK?"

"OK," Beth said easily.

After they sat down Jeremy added, "We are in no rush, no pressure; we will proceed at the speed we choose. First, we eat; then, we can have our long needed conversation. Does that suit you?"

"Suits me."

"You are so agreeable," he said quietly.

"Why not? Still no risk," she smiled at him affectionately.

The time passed slowly. They carefully told each other about their current life status. Neither one of them had ever married. They had both been engaged, but unable to go through with it because the past had never been settled. It seemed that both of them were hesitant to bring out the really essential question — what happened in November 1973?

When they entered her living room, Beth vividly recalled the first time they had made love — how she had to persuade him to go further; he had not wanted to hurt her then, and knowing Jeremy, she expected he had not changed.

When they arranged this meeting three days earlier, neither one of them could have expected what followed. Once their bodies touched, the old electricity between them was awakened. It was clear that their bodies craved a different language — a familiar language that did not call for words. Beth's difficulties with intimate relationships ever since 1973 evaporated.

She moved closer to him and there was no misunderstanding about her intention. "Beth, are you sure?" he whispered gently in her left ear. Her right ear was resting on his chest — his heart was racing. There was no doubt in her mind that his body desired her as much as she wanted him. Her earlier concern had been confirmed — Jeremy was going to be rational about this.

"Does that question ring a bell?" she whispered back.

". . . and the answer?" he asked, unbuttoning her blouse.

"The same as it was in July 1973."

Silence Broken

New York, New York, June 1991

Chapter 47

"Jeremy, why didn't you call me as soon as you came back from the war?" Beth asked the question that had been on the top on her mind for years. Now that she had no doubt about Jeremy's feelings toward her, she could finally ask.

Jeremy took a deep breath. "I called you many times. Each time I called your mother told me that you were not home and you would call me when you returned. I might even add that your mother became annoyed at my persistence." He looked at Beth and added, "I heard from Effrat about the calls you made after leaving. If only you had called just once more, the last eighteen years of our lives could have been completely different."

"When did you call?"

"When I was able to get out of bed."

"What do you mean 'able to'?" She looked puzzled and for a second, he noticed that she became pale. It hit him that she still was not aware that he had been wounded. He reached to hold her hand and began again.

"Let me start at the beginning. The day you flew out, the Egyptians had returned the prisoners of war. Some of us were wounded on the battlefield and for one reason or another were sent to the prison rather than a hospital. I was lucky that our field medical officer had enough time to clean my wounds and set my leg and hand in temporary casts. I was also fortunate to have been captured toward the end of the war, otherwise my fate would have been like many others. Once in prison, we were at the mercy of the guards. I didn't get any medical attention until the Red Cross team came to visit the prison. I guess I was lucky for my timely release; otherwise I could have lost my leg and my arm to the infection. When we landed in Israel, they transported me directly to the army hospital and I began my five month long medical ordeal."

"I did not know." Beth could barely utter the words.

"How could you?" He sat quietly for a few minutes. Then he went on to tell Beth about his torture in prison and the long journey back home. "I don't want to remember those days. Nonetheless, I remember very well how I looked for you amongst the crowd that came to the airport to welcome me, but I didn't see you among them. Ben told me that you left Israel just before the announcement about the prisoners' return and that you had called the kibbutz as soon as you landed in New York.

"I was devastated. I did not know why you left. I asked him to search my room for a letter, some explanation. I told him to bring to me any mail that might be from you. He found nothing. I started wondering if our relationship had meant something different to you than it had to me.

"After several operations and skin grafts, they sent me to a rehabilitation center for a few weeks, then home, and finally back to my unit.

"I did not find your letter for about five months; but I did everything else possible during that time. I wrote to Rami, asking him to check what was going on with you and I asked Ben to send me your address and telephone number. Once I got them, I wrote you many letters. Once I was able to get out of bed, I attempted to call your house — but you never called back. Your mother promised that she would deliver the messages; however, she made it clear that it was up to you whether or not you wanted to speak with me. My letters were all returned unopened; I could not understand why. After a while, I felt that you did not care and I stopped.

"Then I found the letter you left behind. I realized that you probably assumed I was not interested since I had not responded immediately. Your letter prompted me to renew my efforts. Rami tried to reach you again at home, but your mother was not receptive to his inquiries. He also mentioned you were away at college, but it was a big mystery to locate which college; your parents were uncooperative. When I finished my time with the army, I decided to come and find you. I thought that if I could see you we can resolve any misunderstanding.

"When I was preparing for the trip, Rami wrote to me that your father had died and your mother had sold the house and moved. His efforts to locate you were futile. As time passed and I didn't hear from you, I began to believe that you gave up. I never forgot you; you were always on my mind."

"Even when you proposed to others?" she asked awkwardly.

I feel so ashamed. I am so angry at my mother. He never gave up on us. Oh my god. I messed it all up, me and pride! He persisted despite the lack of response from me. I love him so much. Our lives could have been different if I had called once more.

Jeremy gently smiled at her. "I see you know all about my love life. The fact that I didn't marry any of them should speak for itself. I didn't marry them because I loved you. They were wonderful women, but since I could not get you out of my mind, I felt it was not fair to them. For the record, I didn't propose in either case — but I went along with it in both times." Jeremy stopped, looked at her, and continued, "You were the only one I was ever ready to propose to. I rehearsed it daily at the Egyptian prison."

"I don't know what to say. All these years I never thought about the possibility that you actually couldn't get in touch with me. Jeremy, believe me, I would have given anything to . . ."

"I know! I found out from Effrat that she never told you about my injuries. Nobody wanted to alarm you. Everybody was expecting you to return immediately."

"Of course, I understood what had happened once I had read your letter. I could only imagine what you must have been thinking at that time. What I didn't understand was why the letters returned unopened and the phone messages ignored. It made me believe you wished to forget me."

"I am so, so sorry!" she managed to say repeatedly throughout the unraveling tale of his efforts to locate her.

"I can't blame you." She was crying uncontrollably; he held her tight. "You didn't hear from me for months." He took a deep breath and continued.

"What's puzzling me is your mother's reaction, not just to my inquiries, but also to Rami's. Did she even know about me?"

"I guess from my earlier letters, but she didn't know we became involved . . ." Again, she stopped.

"My God, I never knew about your calls or letters." She was still crying. "My mother was probably trying to protect me; she was glad I returned home alive. She told me that while I was in Israel, she had nightmares that she lost me, too. She never recovered from my brother's death in Vietnam."

"I'm sure she guessed why I kept postponing my return home. She didn't want me to go back to Israel . . .certainly not after she knew . . ." She stopped short

He was aware of her discomfort throughout the conversation. "I do want to know what you meant when you wrote...."

Beth's face turned white. He could not finish his sentence.

"Why don't we continue the next time I see you," he suggested.

Silence Broken

New York, New York, July 1991

Chapter 48

Jeremy noticed that Beth was curt on the phone when her secretary had called.

"No, I will not be there tomorrow . . . Look, I asked her not to schedule me for Wednesday . . . No I cannot cancel my plans for tomorrow . . . No! Absolutely not . . . You'll have to call Mr. Timler and explain it . . . He'll have to find other arrangements, I will not be able to cover for him on Wednesdays anymore . . . Yes, every Wednesday . . . I am sorry to dump it on you, but Mrs. Block told his secretary two weeks ago . . . Yes, two weeks ago . . . Yes, that's best, talk to him . . . Good night to you . . . No, it's OK, you did not interrupt anything . . . Bye."

Beth replaced the receiver, took a deep breath, and made an effort to regain her composure. Jeremy, though surprised, chose not to ask any questions regarding the conversation.

After a few minutes of silence, Beth asked, "Did I tell you about the new program I am involved with?" Not pausing for a response, she continued, "I will be working with a different population of clients than I usually have . . . they were absolutely desperate . . ." She paused again. "They said they had called every firm in the surrounding area. It's really is a shame . . ." She sighed. "Anyways, tomorrow is my first day. I felt excited about it after I visited the place."

"What kind of a program is it? What do you mean 'different' population?" Jeremy was curious.

"The Clinical Director said the adolescents are diagnosed with 'Conduct Disorder'. The Courts or the Department of Social Services placed them in the Center. My only concern is the drive to and from The Center."

Beth's words sounded very familiar. He recalled Doctor Stone's comments about the resemblance between Beth and Karen and she had been the one to give him Beth's office number. Just then he realized that Doctor Stone may have met Beth about the job offer. He suddenly felt anxious; he had hoped he would have more time before he would have to approach Beth about Karen.

"Where is this place?" he asked slowly, making an effort to stay calm.

"It is on Long Island and it's called The Reach Residential Center for . . ."

". . . Emotionally Disturbed Adolescents," Jeremy finished her sentence.

"I'll be dammed, Jeremy Offir, you never cease to amaze me. How do you know about that place? Have I mentioned it to you before?"

"No. I dealt with The Reach Center before you returned from California." Beth looked puzzled. "Since Sharon knew that I was coming to the States to find you, she asked me if our affiliated firm in New York could do a personal service for her. It involved The Reach Center."

"What a coincidence!"

"Many things in my life are coincidences, but this isn't one of them."

She wondered what he meant. He ignored her expression and went on to ask her several questions. After each question, he looked straight at her, paused for a few seconds, and presented the next question. Beth chose her words very carefully, but didn't get a chance to reply fully because the next question followed very quickly. There was a common thread to the various questions; they dealt with events that had occurred almost eighteen years ago. For years, Jeremy had so many unanswered questions, and he felt she owed him an explanation. He already told her what had happened to him years ago and how he had made repeated efforts to find her. Now he needed to know her side of the story. Beth was not opening up, or at least not yet.

Silence Broken

In the last two weeks, she had been very happy merely to being with Jeremy. They spent every free moment together, the same way they had done in the summer of 1973. Their relationship renewed almost to where it had been before Jeremy was called to the battlefield — almost, for neither of them succeeded in fighting the intruding memories of the intervening years.

One evening, in the middle of the conversation, Jeremy realized that she was no longer listening and repeated his last question, "Beth, why did you leave Israel and why didn't you return to the kibbutz?"

"Why are you asking me all of these questions? It is in the past! We've already agreed that we cannot change the past."

"Trust me; I have a reason for asking. Please, try to answer my question. What did you mean in your letter, 'I have other news for you, but it can wait until you have thought things through?'"

Her hands moved through her hair nervously. She started to pace the room. *That miserable sentence has haunted me since my daughter was been born.* After almost eighteen years, she was finally being asked for an explanation. Both her parents were dead, nobody knew about her pregnancy. Yet she didn't see any way out of answering his question.

Jeremy recognized the signs; he knew Beth was hurting. He felt bad pursuing the issue, but he was also aware that he couldn't delay any longer. Although he assumed that Beth and Karen had not yet met, it was inevitable that she would see her the next day.

* * *

Jeremy was painfully aware that Karen still needed a great deal of medical attention. Although she was back at The Reach Center and was attending summer school, she had a full leg cast and was taking medication daily. Jeremy smiled as he recalled the tremendous pressure Karen had put on all the medical staff at the hospital to have her discharged so she could attend the summer program. In the hospital, she worked diligently on her play for the Center's competition. Dr. Stone told him that he had a great effect on Karen, but he did not feel the changes had anything to do with him. He felt Karen's progress came from within Karen — although her friend learned to accept her, the most important was that she accept herself.

* * *

There was no time to waste. He needed answers and fast. He decided to try a different approach. He took out the picture that he had received from Karen and placed it in front of Beth. "Does this picture mean anything to you?"

Her expression was blank. She stared at the picture for a while to gain control over herself. "She looks like my mother. Where did you get it? Who is the little girl?"

"You tell me! She's with your mother."

"I said she looks like my mother." After a while she added very carefully, "actually, I'm quite sure it is my mother. I remember her in this dress on New Year's Eve just before she died in January 1983."

"Does the child look like any of your relatives?"

"Not really. She looks like I did in a picture my parents had of me when I was about seven or eight years old. It is very interesting. Where did you get this picture?" She held the picture closer and then turned it over. On the back was written December 1982. "Where did you get the picture?"

"I received the picture from a teenager at the Reach Center. She kept it for the last eight years. This is the last time she saw the woman, she said, and it was the only picture she had from her childhood. The lady used to visit her regularly, bringing gifts and small favors. The picture was taken by her foster parents on Christmas day in 1982. On that visit, the woman brought some gifts for the foster parents and the girl. She hugged her tightly while crying and said, 'These hugs have to last you for a long time. Be happy, my child.'"

Beth could barely utter the words, "The child remembered it all from that year, for eight years?" It was the only question she could manage while trying to control the rising emotional turmoil inside her.

Jeremy nodded. "Based on the picture and some searching Sharon did, she came up with an interesting puzzle."

He hadn't noticed, but at some point while he was talking, Beth had stopped listening. *Why is the past haunting me now that I finally have the opportunity to be happy?* All the clues she had received in the last few weeks added up to the same conclusion that. . . *No, it could not be.*

She trembled from the thoughts that crossed her mind. She had signed the adoption papers as soon as the child was born. Her mother swore that the adoptive family would pick up the baby two days after she left the hospital. Both of them were not supposed to know anything about the adoptive parents.

"Beth, is there anything you can tell me that might help? . . . Beth, are you listening?" He looked at her when he got no response and finally touched her arm lightly. "Did you hear what I asked?" He looked at her more intensely, she was pale and her entire body was shaking. **Shaking.**

It could not be . . . it is impossible . . . it's my own imagination . . . I dreamed about it and wished it so much that I am thinking it is real. I must get a hold of myself . . . what will Jeremy think . . . I'm falling apart . . . what is he saying?

"Would you like to get some fresh air?" Jeremy asked. *What for, I have to know more about the little girl, there is no time to waste. There is no more running away.*

"How old was she at the time?"

"She was almost nine." Then he insisted quietly, "I suggest we go out for a walk. You could use some fresh air. I am sorry to put you through this but it can't be postponed any longer. I have a number of questions to ask you; I need you to . . ."

I can't not tell him that! For years, I had nightmares about giving up my daughter for the sake of my career. How could I tell him whose child my daughter was? Who would understand what I have gone through since I decided to give up the child. The regrets I had and still have even though I knew that for the child's sake, under the circumstances, I had made the right decision. Nothing can change the past! Could it be that this little girl has anything to do with me?

How could I explain it to him? We had just found each other. I'll lose him forever if he knew the truth. How could he understand?

"Tell me more about this teenager. Why did she give you the picture and what have you got to do with her?"

"That is what I am trying to find out . . ."

"Tell me what you know!" Beth was adamant, trying to suppress the turmoil.

Jeremy gave in. He told Beth everything from the time he saw the TV show and newspaper article about a 'Mysterious Rescuer' . . . He went on to tell her about the chain of events that took place before and after to his decision to come to search for her. Beth did not hear any of the details beyond the part about the photo of the girl on TV and in the article. She was shivering again. *There was no way out of this.*

Silence Broken

New York, New York, July 1991

Chapter 49

"OK, you asked for it," she sighed deeply. Jeremy started to say something, but Beth motioned for him to wait.

"Please don't interrupt me until I've finished, otherwise I'll never get it out."

She took a deep breath and began. "When you were in the war, I found out that I was pregnant." Jeremy's face lit up. He was going to say something, but again she motioned him to let her continue. "A girl from the U.S.A. not on the pill! Surprised? You see, despite all my love for you, at the time I did not think there would be any sexual relations between us and certainly not in the spontaneous way it happened. My lack of expectation had nothing to do with you — it was me.

For months, boys in school had tried to approach me sexually and got nowhere. I couldn't stand their touches and kisses. They all told me that I was frigid and would end up a nun. With you something very different and it happened. I felt good, warm and safe. I wanted to get closer and closer. I don't know if my reactions to you were surprising to you, but they definitely came as a shock to me. There were many times when I had to overcome some images that intruded on my mind. I had to forget events I was trying to run away from. I had never felt such a strong desire to be close to anybody before I met you . . . and never again since I came back to the States. You probably assumed from the way I approached you that I was experienced in this area and was probably taking the pill, especially since there was no question that I seemed to be the initiator."

Jeremy didn't care about all of that. He wanted Beth to get to the point. He started to say something but she stopped him.

"I remember you kept asking me, 'Are you sure that this is what you want to do?' I was sure about my feelings for you and I was sure about my desires to be as close to you as possible, but I wasn't sure of, or thinking through, the consequences. You might say that I was a hundred percent emotion and zero percent reason. I thought, at the time, that you assumed that I was not a virgin and had experience with other boys."

Jeremy started to object. He felt she was wrong in her perceptions and interpretations of what they said and inferred during those beautiful weeks that they spent together eighteen years ago. Beth would not let him interrupt.

"You tried to comfort me. You said that it didn't matter and that you loved me anyway. You said you didn't care what had happened before and you just wanted me to be open with you. I could not, however, admit to things that I didn't do. Even though virginity might have gone out of style, trust seemed to me a basic element in a relationship."

"The days and weeks that followed were so beautiful and I was so sure of our feelings toward each other. Then you went to the war and I was left waiting. During the first few days I thought that it was important to tell you the truth about my past. You were out of my sight and your reassuring words were not there. I began to be less sure and I knew we had to talk about it, for my sake at least.

"During your first leave, which was for only a few hours, I tried to tell you, but you stilled my mouth with kisses and we made love. Your actions and your words reassured me of your love and I have cherished those hours since. When we kissed beside the truck you said, 'I heard what you were trying to tell me. I want you to believe me; I don't care about anybody or anything that happened before we met in the kibbutz.'

"I was afraid you might react differently if you knew who the 'anybody' was and what the 'anything' had been. I was willing to risk it by telling you, but not by writing to you. I could not have written those things to a soldier at war; so I waited, hoping you would return soon and we would have the chance to talk. Your letters, which meant everything to me, stopped coming. I waited

Silence Broken

for mail constantly; I waited as long as I could in Israel. When your letters stopped coming, your friends joked that the army censor probably kept them for himself as a souvenir. Then I heard from the States that I had graduated with honors and got accepted at a number of colleges. I made up my mind to stay at the kibbutz and wait until you finished the army. Then I found out that I was pregnant."

Jeremy reached out to hold her hands. She pulled back, feeling that she needed all her strength to continue.

"I was so happy that it was your child. I decided to tell you about my 'previous sexual experiences' and see your reaction. If it still didn't matter, then I would be yours with an additional bonus — the fruit of our love; if you felt that you couldn't handle my past, I would leave for the States and get an abortion." She took a deep breath.

"I began to worry as time passed and most of the soldiers were accounted for. I was running out of time if I was to have an abortion, and my parents were pressuring me about school. Everything became compounded when the news came that you were missing in action. I prayed you were alive. I didn't sleep at night and was restless during the day. I did not know what to do, but I had to act fast. Efrat suggested that I go home for a short time and I thought that it was a good idea. As I was packing to leave for the States, I heard the news that Israel and Egypt were going to exchange some prisoners of war. No names were given and, although I did not know about you, I was optimistic. I held to the promise you made to me that you were coming back and I believed you were safe. I was confident that everything was going to be fine and I felt that the sooner I went back to the United States and dealt with my responsibilities, the sooner I could return and we could settle down and wait for the baby's arrival. I wrote you the letter, but I hesitated leaving it just anywhere. I finally left it in your book of poems, which I believed you would be reading as soon as you came back home."

"I called Effrat from the airport a few times, but there was no clear news about the names of the prisoners of war. On the plane, I was sick. I couldn't believe the way things had turned out. At times I felt disappointed, confused, and regretful, but at other moments I was very optimistic. I didn't know if I had done the right things — leaving before I saw you, writing the letter — but I told myself that you had to know. If it was going to affect your feelings, it was better sooner than later. My main concern was that you were alive and safe."

"In New York, nobody knew about the flight, my arrival, or about my condition. At that point, I had not yet decided how to deal with my family. One way or another, they would go through a period of shock. I feared what might happen. During the stopover in London my anxiety level was really high. I felt I had to call Israel. However, they did not allow us out of the boarding area and there was only one telephone in that part of the airport. By the time it was almost my turn to use the phone they were calling us to board the plane again. I was shaking, my heart was pounding and I felt as though I was about to faint. Back on the plane, I fell asleep. I had a terrible dream that you were hurt and calling for me and I was not there to help you. The dream woke me up and I started to cry." She paused, crying.

"As soon as I landed at Kennedy Airport, I called the kibbutz and they told me that your name was on the list of prisoners and you were returning that day. I cried and didn't care that people looked at me. I missed you so much already that I was ready to buy a ticket on the spot and return to Israel. I said to myself, 'Let's face it; you have to settle things here. So be courageous and go do it.'" She paused again.

"Courageous!!! That was a joke. I was anything but courageous. I dreaded the moment I would see my father. I dreaded my family's reactions to my hopes to marry you, settle in Israel, and live on a kibbutz. Then the memories of the letter and the decision I left for you haunted me again.

"On the way home in a cab, I realized that I hadn't even missed home. The cab stopped, I took a deep breath, and entered the house. My mother was surprised to see me. She asked why I didn't let them know that I was coming home, they would have come to the airport. She was relieved I was back and 'out of the battlefield.' I told her that apart from the reactions as the war broke out and the silence following the outbreak of the war, there was nothing to worry about.

"I felt a sense of pride in Israel's accomplishments. I had the feeling that Israel was my home and I just happened to be visiting on Long Island for a few days. I wondered if love could have done all that or if there was more to it — if it was the kibbutz or Israel as a whole? My mother told me that my father was furious each time I delayed my return. My love for you was a source of strength and I knew I could face everything when the time came. In the morning, I called the kibbutz and talked to Effrat. I asked about you and she said that the prisoners of war returned and that you were among them. Now that I think back, she didn't say that you had returned to the kibbutz, but rather that you were 'back in Israel.' Anyway, after talking to Effrat, I decided to wait to hear from you." She took another deep breath.

"The way I left it in my letter was unmistakable — if you contacted me it meant that everything was OK and that you could cope with my nightmares as well as my love for you.

"Two weeks had passed and I didn't hear from you. I tried to accept the meaning of your silence. I assumed that your feelings toward me had changed. I felt that since I had set the conditions in my letter, it was not your fault. I didn't blame you, but I felt unloved and rejected. I convinced myself that any man, who heard my secret, would react the same way as you did. I was desperate. I wished I had stayed in Israel and explained, instead of using the letter." Jeremy gently placed her hands in his and through her fingers he sensed her pain. Slowly, her hands relaxed and felt tender to his touch. She responded to his reassurance, but he himself was in turmoil at all the misunderstandings.

"Time was getting to be a factor. I knew I needed to have an abortion and the sooner I had it, the better. I tried to forget about our whole affair. I finally talked to my parents about my situation. My mother took it worse than I expected. She emphasized how she felt about abortions and she wanted to know who the father was and why I wasn't getting married. I reassured her that it was not an option.

"The worst reaction I got was from my father. What followed was a disaster for which I blamed myself for years. Privately, he said things in the heat of anger that shed a different light on the situation. Suddenly I was no longer sure about the baby I was carrying. His comments confused me."

Jeremy was pale. He felt as though someone had sheared his heart into pieces. All along he assumed that if Karen was Beth's daughter, then she was his daughter, too. Something in the words Beth selected so carefully pounded in his head.

"What do you mean?" he managed to whisper.

She looked at him, scared, and debated the benefit of telling him the rest of the story. She was not ready for full disclosure, so she merely concluded, "To make a long story short, I had a baby girl. I gave her up for adoption as soon as she was born. My mother saw to the arrangements and I never saw her."

Beth hoped he was not going to ask any more questions. She decided to leave the room and call the hospital in which her daughter had been born and see what information she could get. She identified herself as the lawyer representing the girl and persuaded the medical records office to retrieve information from the archives. They only gave her limited information, but it was enough. She was shocked at what they told her and when she put the receiver down she was shaking, for now there was no doubt in her mind that the girl in the picture was her daughter.

Beth had mixed feelings, but the one thing she was sure of was that she wanted her daughter, regardless of who the father was.

Jeremy didn't overcome his initial reactions to the end of Beth's story. He assumed that since she didn't elaborate, either he had misunderstood, or . . . "I guess congratulations are in order; I'm a father." He tried to lighten the mood when she returned back to the room.

Silence Broken

Very painfully she said, "My daughter was not your daughter. I wish she was. If she was your daughter, I wouldn't have given her up for anything, despite the fact that I did not hear from you. I did not sign the final papers for the adoption until after she was born. I signed only when I was sure that she was not yours."

Jeremy wished he hadn't asked. He felt tormented. Beth tried to explain.

"Jeremy, my daughter was born on February 14th, which was less than nine months since you and I met in Israel. I apparently became pregnant before we met, maybe during my last few days in the United States." Beth saw the agony in his face. He wanted to scream but did not have the strength or will power.

"You had sex with another boy before you moved to kibbutz? Who was it?" He managed to say.

She couldn't bear to see his pain. She wanted to console him. All of a sudden it occurred to her that he might be thinking that she knew she was pregnant before they became intimate and that she hadn't told him.

"I did not know I was pregnant until after you left for the war. It came as a surprise to me when the kibbutz doctor told me I was." She surprised herself from the way it sounded. "Jeremy, you have to believe me. When I wrote you the letter I was sure it was your child. I didn't know about the. . . I was not aware of the things that happened to me sexually before I came to Israel. I tried to tell you that . . . but you didn't want to listen . . . you were the first love I had."

Jeremy did not move. "I don't understand any of it." He didn't give up; all the evidence was there, regardless of the date of her birth. "You had sex with a boy before you left for Israel. Is that what you were and still are trying to tell me? I need some fresh air. I am...I am..." He rushed to the door.

Beth followed him. His pain was too much for her. She took a deep breath and told her story again — this time, a complete story.

Rivcka Edelstein

New York, New York, July 1991

Chapter 50

"I never talked about it before. My father and I, as far as I can remember, were always very close, physically as emotionally. He bathed me ever since I can remember; he was there to put cold wet towels on me when I had a fever and he was even there when I was trying on new clothes. Our closeness grew even more after my brother Kevin went to college. We cuddled on the couch while watching TV and he would touch me in such a way that I felt loved. I was happy that he allowed me to be close to him; I loved him a lot and I did not see anything wrong with it.

"As I became older, I felt an increased need to be with my friends. As usual, I continued to share experiences with my father; I told him about everything. He constantly warned me about the outside world, especially about men. I viewed our close relationship as special.

"This all changed when I reached puberty. The more I sought outside activities, the more my father resisted my changes. He emphasized the need to devote my time to my school work. He made more and more demands on my academic accomplishments. He clung to me even more after my brother was killed in Vietnam. I understood and accepted his concern for me; he was afraid of losing me too. At that point, I had no interest in changing my relationship with him and I wanted him as my best friend. I also sought to expand my social circle. My mother accepted the changes in my social life as normal development and encouraged me to date. She joked about my father's resistance, saying that he had to learn to let go, that there were attractive young men out there so 'Why should she settle for a middle-aged man who is over the hill?' My father was hurt every time she said it. As a result, he added to the demands regarding my academic work.

Silence Broken

"Since my brother's death, my mother seemed to make maximum efforts to be out of the house, with her friends and different charities. Even when she was at home, she was tired and went to sleep. She ended up abandoning both of us, my father and me, in her attempt to cope with my brother's death.

"We no longer had dinners and trips with friends of the family. I found myself wanting to go out more with friends my own age. Although this was against my father's wishes, he never actually stopped me from going. When I returned, my father and I would sit on the couch or in my room and talk about the evening and my friends and who said or did what.

"By the time I was fourteen, things gradually changed and before I knew what was happening, it became a nightmare. It started with gradual touching and comments like 'It's OK between a father and his daughter,' 'It's normal.' He would call me to the bathroom to bring him soap or towels and when I entered he was naked. When I was young, it felt natural to me, but later it felt strange. He would come to the shower and offer to soap my back or dry me off. I knew it was not O.K., but I didn't see how to stop it without hurting his feelings."

"My mother used to joke that my father treated me more like a lover than a daughter. Yet, she never set limits or redirected his inappropriate behavior toward me. I wasn't sure if she was aware of what was happening and I couldn't tell her. My father needed somebody to accept his absolute authority and give recognition to his power as the head of the family — to love as well as to obey. He certainly didn't get it from my mother. I was the perfect tool through which my father met his own needs, under the disguise of love. He tried to convince me that it was for my benefit. He said that he was satisfying my needs for love and warmth that my mother didn't give me. He also said that it wasn't healthy to look for it from strangers who might use me.

"He seemed lonely, deserted, and desperately in need of being loved. He was so tender and caring that I was afraid to hurt his feelings. He used to give me small gifts and frequently pointed out how my beautiful body was so attractive that it 'does things to him.' He suggested that I should not mention anything to my mother in order not to hurt her or provoke her jealousy." Beth took a deep breath.

"His demands in the relationship gradually increased and he kept inventing new excuses for touching me here and there as well as why I should enjoy touching him. He would say 'We are both having a good time and nobody is getting hurt.' 'I would never do anything to hurt you, my love, not you, and I know you would not do anything to hurt me. As long as we are both happy, your life outside should not affect our life in our own world.'

"Well, I felt trapped in this vicious cycle. The more I agreed to go along, the greater his expectations and demands to go further became. It seemed like there was no way out. The more I felt responsible for letting it continue, the more I felt shameful and guilty, the more I made sure I didn't disclose anything to anybody." Beth sobbed.

Jeremy was very uncomfortable. His throat was dry and tight. He was not sure that he wanted to hear all of this. He definitely did not want Beth to go through the torture of relating all of those horrid times. However, there was no way of stopping her now.

"I felt powerless and betrayed. I feared the stigma I'd gain if it became known. I loved my father and I didn't want to hurt his feelings, yet I knew it was wrong and I didn't want to do it. I didn't have anybody I could turn to. How could I get out of it without betraying him? I discarded the option of talking to my mother; she wasn't even available to me in less emotionally demanding situations, why would she be available for this? I felt that she would blame me anyway. I decided that I couldn't seek an outsider. How could I expose my father? How could I expose myself? After all, I was part of it. I was to blame; it was my fault because I went along with it. Nobody would believe me. I believed I was the only one to ever be in such a situation. Why should anyone understand what I was going through?" She paused.

"The ironic part was that the only person I trusted and turned to in the past was my father; I believed he loved me and would help me once he was aware of my firm objections to these activities. However, the more I expressed my objections about it to him, the more persistent and demanding he became. He even accused me of wanting to give my body to strange boys who wouldn't care about me, rather than to the father who loved me. I had no recourse, nowhere to turn; I didn't know how to get out of it. Where could I go, what could I do?" Beth was crying but continued on.

"My world became one big nightmare. I tried to escape my thoughts and disgust, but there was no way of forgetting it. I thought that working hard on my schoolwork would help, but it didn't. I couldn't concentrate on my school work and my marks did not justify the effort I put in. I took extra credits with the thought that I would be able to graduate early and go to college sooner. I was very unhappy and I constantly sought justification for what was happening. I slowly became socially isolated, afraid someone would find out about my secret. I was a nervous wreck and barely ate or slept, never knowing when my bed was going to be invaded. I blamed myself for accepting the things my father gave me. The fact that I did nothing to stop it caused me to start hating myself and my body. I could not tolerate anyone touching me. Most of the time, I just felt dead inside. I even considered suicide as a way to end it all." Beth stopped momentarily to take another deep breath.

"My guidance counselor called me to her office and discussed my academic and emotional deterioration. I considered disclosing to her, but I couldn't bring myself to disclose the truth and the well-kept secret remained unrevealed. I told myself that it would only cause more pain." She paused.

"She had some hunches about my problem and told me that I didn't have to talk if I didn't want to. If home was the source of the problem, which is what she suspected, she had an idea. She suggested doing a project abroad for an independent study during the summer which would be worth five honors course credits. Her idea was that it would enable me to graduate early and go away to college a year ahead of my classmates. I was elated and relieved; for me it meant temporary peace. It also meant I would be able to sleep at night without hands invading my body." Beth wiped her tears.

"Needless to say, my parents' first reactions were negative. In fact, my father hit the roof. He was sure I was doing it purposely to hurt him. They didn't like the thought of me being away from home — so far and so young. However, after my declining marks, the idea of the honor credits appealed to both of them. My mother finally agreed and said my father had to accept it." She took a long, deep breath.

"The night before my flight, my father and I went out to dinner. My mother had an important meeting at the civic association and she was pleased that my father freed his schedule to take me out. My father made a point of telling me how grown up I was. He said that, although I was only seventeen, I was mature in mind and body. In honor of the occasion, he suggested that we have a toast and he ordered something for me to drink. We drank... a lot; or rather I drank a lot and my father talked. He was into his familiar lectures and tips about men and how to watch out for them. He reminded me of why I shouldn't trust any man." Beth sighed bitterly before continuing.

"I didn't need to hear it, I knew it by heart. My father would have been pleased to know my negative reactions towards any guy's advances. My reactions weren't for the reasons he had tried to brainwash me with. By that time, I felt so disgusted at the idea of being touched at all. I believed that if my own father who loved me had betrayed me, what could I expect from others? I felt contaminated." Jeremy noticed Beth shaking. He didn't know what to do. He tried to hold her hand.

"My father continued his 'warnings' and said that no matter where I am, I should remember that he is the only one who loves me. I barely touched my food and instead escaped into the effects of the liquor. I began to feel detached; the words were coming in, but they had no meaning and I heard them from a distance." She looked at Jeremy, trying to convey how detached she had been.

Silence Broken

"We went home and by the time we arrived I was numb and had little control over my limbs. My father helped me to undress and put me to bed; then he joined me. I was so numb and weak I could not resist or respond and that made him more persistent. I felt that night he went further than ever before. Despite the liquor, it was painful . . . At some point later, I was throwing up and my father quickly moved around the room. He mumbled to himself something, maybe to me too, saying that he approved of how good a girl I had really been! He pointed out that he was going to change the sheets quickly and nobody would be the wiser. I didn't care about the sheets or the mess, but for some reason my father cared. He cared a little too much . . ." Beth stopped for a moment, her hands in Jeremy's, and she felt his tenseness. She knew he was angry, but didn't stop. She already felt relief for finally breaking the silence.

"The next morning at breakfast, my father avoided any eye contact. I apologized for my hangover and my mother made cryptic remarks about people who could not hold their alcohol having no business drinking. She was annoyed with my father for permitting the drinking to even take place. God knows what she would say if she knew he actually encouraged it. My father was very calm and satisfied with himself. He said very abruptly, 'Our Beth is a big girl now and new experiences should start at home.' My mother looked at him strangely and said, 'The fact that we are allowing her to go abroad all on her own does not mean that we are giving her carte-blanche to destroy herself.' He replied, 'Of course not dear, that is why I made sure I coached her along in the new experiences.' I was relieved when my mother said she had arranged to take the day off so she could join us for the ride to the airport." Beth paused.

"My trip to Israel served two purposes. Along with getting some rest, I wanted to do a good job on the project to facilitate my early high school graduation and admission to a good college. My guidance counselor promised to help me obtain a scholarship so my parents would not raise objections about my leaving the house and going away to college. She helped me with the college applications and promised to send the forms. In return, I promised to send her ongoing reports on my progress with the project so I could use it for credit and on my applications."

Beth paused and then added some side comments. "You have to remember that it was 1973. There were no mandatory rules about child sexual abuse. It was a lot different from what it is now. Thus, the guidance counselor did whatever she could to extract me from the situation. Now we know that, unfortunately, child sexual abuse is more common than I thought. At that time, I figured I was the only one in the world being tortured in this way."

"During the first hours on the plane I tried to sort things out. The facts just did not fit the image I held of a child molester. I could not believe that my father, a law-abiding citizen, a traditionalist when it came to religion, an educated person in matters of mental health, not under the influence of alcohol and not a violent person, would participate in such a despicable act and to his own daughter! I saw him as two different people — the image he held to the outside world, among his colleagues, relatives, and friends and the one I met and learned to know within the walls of our own house, within the confines of my bed.

"The images that kept coming to me from the night before were very confusing. I couldn't distinguish between my nightmares and reality. The only true physical sensation was a vague sense of pain from below. At first I dismissed my doubts with the honest belief that my father would not do anything to hurt me. The more I tried to sort the emerging images about the night before, the more I doubted my convictions about my father. The fact that I was drunk and physically incapable of resisting did not alleviate my sense of guilt. I felt contempt for him and the hypocritical principles he stood for. I hated him as well as myself. He was a rapist — not a stranger, but one who raped his own daughter."

Beth felt as though she couldn't go on. She paused, took a deep breath, and forced herself to keep going. "Being raped in the safety of my own house by the same person that claimed to love me was too much for me to bear. If I could not trust him, who could I trust? I felt that if my own father saw me only as a sex object, every man would see me that way. I could no longer perceive the loving father I had until the age of thirteen and the monstrous person in my house who now called himself my father as the same person. I actually hated him for spoiling my youth and for using me. I hated myself for allowing it to continue no matter what the consequences of disclosure could have been. My tears poured out; all of those tears which I had not been able to shed for years, tears of doubt and helplessness. I didn't make any effort to hold them back. I cried for hours. The way he lured me into the final episode hurt more than the physical pain it caused. Later I believed that I had tried to resist his advances and that was the reason for the pain and bruises I had. Yet, nothing helped to reduce my sense of despair, feeling of loss, and betrayal." She paused. Jeremy suggested she stop, take a hiatus, but she insisted to go on.

"The stewardess made a number of efforts to comfort me and asked why I was crying. I wondered what her reaction would be if she knew why I was running away. I felt emptiness inside, a huge void. My need for survival was my only guide at that point. For my own sanity, I knew I needed to rebuild my faith in people and to give the world another chance. I decided to start right then and there — as the plane successfully landed at Lod Airport."

Beth took a deep breath and wiped her tears. Jeremy put his hands back on hers. She raised her eyes and looked at him.

"So now you know it all."

"In my worst nightmares, I could not have guessed this. Your letter gave indications of abuse and my imagination worked on all sorts of possibilities, but not to this extent. I could never have figured that your father was . . . "

"A rapist!"

"He didn't look the type. . . "

"I have learned that anybody could be the type. Children in school are finally being taught to be aware of any type of abuse, by anybody. I wish they had this training in my time. You know, the ironic part was that although I never forgave my father for what he had done to me, as the years passed, I found my anger toward my mother increasing." She started to cry again.

"My father and I never talked about that night and I never mentioned who I believed was the father of my child." She looked at Jeremy.

"I was in a rush to wrap up unfinished business in the hope of going back to Israel. I was just waiting to hear from you. In the meantime, I received my High School diploma and a scholarship for college. All the honors and achievement meant nothing to me; my only desire was to hear from you. My hopes and dreams were to be away from all of it, back in Israel, back in a place which I felt was home."

"After telling my guidance counselor about my advanced pregnancy, she made a number of phone calls to the Dean of Students at the college I was about to attend. She obtained special permission for me to live off campus for the first semester. My mother agreed to take some days off and help me search for an apartment."

"As the days passed and no letters or phone calls came from you, I went along with my college plans. I had difficulty accepting that once again I had trusted and loved the wrong person. I felt betrayed and hurt; first my father used me and then you rejected me.

"Five weeks after my return to the States I left for college to start my freshman year. My mother started checking into adoption agencies, despite my objections. She said that it wouldn't hurt to be ready in case I changed my mind. I was not eating well and instead of gaining weight I was losing it. The doctors I visited in the college town gave me contradicting information about the stage of the pregnancy. They said the same thing that the doctor in the kibbutz had told me — it was not unusual to miss a period when you are stressed.

"I made my final decision to give the child up for adoption when my water broke two months early, according to my calculations. I called my mother before I left by cab. She said 'I guess you are ready to deliver,' and I said, 'It couldn't be; it's too soon.' She said quite coldly, 'Apparently not.'

"That was the last straw. I realized that her words 'apparently not' were appropriate only if my father really had raped me. I concluded that the baby was conceived during that last ordeal with my father. It was less than seven months since you and I made love for the first time and nine and a half months since my father had last abused me. I told my mom to make sure I didn't see the baby. I decided to give it up for adoption and that I didn't want to know anything about it. She said that it might be difficult because of my persistent refusal until that point.

"The delivery was very painful. My mother reassured me that she had made all the arrangements. She kept all the information from me, except for the fact that it was a baby girl. I heard the nurses pointing to me and talking about the 'young mother with the tiny baby.' I guess that my poor emotional and nutritional state affected the size of the baby.

"A week and a half later I was back in classes. Nobody aside from my mother and father, knew what had happened to me; but I was different. By then I was part of a hidden conspiracy. I had delivered a child conceived in an incestuous relationship and I could not forget it.

"When the news reached my father about my delivering a baby girl, he had a serious heart attack. He could count as well as I could. Five days later, my father died. The funeral was very private — only for the immediate family. I cried for him, I cried for myself, and for my daughter who had been rejected through no fault of her own." Beth sobbed, her head nestled in Jeremy's shoulder and her words were barely audible.

"The end of the story you already know. I never returned to my childhood home. A few weeks later, the house was sold and my mother moved to an apartment near her job. I moved onto the campus the next semester and stayed there most of the time.

"I tried to forget. In order to keep a distance between my past and myself, I basically severed all of my relationships from the first 18 years of my life. On holidays, I wrote notes to a few relatives and to Rami, but I never included a return address. But my efforts were to no avail — the memories haunted me all of these years. I couldn't forget my past, my abandoned daughter, my father — and you."

Silence Broken

New York, New York, July 1991

Chapter 51

Jeremy cried with Beth as he held her in his arms. He wanted to be alone, he needed space, but he could not leave her at that moment. He was stunned; ready to explode. He desperately needed to calm himself.

He was at a loss for words and didn't know what to say. He had heard about child sexual abuse through his legal practice, but personally he was not aware of anyone affected by it. He was shocked about Beth's story and its impact on so many people. Never in his wildest dreams would he have thought that the monstrous father Beth had described and the man he had met at the ski lodge during the winter of 1970 were the same person.

He was also hurting from his own loss; he felt a void inside. Although he clearly heard that Karen was not his child, he did not want to believe it. When he first heard about Karen, he believed that if she was Beth's daughter then she was his daughter too. In his heart, he refused to accept anything to the contrary.

For a moment, he wished that he'd never heard the details and that he was simply left to believe that he was Karen's father. But he knew why she had told him — Beth was always honest with him. That was one of the reasons why he loved her so much. Still, a part of him wished she hadn't told him.

Hearing her story, seeing her struggle through her painful old memories from 1973 and her reactions made him want to move closer to her. Now he understood what had happened. He also remembered all the times Beth tried to tell him about her past and he didn't want to hear.

He realized that a new chapter was about to take place in this three-folding tragedy. He wondered how Beth would cope with facing Karen, a constant reminder of Beth's past betrayal.

What about Karen? She wanted her mom, but could she cope with the atrocity of her birth? Honesty was always his guideline, but here he feared for everyone if the truth came out. He was sure that there was no good reason to tell Karen about this.

It was so ironic. It was all about disclosing one secret and now they would be keeping another secret for the rest of their lives. Finding each other might not be the best thing for either Karen or Beth. He couldn't find the words to express his thoughts. He wondered if Beth grasped the impact of the news she received this evening. He regretted his part in this matter, but realized that in all likelihood Beth would have found Karen at The Reach Center without his help.

Beth broke the silence, expressing her relief at having finally had broken the silence and told the story. She knew he loved her and he could help her approach her daughter. She felt she received a second chance in life.

That night, they cuddled in each other's arms. Beth was too excited to sleep and they spent most of the night talking about Karen. Jeremy suggested that Beth call The Reach Center and explain her situation. He was sure Dr. Stone would not be too surprised. He also felt very strongly that there was no need to mention who the father was and he doubted that anybody would ask.

Beth had asked Jeremy what made him feel there was a connection between herself and Karen. He realized that she hadn't heard any of the explanation he had given earlier.

He told her again about Sharon's visit in Israel, Karen's clip on the TV and her photograph in a New York paper, and the great resemblance that Sharon noticed when she met Karen in the court. "Intuition and facts were put together. Sharon felt it was more than coincidence and from there the wheels began to turn."

"I am curious," Jeremy said after a few minutes, "what did you hear from the hospital that convinced you that Karen was your daughter?"

Silence Broken

"The record showed that she was in the hospital for six weeks after the delivery; she needed some help in breathing and she was put in an incubator. When she was ready for discharge, she was taken by Mrs. Robinoff, my mother, to Long Island. I guess she wasn't adopted immediately as my mother had told me. I imagine she wanted to spare me the details."

They were still talking when the alarm clock rang.

Rivcka Edelstein

New York, New York, July 1991

Chapter 52

Earlier that morning Ms. Robinoff showed up for her first day of work in The Center. Initially there was a scheduled 'Welcome aboard' session, introducing Ms. Robinoff to the therapeutic teams. However, Ms. Robinoff called saying something came up and it was essential for her to speak with Dr. Stone as soon as possible.

In the waiting room, Nellie noticed that Ms. Robinoff made an effort to remain composed, but it was clear that she was nervous. She fidgeted in her seat and kept playing with her hair.

After a few minutes the phone rang, startling her; Dr. Stone asked Nellie to send Ms. Robinoff in.

The two of them had been in Dr. Stone's office for more than two hours. When Ms. Robinoff arrived, she had introduced herself and stated that she was there to meet with Dr. Stone. Nellie recognized the voice because she had spoken to Ms. Robinoff on the phone on a number of occasions. When Nellie saw the face that belonged to the familiar voice, she realized what had haunted her for weeks; she felt a special acquaintance with that voice, but could not pinpoint from where. When she saw Ms. Robinoff for the first time she was struck with how familiar she seemed, but she still couldn't place where she might have met her.

At 10:30 AM the loudspeaker sounded in the English class and Karen was called to Social Services. She, along with the others in the class, looked puzzled; Karen wasn't involved in any serious offense for quite a while. Her classmates stared as she walked out of the class dragging her left leg, still having difficulty walking with a full-length cast.

She walked slowly to the main office in Social Services. She was very aware that nobody got called during the middle of class unless it was serious. *What could it be?*

Silence Broken

"Dr. Stone paged me," Karen announced.

"I'll tell her you are here," the secretary smiled at her and motioned for her to sit down. Nellie had a soft spot in her heart for all the residents, but she was especially fond of Karen. At first, Nellie felt that Karen was a rude trouble maker, but as time passed, she agreed with Dr. Stone's optimism about Karen's potential. Since she typed all the records she was quite familiar with the hurdles posed by Karen's adoptive parents.

Nellie called Dr. Stone and while she was on the line with her, she motioned for Karen to go in.

* * *

Beth sat down on the couch beside Dr. Stone, sobbing. Karen walked into the room and looked confused.

"Karen, I called you in because Ms. Robinoff wanted to clarify something before accepting our offer to be our lawyer."

"But Mr. Offir is my lawyer!" Karen said defensively.

"Yes but please hear me out. You see, Ms. Robinoff recently discovered that the daughter she gave up for adoption is here…"

"Wait a minute!" Karen exclaims, cutting Dr. Stone off. "As far as I know, I am the only adopted one here… Does this mean . . . ?"

Dr. Stone nods her head.

"Oh. My God. No way! You mean…seriously? But how?" She turned to Beth crying, "Why? And where have you been this whole time?? Oh, that doesn't matter, I'm just so happy you are here!" Karen burst into uncontrollable cry.

"How did you find her?" Karen turned to Dr. Stone trying to overcome her unexpected shock.

"Huh? Come again? What did I do?" Karen wiped her tears. Her voice was very shaking.

"It started with the TV clip of 'The Mysterious Rescuer' and the picture you gave Mr. Offir. He helped piece the scattered bits together."

"Huh…who would have thought? But the more important thing is that I got my reward after all!"

Dr. Stone nodded her head.

At this moment, Beth stood up and hesitantly said, "I am so sorry for all the distress I have caused you, can you ever forgive me?"

"Are you kidding? I am just so happy to see you," Karen exclaimed, ignoring her deep-rooted anger and resentment.

"Can I hug you?" Beth asked meekly. Dr. Stone slowly slipped out of the room, unnoticed.

* * *

No sooner had the door to Dr. Stone's office opened, when Nellie heard Karen's screams and cries. Dr. Stone came out to the main office with tears in her eyes.

"Is she related?" she asked.

"Very much so!" Dr. Stone said, wiping her tears.

"Her mother?" Nellie asked in disbelief.

"Yes, she is."

Nellie was confused, but Dr. Stone was on her way out as she said, "It's not by my doing; Mr. Offir found her."

After a long time, Karen stepped out of the Clinical Director's office holding hands with Beth and dragging her behind. Both Beth and Karen's eyes were red.

The lunch bell rang and the residents passed beside Social Services on their way to the dining room. Karen flung open the door, led Beth into the hall, and loudly declared: "Hey everyone, meet my mother. My real mother."

Silence Broken

There was no way to stop the commotion that took place following that statement.

Rivcka Edelstein

New York, New York, July 1991

Chapter 53

At her next session with Dr. Noble, Beth told her about disclosing to Jeremy and her meeting with Karen. The psychologist listened to the detailed account of events that took place in Beth's life more than eighteen years ago. Beth sobbed throughout the entire session. Jeremy's supportive reaction had helped her to see that it was OK to tell. Her fears of losing his love for her were proven to be unfounded. Now she took the risk of telling Dr. Noble. She found it easier the second time even though it was still very painful.

To her amazement, Dr. Noble wasn't surprised by her disclosure. Indeed, she had long ago suspected it. Dr. Noble suggested that they deal first with her sexual victimization and leave the concerns she has about Karen for a later date.

Beth apologized for not telling Dr. Noble about it before. Dr. Noble assured her that it was very common for child sexual abuse victims not to disclose for a long time even to their own therapists.

"I was afraid you would not like me."

"There is no reason for me to dislike you; you didn't do anything wrong."

Dr. Noble asked Beth why she didn't disclose to somebody while it was going on or soon after?

"It seemed important to me to keep it to myself. I didn't want to betray my father."

"He betrayed you; what he was doing to you was wrong and he needed to be stopped. By talking about it, you would have received help."

"I was too ashamed; I was partly to blame."

"It wasn't your fault! He was the adult and you were the child; you were trapped. You were the victim. You have nothing to feel shameful or guilty about."

"It is 1991 now; things are clearer. It was not so in 1972," Beth said.

Dr. Noble nodded her head in agreement. "Yes… since then, we have come a long way in protecting children."

* * *

In subsequent sessions, Dr. Noble had to frequently repeat the fact that it was not Beth's fault and rather it was her father who was to blame. It was her father who was the adult, the one responsible for his actions. Although Beth understood it on an intellectual level, it was very difficult for her to accept that she was not partially responsible for what had happened. Beth was confused and unable to understand how she could have conflicting feelings of hate and love toward her father. Dr. Noble and Beth talked about it.

Dr. Noble and Beth discussed the effects the abuse had on her since she was 17 years old. It took a few sessions to go through the various long-term ramifications of the abuse. They talked about the guilt and shame that Beth felt when she was with others. She was afraid that they might find out. She was very anxious.

Beth was afraid to trust anybody. She cried when she put her feelings into words. She felt used and damaged. She believed for a long time that nobody had, or ever would, love her. She described her fear of closeness, how she reacted to any type of intimacy, and how she had to fight her initial reactions of running away from the approaching hands or body of someone else.

". . . Except for Jeremy," she concluded.

"What was different with Jeremy?" Dr. Noble asked.

"That is the part that I don't understand."

"What do you mean?"

"In the beginning, I froze whenever he attempted to get closer. Don't misunderstand, I wanted him to, but something in me stopped him . . ." Beth stopped. She was reliving those evenings with Jeremy. She sobbed, remembering how patient he was with her.

"He was a real angel about it."

Dr. Noble was listening.

"All those images would come to my mind so vividly, as if they were happening right then and there. They would make me freeze."

"And?"

"And what?"

"Eventually you overcame them. You won."

"That is what I don't understand. What happened? One evening I was free from the images, at least for a short while, and I actually seduced Jeremy." She smiled mischievously.

"Maybe Jeremy's love helped you through it."

"No. I don't think it was Jeremy because, at one point, I hesitated. He stopped and I persuaded him to go on. I can't believe I am saying this." Beth said shyly.

"Tell me about that time."

Beth told Dr. Noble the circumstances that led to the first sexual relationship she had with someone other than her father.

Dr. Noble suggested that her ease with Jeremy was because the setting was different. It was not in the confines of a bedroom. The similarity between her father's and Jeremy's attempts to get close to her was weakened. This, plus her desire to get closer to Jeremy, helped her take charge of her mind and body and she overcame the intruding images.

Beth was mesmerized. She had tried to figure it out for years.

"But why was I able to do it afterwards in a bedroom?"

"By then you had new positive images with Jeremy. Each time you had sex with Jeremy those old images lost some of their power over you. You were able to fight them."

Beth left that session feeling more in control over her life. She had never felt in control over her body or mind before. On the contrary, she had felt powerless and weak. Things happened to her not by her own design.

She discussed the fear about her lack of control over her life. The doctor helped her to see that she did have considerable control since she left her home to go on the project and she used it well.

Beth was able to see that, even though she had no control over the 1973 war and her father's death, she was strong and made decisions in her life that dealt with all of the consequences of the two events. Beth became eager to move on with the therapy, so she started seeing Dr. Noble several times a week.

* * *

"Tell me about your father," Dr. Noble asked.

There was a long pause. She tried to talk a couple of times, but stopped herself.

"He was a hypocrite," she finally said in anger. "Yes, that describes him best; a hypocrite!"

Dr. Noble did not say anything.

Beth was disappointed; now that she disclosed everything, she thought she would be instantly cured. She didn't want to talk about her father. She wanted a magic pill that would heal her wounds instantly and free her of those damn memories. She didn't want to talk about her father, his hypocrisy, and his double standards for boys and girls. She didn't see what purpose it would serve. She remembered, in detail, his preaching against condemning others who looked for their own sexual pleasure while he himself was satisfying his own sexual desires with a child, his daughter. How could defining her father's personality help her in the cure she was seeking?

". . . His patients liked him, but they didn't know him, at least not the way I knew him. He believed that nobody could care for him if they really knew him."

"What do you mean?"

"I don't know. He had a hidden secret. He was ashamed of something, aside from what he did to me. He referred to it a number of times when I was inquisitive and asked questions. He always said that he couldn't tell me even though he loved and trusted me."

In following sessions, Beth talked about the relations between her mother and father. "They were never angry with one another. It was as though there was nothing between them. When my brother was killed, the indifference between them became even more obvious . . ."

Dr. Noble asked Beth about her father's parents. She described her grandmother as "a very controlling and punitive person." She was a highly-educated woman and wanted him to become a doctor.

"Grandma insisted that Dad go to medical school, but he was interested in psychology. He ended up going to medical school and chose to specialize in psychiatry." She paused for a moment.

"He was afraid of his mother and he especially avoided his uncle, his mother's older brother."

She remembered that when they were young, her grandmother used to take her and Kevin to play and shop in the city. She was never interested in what they wanted to do. They did what she planned for them.

Later on, she talked about her grandfather.

"He left my grandmother when my father was about six. As soon as he remarried, he severed all ties with her and my father."

Silence Broken

"You said something about your grandmother's older brother and your father."

"Yes. I never understood that, but my father hated him. He felt the guy was a fake scumbag. My great uncle never got married. When I asked Grandma about her brother and Dad, she said, 'When your father was young, my brother was the only man who spent time with him. He was like a substitute father and partook in all typical father-son activities. They were inseparable; but then then your father withdrew from my brother and from other people.' She said she never understood what had happened."

* * *

From one session to the next, issues were addressed and became somewhat clearer. Beth was able to express her anger toward her father, a freedom she did not allow herself until now. In one session, Beth told Dr. Noble that neither her mother nor her brother liked to spend time with her father.

"They avoided him." She cried and tried to continue; through the tears Dr. Noble was able to hear parts of her words.

"You don't know how much I loved him. I trusted him. I looked up to him. I thought he accepted me and liked me, but all along he only wanted me because of his sexual desires. I still don't see how he could have done that to me. I'll never forgive him for doing that. What did I do to deserve it?"

"You did nothing to deserve it; it wasn't your fault. You have to accept that."

* * *

"My father is dead. Why is it so important to talk about it at all? What good is it going to do?"

"You are alive and you have much of your life ahead of you. You need a chance to live it without the excess baggage you have been dragging around."

"If it is good to talk about it, why don't all the victims out there tell someone?"

"There are many reasons why victims tended, in the past, not to talk about their sexual traumas. Children who are victims are especially afraid of what might happen if they disclose."

"I guess that's what I was doing. What could have made him sick in that way, so twisted that he did that to me?"

"Don't try to find excuses for what he did. Nothing made him do it to you, but . . ."

"Yet, he did it. Why?"

"Although I must emphasize that most sexually abused victims do not turn out to be abusers, we now know that most of the abusers were victims of abuse themselves. A person does not have permission, authority, or an excuse to abuse others just because he or she had been abused."

"I always wondered about my father. Until recently, I wasn't aware that boys were being molested. I remember some comments and incidents my Grandma made and mentioned, respectively."

"We don't know what caused it in your father's case."

"My father's uncle! That's what happened, I'm sure about it," she said suddenly, surprising herself as though not even hearing Dr. Noble, who didn't respond. Beth went on. "I remember a conversation between my brother and my father. My father said to him, 'My father was not there for me. I felt a void inside, a hole that nobody could fill. I searched for a substitute in different people and activities, but there were no good replacements. My uncle tried to be a father figure but he turned out to be a sick replacement.'"

"It doesn't mean he was sexually abused."

"I'm sure he was abused. In the letter he left for me, that he wrote after his first heart attack," her voice cracked, "he said that he was betrayed by someone he trusted in his childhood and he was sorry that he had betrayed me. He wrote that he shouldn't have done it especially since he knew the pain he suffered. The letter was evasive in case someone else might read it."

"From the letter, you know your father was accepting responsibility for what he did to you and he was aware of the harm done," Dr. Noble pointed out.

"I still can't see how he could have recreated the same situation with me. I trusted him and it was a really dirty thing to do. Just because it happened to him, it didn't give him the right to do that to me."

"What he did was inexcusable and he was wrong. He knew it and apparently, through his letter, he was asking for your forgiveness."

"Never!" Beth was not ready to forgive, not just yet.

* * *

After a few more sessions Beth said, "I always felt betrayed by my father. I also know that I was angry with my mother. She should have been there to protect me. I couldn't forget it all of these years. I am glad that I am finally talking about it." Beth looked at the poster hanging on the wall as she had done several times before. *The truth will set you free, but first it will make you miserable.* She thought to herself how true that was.

"I am glad too!"

Rivcka Edelstein

New York, New York, July 1991

Chapter 54

During the days that followed Beth's story, Jeremy continued his focus on the legal issues concerning Karen. Now that mother and daughter reunited, it was urgent to facilitate the process of rescinding the adoption.

A few months earlier, Adela and Max Burgs heard from their lawyer that they might have to pay child support for Karen for the next few years. They were very happy with Jeremy's progress and were very cooperative since they were eager to clear up the legalities. They cheered up when they heard that they didn't need to pay any child support. Not once did the Burgs ask what was going to happen to Karen.

Jeremy and Beth had a date to meet at a restaurant across the street from Lincoln Center. He was reading a newspaper when Beth came in; she started to talk before she even sat down.

"I am so excited that I'm about to burst. I don't like talking about clients outside the hospital, but I must share my excitement with someone."

"Do I count as someone?" he asked, smiling.

She looked at him with amusement in her eyes. "I guess so. I don't have a choice now," she said, partially smiling.

"Go ahead, I'm listening."

"We had an emergency case this afternoon, a young man who tried to commit suicide by overdosing on sleeping pills. His roommate had found him. We were called to observe and make sure the rights of the young man were protected. She went into the details of the case; Jeremy was trying very hard to follow along. He was so proud of her and her commitments to young people.

Silence Broken

"What leads a person to want to commit suicide?" Jeremy asked after she finished relating the case.

"I always wondered about it, at least since my adolescent years . . ." She stopped, remembering she had already told him about her experience.

Beth mentioned what Dr. Noble told her when they spoke about it. Then she looked at him for a second and wondered, "Are you surprised that I go to therapy?"

"Not at all. Anyway," he added jokingly after a pause, "I thought that in this country it was the 'in thing' to do." Jeremy was aware that Beth was seeing her therapist daily since she met Karen. He was very pleased with the changes he saw in her.

"I never do things because they are 'in.' I desperately needed it. In retrospect, I can say it was the most sensible thing I've ever done." She looked at him, emphasizing that she meant the last comment seriously. Again, she noticed how relaxed and close she felt with him. "I feel as close to you now as I did that summer in Israel."

Again, he reached his hand to hold hers and, looking straight in her eyes, he said, "I feel the same way."

She then proceeded to tell Jeremy about her treatment. "Speaking about my therapist — she is wonderful. In the past, I convinced myself it was my fault my father died, that I lost the baby, and that I lost you . . . I concentrated on all the mistakes and problems I caused. Worst of all, I didn't see how it could be any different in the future. I had no joy, no satisfaction, and I functioned like a robot."

She looked at him, and then continued. "Dr. Noble showed me how to challenge and dispute the validity of some of my erroneous beliefs. We solved problems together, as partners. Now I can see more clearly what was happening. I learned to change the rules by which I live and by which I view the world."

Beth talked freely and with excitement about her progress. Jeremy listened attentively and asked many questions. *I would love to sit and listen to Beth for many more years.*

Silence Broken

New York, New York, July 1991

Chapter 55

Sunday evening Jeremy and Beth drove to New York City after returning Karen to The Reach Center, wrapping up a weekend that the three of them had spent together.

"She's got guts, something I didn't have," Beth said in response to Jeremy's detailed description of the Burgs and his discussion with them. "From what I've heard, at times her choice of actions were not socially desirable and even quite dangerous, but she's got guts!"

"Well, that's not the way the Burgs saw it!"

"Yeah? How did they see it?"

"As 'rotten to the core' and I quote."

"I have to say, the more I hear about their actions and their twisted values, the more I'm proud of Karen for rebelling. I am glad that she didn't think that just because they were older they knew better. More kids should have the sense to question the appropriateness of some of the actions of the adults in their environment."

"What do you mean?" Jeremy was confused.

"Children are taught to believe that the adults - parents, teachers, doctors, ministers, etc. know what is best. The fact is that sometimes they don't necessarily know. Sometimes, knowingly, they do not act in the best interest of the child at all."

"You cannot take a few bad examples and decide all authority figures don't care about the welfare of the younger generation," Jeremy argued.

Beth got quiet. She was aware that she spoke out of her own personal pain and experiences, but she also knew it wasn't just her. Every day she read in the newspaper or saw on TV incidents of child physical, sexual, and emotional abuse; it was being reported with higher frequency and intensity than anybody could believe possible.

Jeremy noticed that Beth was not listening and he remained quiet for a few minutes and just stared at her.

"It's good for a child to question adults' motives and actions; parents who mean well will not mind it and they should encourage it." Beth concluded.

"You might be right, to some extent. Still, I hate to think about the effect it would have on the children. They would need to be on constant guard for adults' motives and actions. Just because of a few cases . . ."

"Don't underestimate their percentage in the population; it's higher than reported and, unfortunately, it seems to be a growing phenomenon. Don't forget that when there is abuse it is usually not limited to one member of the family. Also, males who tend to sexually abuse children don't necessarily do it only to their own children or relatives." She went on to quote some of the statistics she had read in the research and heard from Dr. Noble. Jeremy was shocked. "It wouldn't hurt lawyers and judges to become more aware of the data available; then maybe they wouldn't agree to or suggest the kinds of plea bargaining which perpetuates the problem rather than try to wipe it out," Beth said angrily.

"I agree with you," Jeremy said quietly.

Beth's comments refreshed his memories. He recalled a party he had attended in Israel where one of the psychologists among the guests became infuriated — she pulled out a newspaper clipping about a girl who charged her stepfather with sexual abuse. The man admitted it in court and then said that he was sorry and the judge let him go home. The psychologist argued that the real issue was not addressed and a destructive message had been delivered to the victim and the public. The stepfather was not getting the treatment he needed to stop molesting minors. The victims were getting the message that it did not do any good to disclose or report the incident.

Silence Broken

Beth's comments a few minutes earlier shed more light on what the psychologist had said at that party. It was a serious issue which could no longer be avoided.

"You're quiet," he heard Beth say.

"I was just thinking about what you said."

Rivcka Edelstein

Long Island, New York, July 1991

Chapter 56

Beth drove back from The Reach Center. She was tired and restless after her long meeting with Dr. Stone. During the past few weeks, she welcomed their talks.

In addition to her duties as the new lawyer for The Reach Center, Beth also met privately each week with Dr. Stone to deal with her own relationships with Karen. Her time with Dr. Stone had been very productive, but today's visit was extremely painful.

Dr. Stone pointed out the conflicting feelings of love and anger Karen had toward her. Moreover, those feelings were to be expected. For years Karen had prayed for her real mother to appear and rescue her, and yet, at the same time, she harbored anger and resentment for being rejected. Although Karen didn't express herself openly, she constantly raised the question of why Beth had been willing to give her up. She was unwilling to accept "education and career" as an explanation.

Beth knew that Karen was right. How could she share the truth with Karen? How could she tell her why, after her initial resistance, she decided to give up her child for adoption? Beth wondered whether she should have opened up to Dr. Stone about Karen's father.

Dr. Stone had sensed there was more than Beth had told her, but she had not pursued it. Beth wondered if there would be a purpose to disclosing. There would never be a time when she would want Karen to know the circumstances under which she was conceived and why Beth rejected her at birth. Even though Beth understood why Karen was angry with her, she felt very uncomfortable and hurt. She felt overwhelmed with self-pity. She loved Karen, but seeing her was a constant reminder of the horrors and pain she had tried so hard to forget. Beth was angry for what was done to her and felt guilty for what happened to Karen.

Who am I kidding? How could I even think that I'd erase those feelings? she reprimanded herself angrily while driving home. Dr. Stone encouraged her to give the new relationship time. Time she had, but would it heal the scars? Tears rolled down her cheeks and tickled her lips. Her initial joy at locating her daughter was weakened with fear and doubts.

"Self-pity wouldn't do this time," she said to herself as she approached the Tri-borough Bridge to Manhattan. "I am not going to run away from my troubles this time. Here is my chance to make it up to Karen for the last seventeen years." By the time she passed the toll booth she felt better. She decided that although Karen had made spiteful and hurtful comments to her, she could not blame her. She prayed that the therapy Karen was receiving and the sessions they had together would ease some of the pain they both felt. She was glad Dr. Stone had enlightened her about Karen's conflicting feelings. "Now it all makes sense."

She would talk with Jeremy about this; aside from her therapist, he was the only one who knew the truth.

* * *

In the last couple of weeks, Jeremy approached her about making the commitment and what it meant. She felt that she needed more time. He knew that he should tell her about the pressures he had from his law partner, Ben. He needed to return to Israel to deal with his client.

Rivcka Edelstein

Long Island, New York, August 1991

Chapter 57

Karen paced the dorm's living room and repeatedly dialed a phone number. Beth walked in.

"Good, you're here." Karen welcomed Beth at her next visit. "I was trying your number for a long time and they couldn't find you." Karen burst out with tears of relief pouring down her cheeks.

"What's the urgency?" Beth smiled. She was happy to know that Karen had been looking for her. "I told you I would be here today. I would have called you otherwise. Am I late for our session?"

"No, but there is no time to waste. You must do something to stop him, you simply must." Karen was out of breath.

"What are you talking about?"

"I am talking about him; he's leaving."

"Who? Who is leaving? Mike?"

"NO! Jeremy! Are you playing a game?" Karen went on, obviously impatient, and her remarks reminded Beth of herself. "He was just here. He came to say good-bye. He is leaving for Israel tonight. Stop him, please stop him."

Beth caught her breath at the last second, preventing a scream from escaping. She was not aware that he was about to leave or that it would be this soon. He had urged her to make a commitment, but she did not realize he meant it as an "either/or" proposition. She needed more time. She loved him and wanted to be with him in Israel, but she could not make a decision about moving out of the country just like that. What about Karen? She didn't communicate her feelings to him. When she last saw him, he asked her to call him. In the last three days, she was so involved with several clients, that she barely had a chance to think. How could he leave without calling her or seeing her? Beth, who was caught in her own thoughts, heard Karen's pleading voice.

"Do something; you know you can stop him."

Do I? She thought that they were going to work things through and now, once again, she wasn't sure.

"Jeremy is an adult and he has his reasons. He also has commitments." Beth said, hoping she sounded convincing. She uttered the words more for herself than for Karen. Inside she was shaking.

"You know you love him and everyone knows it."

"What I don't see is how this is a concern of yours." Beth snapped back and immediately regretted her outburst. Everything was moving too fast.

"He saved my life." Karen started defensively. "I feel very close to him; he accepts me for who I am."

"I'm sure that's true. I'm sorry I snapped at you, Karen. Give me some time." *Time is the only thing that could help. Did I hear accurately a moment ago?*

"What do you mean, he saved your life?" she asked.

"Didn't he tell you? You didn't know? I cannot believe he didn't tell you! Boy, what a miracle it was!"

"Didn't tell me what, Karen?"

Karen looked at her watch impatiently. "Is it important now? You should think about how to stop him rather than…"

"It's obviously important to you; you just brought up the fact that he saved your life as the reason you want me to stop him."

"Stop him for all three reasons."

"So, tell me, how did he save your life?"

Realizing that Beth was not about to budge until all of her questions were answered, Karen started to explain. "When I was taken to the hospital, I had lost a lot of blood..." Karen described the details as told to her by the attending doctor. "The doctors were very worried because I have a rare blood type and it was not available in their blood bank. They called various places multiple times; as time was running out, I was starting to lose hope. Then Jeremy walked in to inquire about the status of the situation and offered to help in any way he could. The doctor told him that they needed a large supply of fresh blood matching my blood type. He was willing to donate blood if they could use it. He was immediately tested for compatibility. To make a long story short, the doctor later said to me, 'You are a damn lucky young lady. He basically saved your life . . . Without the ample supply of blood that he was so willing to give you might not be here right now.' Later, Jeremy explained to me that he was able to donate because he is a universal donor."

Beth's mind was racing and she made an effort to ask her the next question without showing any signs of her inner emotional turmoil. "What blood type are you?"

"O minus. The doctor said that the chances of finding a donor were very slim . . ."

"What was Jeremy's type?" Beth interrupted.

"He's an O minus, too, and not just that, the doctor added that 'the match was perfect,' whatever that means. You probably understand more than I do," Karen said as she practically pushed Beth out of the door.

Beth felt weak and tried not to show Karen how revealing this conversation was. She didn't want plant any false hopes in Karen until she had a chance to verify its accuracy against hospital records and talk to Karen's surgeon.

"What is your blood type?" Karen asked her mother as she was directing her toward the car.

"I'm A positive," she answered. *Same as my father...*

If Karen was correct in recalling the conversation with the doctor, then the aforementioned information had the potential to drastically impact their lives. She prayed silently. *Let it be so.* Beth realized that she was no longer paying attention to Karen's remarks.

"Would you please try to stop him from leaving? Maybe he can delay the trip for a little while; it will give you more time . . . The last time I saw him he didn't mention anything about leaving and then he came today and said, 'Good-bye, Karen, I must return home . . .'" She turned to Beth, "You must agree it was a sudden decision; it came as a surprise to you, too? Have you forgotten how to speak? Say something!" Karen was becoming irritated.

"I cannot answer all of these questions; it is quite a surprise to me, not that he is leaving, but the timing of his departure." Beth paused. "You do understand that he has a full practice in Israel and he has obligations to the partnership. He already stayed longer than he originally intended to."

"Well," said Karen teasingly, "in the original plan he did not intend to fall in love . . . or come to think of it, maybe he did have it in mind."

"What are you talking about?"

"You can continue to deny it, but you're not fooling anybody but yourself. He's in love with you; he told me so himself, as if it were difficult to guess! You know he's a wonderful guy and I don't say that about many people in this world. Anyway, you'd be getting a wonderful partner considering what's out there; he's a good catch."

"Go already!"

Beth was quiet. Her mind was racing, figuring what steps she had to take before she headed to the airport. The only noise that could be heard was the sound of the ignition.

"Please tell Dr. Stone that I'll not be able to make our session today." She kissed Karen on the cheek. "I'll run to the airport to find Jeremy before he leaves. I don't intend to make the same mistake twice."

"What do you mean 'the same mistake twice?'" Karen asked, as Beth started the car. She received no immediate answer, but Karen didn't mind. She knew Beth should go before it was too late.

Silence Broken

Brooklyn, New York, August 1991

Chapter 58

Jeremy was sweating profusely. He didn't want to leave like this, even though he was urgently needed in Israel. He knew he would return back to the States as soon as he could, he still didn't want to leave before he talked to Beth.

As he stood, for the seventh time, in front of the phone booth, he questioned the fairness of his request to Beth. He should have given her more time to think and sort things out; after all, a commitment on her part meant a commitment not just to him, but to a different life style. Would he have been willing to move to the U.S.A. if needed? How can he leave without seeing Beth? Time was of the essence.

In the past few weeks, Ben had repeatedly asked him to return to Israel right away. Jeremy knew he should be there. Last time he talked to Beth, he told her about the pressure he had from Ben to return. At that time, he did not know that he was needed immediately. He just got the call this morning and had been trying to reach Beth ever since. He hadn't heard from Beth for two days. He wondered why she had not returned his numerous messages at her at her office in the firm.

On the way to the airport, he stopped at The Reach Center to say good-bye to Karen. He felt a lump in his throat and a knot in his stomach when he thought about leaving her. He had become so attached to the "young lady." Karen had begged him to wait, knowing that Beth was supposed to arrive for their session later that evening. He couldn't wait any longer if he intended to catch his flight. He explained that it was urgent for him to take the first flight back to Israel. He promised to return soon, but he did not know exactly when. He gave her his address in Israel in case she wanted to get in touch with him. He also explained to her that Judge Levi had all the information that he had gathered about the legal process in rescinding the adoption.

Before leaving the Reach Center, he attempted to call Beth one last time. He tried both at the office and at her apartment. He hoped that maybe this time he could get her, but alas his efforts were to no avail.

What he really wanted and needed from Beth, before he boarded the plane, were some cues regarding her perception of their future. He needed to know where things stood so he could plan ahead. He knew that all they needed was more time and patience. On the other hand, he also knew that time was of the essence now. He was sorry that, in their last meeting, he had pressured her for a decision. He did not want to lose her again. Jeremy started to became alarmed.

When he arrived at the airport, he immediately went to check if Beth had received the messages which he left for her earlier. He reached for the phone in the booth and started to dial the very familiar number of Beth's firm. The operator answered his questions with a cold voice. "No, Ms. Robinoff did not pick up her messages; no, she did not leave a message for him; and no, they don't know where she is - he should call later."

Jeremy trembled as he replaced the receiver. *I'm leaving without saying good-bye and Beth didn't even get the messages. I want her to know that I will be back soon. She needs to hear that before I board the plane.*

A few minutes passed and the loud speakers were announcing the check-in for his flight. Jeremy made another attempt to contact Beth. No, she didn't pick up her messages. She was in court the whole day.

He paced around the phone booth, hoping to find something. Again, the loud speakers were announcing the check-in for his flight. He picked up his suitcase and walked into the departure gate. As he walked through the gate, a flight attendant ran up behind him. She taped his shoulder and whispered something to him. Jeremy backed off and approached the El-Al service counter. A flight attendant gave him the phone. "I am glad you called, Beth," he said, relieved.

"Jeremy, its Sharon." He heard the voice on the other side. He was disappointed. He listened for a couple of minutes, his stressed face gradually seemed to calm down and his body relaxed.

"Are you sure?" He listened for few seconds more and said, "Sharon, thanks for calling. I'll call you later." Jeremy sighed with deep relief and turned around and whispered something to the flight attendant. He placed his ticket on the counter. The attendant marked it with a pen. "See you soon," she said with a smile.

Jeremy picked up his suitcase and walked towards the phone booth. Jeremy dialed the office number again, this time directly to Beth's department. He got Ms. Block.

* * *

"Saying good-bye to someone, mister?"

"Trying to," he said absentmindedly. He turned around. His eyes widened at the sight of her. Beth stood beside him, flushed and out of breath.

"I was just trying to reach you one more time. They told me . . ."

"How could you even think about leaving without saying good-bye? Walking out like this?" she burst out without waiting for his explanation.

"My father had a heart attack…"

"I am so sorry. When?" Beth said with obvious remorse for her verbal attack.

"My mom called Sharon this morning. I need to be there for them…"

"Of-course… When Karen told me you were leaving I was very angry and hurt. Jeremy, I understand the urgency. I'm so sorry about your dad." She felt embarrassed.

"I would never have left you for a second if I had a choice. I have been leaving you messages for the last two days, continuously calling your home and office to explain my necessity to leave. I already know that you did not get them." He took a deep breath, "Beth, it's not like I wasn't going to be gone forever! However, I'm still happy that you came to see me off."

"Aside from coming to see you off, I need to tell you something. I've been trying to think of how to word it."

"Beth, aside from the emergency about my father I was thinking about how unfair it was for me to pressure you to make a decision about us. I understand that you need time to decide and..." He stopped.

"I didn't come to say good-bye and you are not getting away from your obligations that easily." She smiled.

"What obligations? Look, Beth, forget all I said to you the last time about commitments and obligation. I understand you need more time. I am not running. You know where to find me and I know where to find you. I'll be back soon."

He was relieved that Beth had come to see him before he left. He was happy they could have a chance to talk. He looked at her and from her facial expression, he realized she said something that he missed.

"Sorry, Beth, could you repeat the question?"

"It was not a question, it was a statement: you're Karen's father."

"What?!"

"What I said before was that I have just learned that you are Karen's father."

"I see, you were talking to Karen and she told you that she considers me as the father she did not have. She told me that, too."

"I am not talking about how she feels; I'm talking about biological facts."

Silence Broken

"We might as well sit. I'm very confused."

"I hope you don't mind that I gave you the news more than seventeen years too late, but consider it fair, since I just discovered it myself."

"This doesn't make any sense to me. Didn't you tell me over and over again that there was no chance that Karen was my daughter? And you did such a good job of convincing me that at last I believed it..."

"Tonight, when Karen told me that you gave her blood..."

"I'm a universal donor. That's why they could use my blood!" He wished it were true, but Beth wasn't making any sense. How could she have just learned about it? From whom? How?

"Not your blood type. Hers."

"When Karen mentioned that she was O negative it hit me. You see, everyone in my family has type A blood, so she couldn't be my father's child. To confirm, I went to the Reach center's office and checked Karen's records. She does have O negative. So, she must be your daughter!"

Beth told him quickly, excited about the events which had taken place that afternoon at The Reach Center. She held his hand as she relayed the details of her conversation with Karen, her visit to the hospital where Karen was hospitalized, and about her talk with the doctor to verify the accuracy of Karen's report on the incident.

"I also called the hospital where Karen was born. Now I finally know why she was born premature and why she stayed in the hospital for few weeks after her birth..."

Jeremy was overwhelmed; he had already stopped listening to the details and could barely speak, but when the words finally came out he said, "This is wonderful news." They got up and kissed. Jeremy's eyes were moist. He squeezed Beth's hands. "I should have done a genetic test as soon as you both came into my life again." Beth said apologetically. "I can't believe it! It seems so simple that I'm amazed. With all of your knowledge, why didn't you ask for a blood test to start with?" Although he said this lightly, he was quite angry with her and alarmed at the possibility that he would have been left in the dark about this if it were not for the accident.

"I didn't challenge your explanation at all because it was so clear that you were sure I wasn't the father. I assumed that if there was any doubt in your mind you would have checked it." By now he was even angrier with himself. "I should have..."

"I accepted that she was not your daughter for so many years that I never even thought to challenge the idea. You have to believe me. Although I didn't hear from you, I never would have agreed to the adoption if I knew that she was your daughter."

Jeremy held her hands and squeezed them tightly as the significance of the information dawned on him. "I am glad you used the information Karen gave you as fast as possible — this is wonderful." His voice was hoarse and he made an effort to calm down from the shock of this excitingly unbelievable news. He was happy for himself, for Beth, and for Karen.

"Let's find a private place where I can hold you close. I cannot tolerate this distance any longer," he whispered and she agreed, but the conversation had not yet ended.

The loud speakers were announcing, "Final boarding call for Flight 2044 to Israel."

"Jeremy, for the last few minutes they announced the final boarding of your flight..."

He looked at her. "With all of this information which you just dropped on me, you must be kidding! There is so much to do . . . First priority is the issue of her release from those so called adoptive parents of hers . . ." He was making plans and talking at the same time.

"What about your flight..."

"I changed my flight to tomorrow."

Silence Broken

"What about your dad?"

"Sharon reached me a few minutes ago. She told me my father's out of any imminent danger. So I changed my flight for tomorrow. I was having a hard time leaving before seeing or talking to you."

"Thank God he is out of danger...!" She reproached herself for being angry with him earlier and kissed him again. "I guess we can spend tonight together."

On the way back to the phone booth, Jeremy said, "Do you know how many times in the last few weeks I have envisioned Karen in Israel, in a normal environment? Now that I know that she is my daughter, it is simpler and more realistic."

"What about her mother?"

"Well, that depends on her mother, doesn't it? Beth, will you marry me and go with me and our daughter to live in Israel?"

"Yes! Yes!" She whispered. "This is an offer that I can't refuse."

Jeremy embraced her, kissing her passionately. He was happy at last. The woman he had always loved agreed to become his wife. "Beth, you've just made me the happiest person in the world and to think that with my stupidity, I almost left. I cannot believe, at last, it is happening . . . after all those years of loneliness and pain."

She cuddled up in his arms.

"She was right, once again. She did say that you are a wonderful person and that I could do a lot worse."

"She? You mean Karen. I'm glad I have my own lawyer to look after my interests."

"You aren't kidding? Karen just told me that she would like to be a lawyer when she grows up."

"You mean she has more growing to do? Sometimes I have the feeling that she is the grown-up, not me," he said quite seriously.

"Shall we call her?"

"At this hour? Do you know it is after midnight? I suggest we let her sleep and go to visit her tomorrow. I hope you can come up with the words you will tell her. I, for one, have to readjust to the fact that I'm her biological father. You know that, biological or not, I loved her as a daughter from the moment I thought she was your child." To himself, he had to admit, it was much more appealing to think of her as a product of their love rather than the consequence of an incestuous relationship.

"I'm sure that together we can do it. We'll simply tell her the truth." Finally, there was a truth that they could openly share with Karen.

"I need to call Ben and let him know I'm not on that plane. It would be unfair to let him drive all the way to the airport to find out I'm not there," he said jokingly.

Jeremy dialed the overseas operator and asked to make a person-to-person collect call. While the operator placed the call, he explained to Beth his plan. It was too noisy, Beth was too anxious to stand there, and she did not understand the language anyway. It was a long call and she saw Jeremy getting excited and punching the telephone. 'Ah, oh, Ben is upset!'

"What do you know?" Jeremy said after he put the receiver down. He turned to her. "Could you believe it?"

She was afraid to ask, not sure she was ready for any bad news. She didn't answer.

"Ben was glad I called. He was calling me all afternoon to let me know that he succeeded, at the last moment, to get a six-week extension for the court hearing. So, once my father's health improves, I can return back here to be with you and Karen."

"Well?" She looked at him while they were hailing a cab.

"Well what?"

"Did you tell him?"

"About what?"

"About us!!!" She was about to scream it, but managed to stay calm. She wanted to hear that she was going to be accepted in Israel.

"I told him that there was satisfactory progress in all spheres."

"What was Ben's reaction?"

"Oh. . . Well, he said that we should name the first child after him because he was instrumental in the current events — he gave himself credit for convincing me to go to the United States. He was excited, to say the least, but I didn't tell him that our first child's name was not going to be Benjamin." He still couldn't believe the good news about Karen — it was so wonderful.

"We should call Sharon."

"In the middle of the night?" Beth asked in a shock.

"Absolutely! She deserves it, after all the times she's awakened me to announce her last minute trips to Israel. Besides, I would like to suggest that she look for a bridesmaid dress." Jeremy said lovingly.

"Yes! Sharon, Effrat and Debbie." Beth smiled.

"And tomorrow we will go visit Karen. Actually, come to think of it, my daughter should be the first to know."

"Our daughter," Jeremy corrected her with a smile.

Rivcka Edelstein

Long Island, New York, August 1991

Chapter 59

Dr. Stone sighed with pleasure. She knew what long hours and intensive effort everyone put into the play throughout July and August. Karen was energetic, despite her heavy cast, and did not allow anything to slow her down. Although the play was submitted by the cottage as part of the competition, everyone agreed to recognize Karen as the sole author. When they made the decision to produce it, everyone worked hard to get it done.

Dr. Stone's reminiscing was interrupted by the loud rhythmic clapping and chanting, "Dr. Stone! Dr. Stone!"

She didn't know how it started or by whom and it wasn't part of the program. The only one who was supposed to be called to the stage was Karen — after all, it was her play and her production. All heads turned toward Dr. Stone and the glances communicated the same message as the clapping and shouting continued. They were calling her to come up on the stage. She looked toward the stage and noticed Karen was still there.

Karen spoke into the microphone, "I repeat, we would like to invite Dr. Stone to the stage." There was no way out, so Dr. Stone proceeded to the stage while the crowd roared. She climbed the stairs and her legs were shaking. She was never short for words, but they really caught her off guard this time. Once she reached Karen, Karen said very clearly, yet emotionally, "We, residents, staff, and parents, would like to thank you for your unrelenting faith in us."

Tears came to Dr. Stone's eyes and she fought hard to overcome them. She did not think she could say a word, but the audience continued to cheer loudly and excitedly. After a while Karen raised her hand to motion that she had more to say.

"To prove, beyond a shadow of a doubt, that we have faith in you, we got this for you." She turned to the side and motioned to two boys and a girl who emerged from behind the curtain with a huge plant. "We felt that your office could use some decoration," she continued.

Dr. Stone unwrapped the huge plant and could not believe her eyes. It was 'The Duchess,' one of the protea family of plants illustrated on a poster in her office. She smiled. While at a professional conference in Hawaii, she had wanted to bring one back, but was discouraged from buying it because of the special climate required. Now she remembered an incident a few weeks earlier when one of the residents had inquired about the poster and asked most casually which plant she liked best.

Karen continued, "The nursery people in Maui told us on the phone, before we ordered it, that it needed a special climate and care. They did not believe it was going to survive in our climate. Of course, they don't know you. We believe that Everything Is Possible; after all, look at what you have done with us in this climate."

Dr. Stone smiled. She was still shaking, but had regained some of her composure. She could barely say "thank you," but proceeded to hug and kiss the four residents.

Some people in the audience began chanting, "Speech, Speech." She took the microphone and called the residents and staff to the stage. When they had all climbed up, she turned back to the audience.

"I would like to say that today's events were the result of the strong commitment and dedication of every single person at The Reach Center. We, the residents, and staff, would like to thank you, our guests, for your continued support and unrelenting faith in our program. Your encouragement is necessary for our work."

The guests cheered loudly. The four residents came closer and hugged Dr. Stone warmly as the rest of the residents and staff hugged one another.

* * *

Unlike at the Easter dinner, this time when Karen left the stage after the performance, she had two happy parents ready to hug her. Jeremy and Beth were really overwhelmed. Her voice was thrilling and they were very impressed with the way she had incorporated their life into her story. Jeremy, who had read an earlier draft, noticed the changes she had made after she found her mother and discovered her father. Everybody came to congratulate Karen and meet her parents.

* * *

No one knew that among the guests was a professional theater critic — Ms. Lori Bard — who had heard about The Reach Center from a friend. Soon after the play began, Ms. Bard became engrossed. She forgot it was a play written by a seventeen-year-old young lady and performed by young men and women. She forgot that they were "sick kids" as labeled by society and she was very impressed.

Karen's face seemed familiar to her throughout the play. After the play ended, Ms. Lori Bard introduced herself to Karen and congratulated her. Karen did not think twice about the name Lori Bard. She graciously thanked her for her kind words. Finally, it occurred to Ms. Bard where she knew Karen from. It was from the picture of the "Mysterious Rescuer" article. Now she understood why the newspapers were not allowed to print her name. She suddenly became concerned. Earlier she had an idea, but did not want to say anything about it until she checked with her editors, but now she wasn't sure. The privacy of the residents must be secured. She decided to approach Dr. Stone about it and the two went to the side of the auditorium.

* * *

The telephone rang continuously in Dr. Stone's office. Each of the callers wanted to know if she read the article in the paper and if she knew the critic had been in the audience and what she thought about Ms. Bard's suggestion?

No, she hadn't had a chance to read the paper. No, she did not know there was a critic among the guests until after it was over. Yes, she met Ms. Bard. She did not know how she felt about Ms. Bard's suggestion because she did not yet know what it was. After a few more similar calls, it seemed essential to get the paper and read the story for herself.

Rivcka Edelstein

Ms. Lori Bard- Drama Columnist

Yesterday off Broadway-

Tomorrow on Broadway

New York, August 31- *Everything is Possible* is an original musical production, presented yesterday at the grand opening of the The Reach Center's new Cultural Complex. Although this production is not currently open to the public, it most definitely should be. Not only would it promote fundraising and benefit The Center, it would be a cultural gift to the surrounding communities. *Everything is Possible* is indeed a cultural gem. It portrays the true story of a group of juvenile delinquents rejected by society and their effort to reenter said mainstream society. For some theater goers, the themes of truancy, crime, drugs, runway youths, and their causes may be depressing. However, the underlying message is that with hope, faith, and inner strength, everything is possible. The play is serious and thought provoking, as well as humorous and uplifting.

One of the most impressive features of the production is the high- performance quality, especially considering that every actor was between the ages of thirteen and eighteen and have no prior theater experience (last names of actors withheld to protect their rights).

Karen, the playwright, co-producer, and one of the actors, is a sensitive and mature girl at seventeen. She wrote the play for a competition and explained that "the play is meant to be an expression and gesture of gratitude towards my fellow residents, the professional staff, Judge Levi, and all who supported me with firmness, consistence, and care." Jim, Tanya, and Mike composed the energetic music to accompany Karen's beautiful lyrics. Though many of the songs are memorable, one of the highlights was the song *Hope*, sung by Karen, accompanied by the cast. The song relates the biblical story of Ruth and her unshaken faith.

Silence Broken

Dr. Stone finished the article, which ended, *"Thank you, Reach Center, for a wonderful evening."* Dr. Stone was pleased that the residents' efforts were recognized and their skills noticed; she had known it all along. The residents deserved it. The article would positively affect their assessment of their own ability. In response to Ms. Bard's suggestion, Dr. Stone thought, it might be a good idea to open the complex to the public.

Rivcka Edelstein

Over the Atlantic, September 1991

Chapter 60

"Now let anyone deny that everything is possible," Karen mused as she stretched out her legs and clasped her hands behind her head. She smiled at Sharon with great satisfaction and winked.

"In the beginning, you didn't believe me. Everybody thought I was out of my mind. Who ever heard about a young teenager longing for her real mother, unwilling to accept mediocre adoptive parents."

Sharon nodded and Karen went on, not wanting to be misunderstood. "You know I don't object to adoption. It depends on who adopts and who is being adopted. I do object to the superficial job done in my case. People's motivation and expectations for adoption should be checked. The adoption agency accepted the empty promises given by the Burgs."

Sharon was used to hearing Karen question the established system. She often had to remind herself that Karen was still fairly young. By and large she agreed with what Karen was saying. Sharon saw both sides; some judges completely disregarded the social workers and their recommendations, while others accepted it without even asking questions. Yes, many injustices were done to youngsters whose needs were overlooked.

To Karen she said, "You do know that adoption of children is usually a very good solution for all three groups — the adoptive and biological parents, and the adopted child."

"I know, but I wish some agencies would be more careful."

Sharon agreed. "Recently, many safeguards have been established to avoid abuse."

Karen, fearing she had brought too much seriousness to the happy atmosphere, shook her head and went on "Forget it; it's all behind me now. Who could have asked for a nicer couple to be my parents? I pinch myself constantly to see whether I am dreaming or whether this is actually happening to me. You dream about something for so many years and then you stop hoping. Here I am! It happened to me! Nothing nice ever happened to me, so it was about time. I'm very happy."

"Ladies and gentlemen, we are approaching the shores of Israel. If you look out the windows on your left, you will see the city of Tel Aviv," the pilot said. There it was!

Karen gazed out the window. Israeli folk music sounded from the speakers and Sharon rummaged in her purse for tissues.

"This always happens to me when I come home," she sniffed. Karen looked at Sharon; her eyes were filled with tears and her voice was trembling. Karen looked around and noticed that Sharon was not the only tearful passenger.

From the languages spoken during the El-Al flight, she knew most of the people were Israelis. Whether or not they were currently residents of Israel, the reaction of coming home was universal. When the plane landed, everyone applauded.

The pilot asked the passengers not to remove their seat-belts until the plane came to a complete stop, but it was as though they had not heard him. Everyone was on their feet before the captain finished his sentence.

Rivcka Edelstein

Tel Aviv, Israel, September 1991

Chapter 61

The music stopped and all the guests looked at the couple as they stood facing each other. The Rabbi stood in front of them, facing the guests and asked them to join hands to begin the ceremony. His words were simple and they added to the special excitement among the guests. Everyone was aware of the love behind this marital union, and many of them knew about the pain. During the past eighteen years, among the members of the *gar'in*, the questions most frequently asked were "What happened to Beth and Jeremy? Why didn't they get married?" Very few of them had answers. The wedding was a happy ending to all of those unanswered questions.

Even Karen was in a daze; she felt like the guest of honor. When Jeremy and Beth were standing on the receiving line to greet their guests, Karen was right between them. "We would like you to meet our daughter, Karen. Karen, this is our friend Ruth . . . David . . ."

Karen had met most of the guests before the wedding, since most of them did not want to wait until the formal wedding ceremony to express their joy. Karen had the chance to meet them earlier in her parents' apartment — friends like Effrat, Yochai, Ben, Jonathan, and Rami. They kept dropping by in the evenings and offering to help with the preparations. Along with her newly found parents, Karen received a large family and a number of new friends. She liked them all and they were super to her. She especially liked Yael, Ben's daughter, and the two of them became close friends very fast.

The wedding as a whole was a new experience for Karen. After a few hours, the guests left and Karen stood beside Sharon. "Did you notice the way my dad looked at my mom? You could read love in their eyes. I don't think I will ever forget that look. How many children are lucky enough to observe their parents' wedding the way I did! You know, it is even more beautiful than the ending I used for the play. Maybe I should change it to mirror reality."

Rivcka Edelstein

Everything Is Possible©

Everything is Possible© 1978, is a psychological therapeutic game developed by Dr. Rivcka Edelstein and published by Reim International Associates in the United States and in Israel.

www.ingramcontent.com/pod-product-compliance
Lightning Source LLC
Chambersburg PA
CBHW061630040426
42446CB00010B/1343